KAKADU

LOOKING AFTER THE COUNTRY — THE GAGUDJU WAY

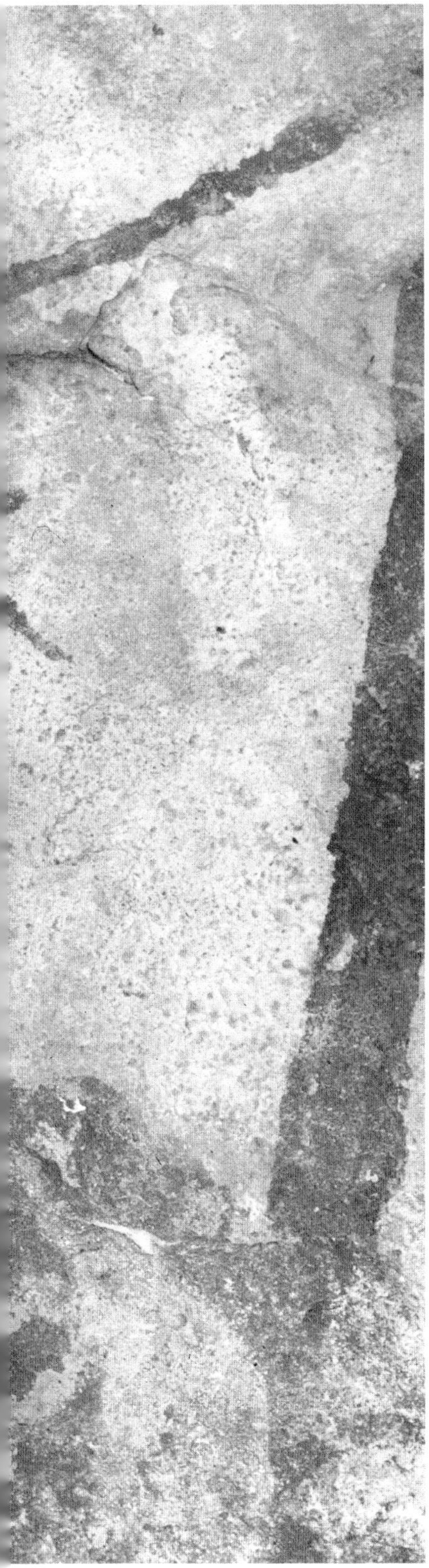

KAKADU

LOOKING AFTER THE COUNTRY — THE GAGUDJU WAY

Stanley Breeden and Belinda Wright

SIMON & SCHUSTER
AUSTRALIA

Half title page
Djawok the koel. This is not considered a painting but a manifestation of Djawok himself.

Title page
A real cave spider beside a rock painting of a spider. © *National Geographic Society.*

Right
Run-off after heavy monsoon rain.

To Big Bill Neidjie, Toby Gangele, Felix Iyanuk, Bluey Ilkirr, Jonathan Yarramarna, Susan Aladjingu and all the Gagudju people.

To the memory of Nipper Kapirigi, George Namingum and Dolly Yanmalu.

KAKADU—LOOKING AFTER THE COUNTRY THE GAGUDJU WAY
First published in Australasia in 1989 by
Simon & Schuster Australia
7 Grosvenor Place, Brookvale NSW 2100

A division of Gulf+Western

National Library of Australia
Cataloguing in Publication data
Breeden, Stanley, 1938–
Kakadu, looking after the country the Gagudju way.

Includes index:
ISBN 0 7318 0020 6.

1. Natural history — Northern Territory — Kakadu National Park. 2. Gagudju (Australian people). I. Wright, Belinda. II. Title.

508.9429′5

Designed by Patrick Coyle & Associates
Typeset in Hong Kong by Setrite Typesetters Limited
Produced by Mandarin Offset in Hong Kong

PREFACE

WHOEVER SPENDS ANY LENGTH OF TIME IN KAKADU, cannot help but come under its spell. I first felt this fascination in January 1972 when I visited Cannon Hill on the East Alligator River. It was the wet season and the wide marshes filled with countless birds, the ancient sculptured sandstone, the freshness and unspoilt wildness of the place were unlike anything I had ever seen. During the next two years I spent five months in the region and became particularly spellbound by the rocky escarpments along the Arnhem Land Plateau. There were no roads or tracks to the stone country then and to see Jim Jim Falls, Twin Falls, Deaf Adder Creek and other places required major undertakings. Although I did not meet any Aboriginal people in the bush, their spirit seemed everywhere; in the exquisite rock paintings, the burial sites and the quarries where they had made stone implements.

Shortly after my last visit in 1973 I left Australia to live in India but Kakadu was never far from my thoughts. I was always looking for an opportunity to go back to what for me remained the most beautiful place in the world. My chance came in 1985 when my wife Belinda and I were asked by the National Geographic Society to make a television film there and to write and photograph a story for the magazine. But how things had changed! Kakadu had now become a National Park run by the Commonwealth Government. It was criss-crossed by new roads. There was a brand new town, Jabiru, of about 2000 people and a uranium mine. Over 150,000 visitors a year came to see its wonders. But Kakadu had not lost its character and amazingly the original inhabitants, the Gagudju people, had gained title to and were living on their traditional lands. For me Kakadu was now complete.

We stayed in Kakadu for a year and a half. Belinda too became captivated by the place and soon formed a close rapport with the Gagudju people. Over the months Big Bill Neidjie, Nipper Kapirigi, George Namingum, Bluey Ilkirr and other Aboriginal people gradually took us into their confidence and gave us their friendship, for which we will always be grateful. They opened our eyes to a very different, and most valid, way of looking at nature and man's place in the scheme of things.

We wish to thank all the Gagudju people for their patience, forbearance and generosity in telling us about their story and allowing us to photograph in their country. We are grateful for the logistical support given us by the Gagudju Association and Pancontinental Mining. Many people, over the long period it has taken us to put this book together, have helped in countless ways. We wish to especially thank Jonathan and Sharon Nadji, rangers of the East Alligator District, Bob and Libby Hall, Margaret Fuller, Andrew Pickering, Kym Brennan and Peter and Patti Manigault. Stephen Davis gave us much helpful advice and patiently answered our many questions. We are indebted to George Chaloupka for his counsel about the rock paintings. Suzanne Venables did an outstanding job typing the manuscript. We thank the National Geographic Society for the use of a number of our photographs that first appeared in their magazine.

Finally, we are especially indebted to Ian Morris for his encouragement throughout this project, for his unstinting and ever-cheerful guidance and assistance in the field, for his generosity in sharing his unique and wide-ranging knowledge of Kakadu and the Aboriginal people and above all for his friendship. We also wish to thank Ian for allowing us to include many of his exceptional photographs.

STANLEY BREEDEN
BELINDA WRIGHT

Topaz, Queensland
31 July 1988

NOTE

The area now known as Kakadu and before that as the Alligator Rivers region, was originally inhabited by Aboriginal people belonging to as many as thirty different clans — the Bunitj, Mirarr, Badmardi, Warramal, Murumburr, Rol and others. The clans, each made up of a number of extended families, were related through marriage, a common belief in the Dreamtime and the rituals that ensure its perpetuation. The people had no collective name. A number of languages were spoken in the area. The Bunitj and their neighbouring clans living on the west bank of the East Alligator, spoke a language called Gagudju. At the turn of the century and some thirty years afterwards, when white people first tried to settle there, this language became the *lingua franca* for the whole region. The catalyst for the widespread use of Gagudju was a white man called Paddy Cahill who had come to live among the Aboriginal people. He first came as a buffalo shooter, but then settled in Oenpelli, in Arnhem Land, just a few kilometres across the East Alligator from Kakadu. Cahill became fluent in Gagudju and encouraged its use by all the clans.

In 1912 the pioneering ethnologist Baldwin Spencer came to Oenpelli and with Paddy Cahill's help studied the Aboriginal people around the East Alligator. He called them Kakadu which was the way he spelt Gagudju. The Gagudju language is now only properly known by one person, the elderly Dolly Yanmalu of the Bunitj clan, and is spoken to a lesser extent by just a few others. The language will die out before too many years. But the name is perpetuated as it was adopted by the members of the surviving clans of Kakadu in 1979. At that time they joined together and formed an association to deal with all the pressures on them and their lands. They called it the Gagudju Association and all the members now refer to themselves as Gagudju.

CONTENTS

KAKADU CHRONOLOGY

50,000 years before present
Aborigines first come to Australia; world's first navigators

35,000 years before present
First rock paintings; simple hand prints

23,000 years before present
First people at Malangangerr and Nawulabila

20,000 years before present
First true rock paintings; large naturalistic figures

18,000 years before present
Edge-ground stone axe; world's first technology

10,000 years before present
Rainbow Serpent first appears in rock paintings
Man first moves into villages and practises agriculture — in the Middle East

7,000 years before present
X-ray paintings first appear in Kakadu — continue to today

5,000 years before present
Egyptians build first pyramids
Rise of Hinduism in Asia

1,500 years before present
Freshwater floodplains form in Kakadu

0 Jesus of Nazareth is born

1788 AD Balanda arrive to begin European settlement of Australia

1818 Phillip Parker King sails up Alligator Rivers and names them

1824 Captain James Bremer claims Kakadu for British Crown

1828 First water buffalo shipped from Indonesia to Northern Territory

1830c First rock paintings featuring Balanda and sailing ships

1838 Military settlement established at Port Essington

1845 Ludwig Leichhardt crosses Kakadu

1849 Port Essington settlement abandoned

1866 John McKinlay crosses Kakadu

1869 Darwin (then called Palmerston) established

1872 Overland telegraph reaches Darwin

1880s Gold rush around Pine Creek
First record of Gagudju people visiting Darwin
Buffalo shooting begins, Paddy Cahill first visits region

1906 Paddy Cahill takes up residence in Oenpelli

1912 Baldwin Spencer visits the area and calls the people Kakadu

1919 Influenza pandemic claims 25–50 per cent of Aboriginal people Australia-wide

1920 Carl Warburton takes up buffalo shooting lease on East Alligator floodplains

1925 Oenpelli becomes a mission

1931 Arnhem Land declared an Aboriginal Reserve

1942 Many Gagudju people removed from their land by the army

1960s Gagudju people working on cattle stations in the Kakadu region forced to leave because of equal wages legislation

1964 Najombolmi paints last major rock painting in Kakadu

1974 *Environment Protection (Impact of Proposals)* Act declared

1975 Fox Enquiry begins hearings

1976 *Aboriginal Land Rights (Northern Territory)* Act declared

1977 Fox Enquiry Report recommends (1) Kakadu National Park be established, and (2) Uranium mining go ahead after consultation with Gagudju people

1978 Gagudju people granted title to their land which they then lease to ANPWS to be managed as a National Park

1979 Stage One of Kakadu National Park is declared
Gagudju Association is formed
Uranium mining commences

1981 Stage One of Kakadu is listed as World Heritage

1984 Stage Two of Kakadu National Park is declared

1987 Stage Two of Kakadu is listed as World Heritage
Stage Three of Kakadu National Park is declared (making a total of approx. 19,000 sq kms)

1988 More than 200,000 people visit Kakadu

Sunrise with floodplain pandanus.

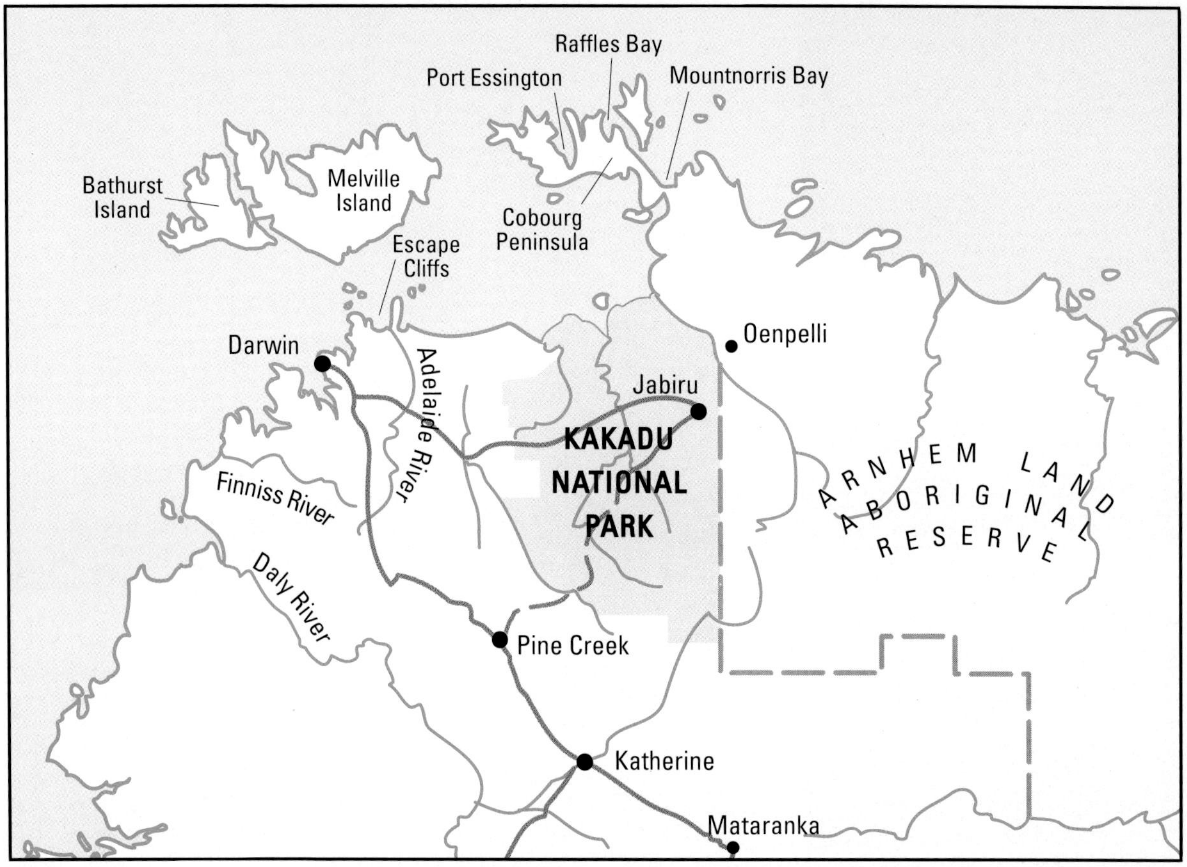
Raffles Bay
Port Essington
Mountnorris Bay
Bathurst Island
Melville Island
Cobourg Peninsula
Escape Cliffs
Oenpelli
Darwin
Adelaide River
Jabiru
KAKADU NATIONAL PARK
ARNHEM LAND ABORIGINAL RESERVE
Finniss River
Daly River
Pine Creek
Katherine
Mataranka

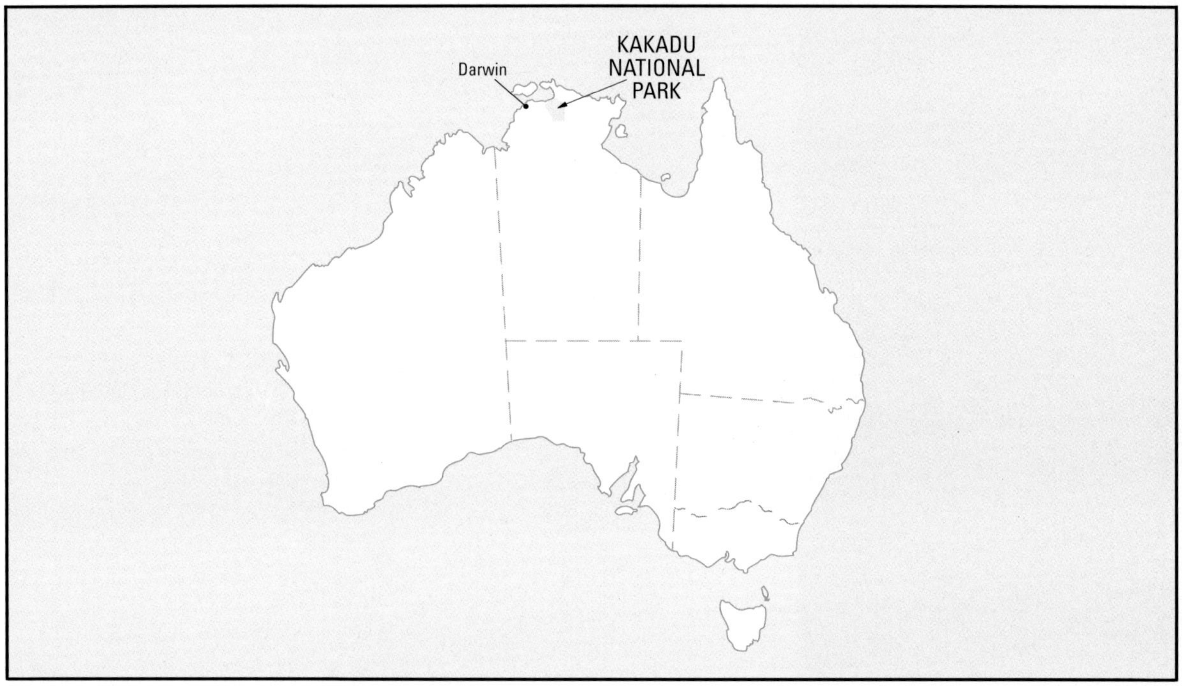
KAKADU NATIONAL PARK
Darwin

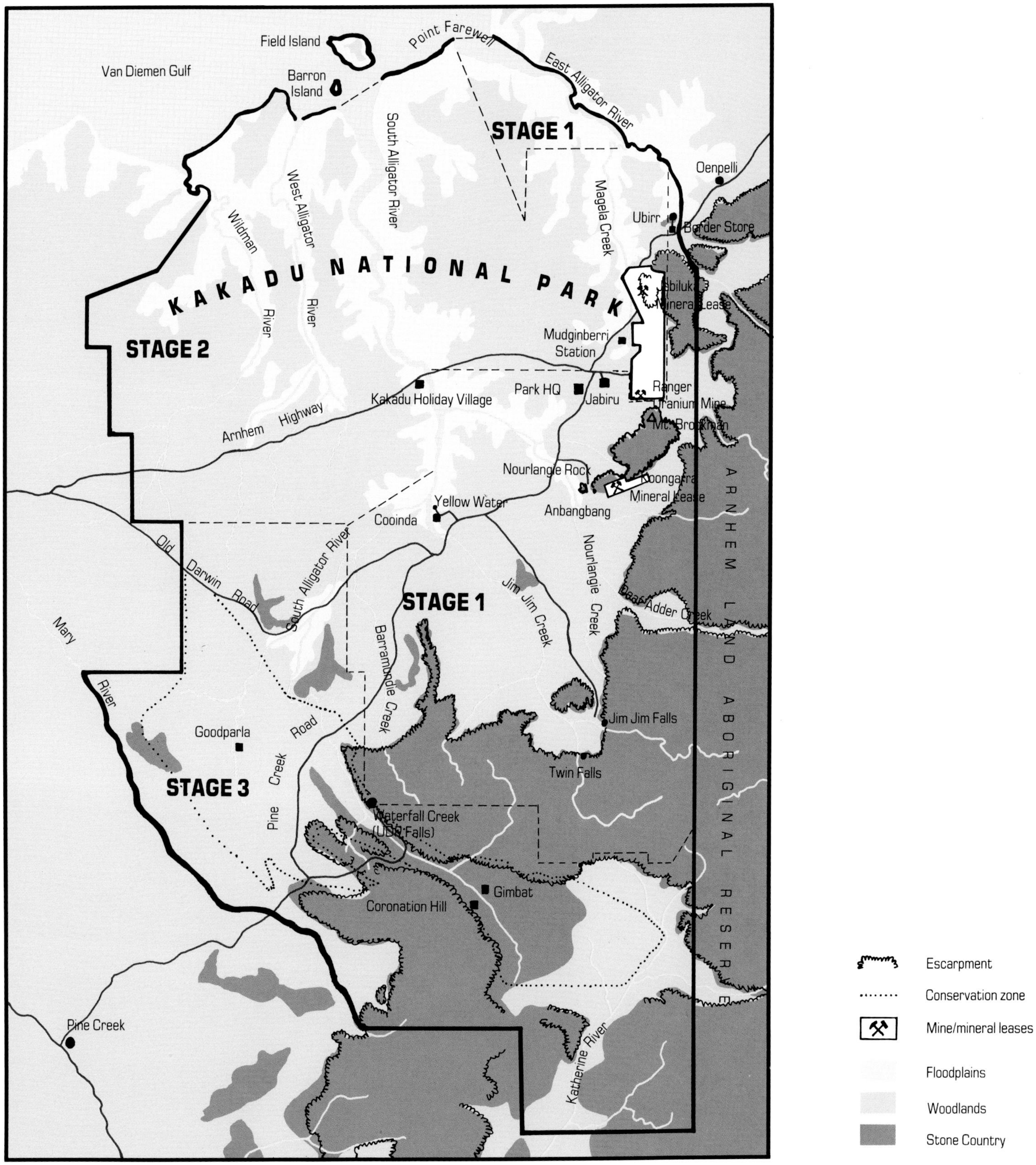

KAKADU NATIONAL PARK
STAGE 1
STAGE 1
STAGE 2
STAGE 3
Van Diemen Gulf
Field Island
Barron Island
Point Farewell
East Alligator River
South Alligator River
West Alligator River
Wildman River
Magela Creek
Oenpelli
Ubirr
Border Store
Jabiluka Mineral Lease
Mudginberri Station
Kakadu Holiday Village
Park HQ
Jabiru
Ranger Uranium Mine
Mt. Brockman
Arnhem Highway
Nourlangie Rock
Koongarra Mineral Lease
Yellow Water
Cooinda
Anbangbang
Old Darwin Road
South Alligator River
Nourlangie Creek
Jim Jim Creek
Deaf Adder Creek
Barramundie Creek
Mary River
ARNHEM LAND ABORIGINAL RESERVE
Jim Jim Falls
Twin Falls
Goodparla
Pine Creek Road
Waterfall Creek (UDP Falls)
Gimbat
Coronation Hill
Katherine River
Pine Creek
Escarpment
Conservation zone
Mine/mineral leases
Floodplains
Woodlands
Stone Country

1~MARRAWUTI'S KINGDOM

A LOW MIST BLANKETS the plain and billabongs on this pleasantly cool May morning. To the south the towering sandstone escarpment looks dark and brooding in the hour before sunrise. The skeleton of an ancient paperbark tree thrusts up through the mist. Hunched in its topmost branches sits Marrawuti the white-breasted sea-eagle, his huge talons gripping the dead wood. Soon a pink glow spreads across the eastern sky, putting a wash of colour on Marrawuti's immaculate white and grey plumage. As the sun rises a light breeze springs up and gently lifts the covering of mist, revealing a vast floodplain stretching towards the north-east. The sheet of shallow water is deep green with aquatic plants and is stitched all over with star bursts of white waterlilies. Strewn across the plain is a loose string of large dark boomerang shapes; these are the billabongs, the permanent waterholes. The rains of the wet season, only recently ended, have been abundant and the waters teem with life.

At this early hour honeyeaters sing and lorikeets screech in the islands of paperbark trees. Out in the open cormorants, egrets, spoonbills and pelicans add strange burping and gurgling sounds. Ducks whistle and twitter and the clanging call of the darter carries far over the water. Thousands of flying foxes, just returned to their roost from their nightly feeding, screech in a grove of freshwater mangroves. As a background to this morning cacophony there is the constant monotone of countless pied geese feeding and squabbling in the shallow water. Raising his head Marrawuti adds his voice to the chorus in a resounding 'ank, ank, ank, ank'.

Nothing escapes the eagle's inordinately sharp vision — from the dragonflies' dancing flight beneath his perch to a crocodile cruising in a distant billabong. He sees a lotusbird walking to his floating nest to incubate the eggs, whiskered terns diving after fingerling fish, pygmy geese stripping seeds from water plants, Burdekin ducks shepherding their brood of ducklings across a patch of open water and egrets poised motionless ready to spear passing prey. But he is especially alert to the movements of fish, his favoured prey, from the small archer fish shooting at insects with jets of water, to giant barramundi striking at frogs or grasshoppers that may have strayed from cover.

These floodplains and billabongs are the very heart of Marrawuti's kingdom and contain an unrivalled throng of animals.

Marrawuti is hungry. He takes off from his look-out perch and with powerful wing beats spirals into the sky. There is no easy prey below, no injured duck or goose nor unwary fish. He glides towards the flying foxes and lands in a tall tree overlooking the colony. The large black bats fall silent and move lower into the trees hiding as best they can in the foliage. The eagle shakes his feathers, preens and waits and waits. It becomes warmer. A crocodile

Billabongs along the South Alligator River during flood.

heaves itself onto a small island and basks in the sun, its enormous mouth gaping open. The flying foxes, in time, relax their vigilance, cool themselves by fanning with their wings, and resume their squabbles. Marrawuti now launches himself and charges into the colony with power and speed. In panic the densely massed bats try to take off, they get in each others' way. In the confusion Marrawuti wheels round, the air whooshing through his wing feathers, and snatches a flying fox out of the air. The black form struggles briefly before its heart is pierced by Marrawuti's sharp talons. The eagle carries his victim to his nest, a huge untidy structure of sticks in a lone paperbark out on the floodplain. His mate joins him in a triumphant duet.

By midday it is hot and Marrawuti and his mate, both now replete, seek the coolness of higher altitudes. The two leave the floodplain on slow wing beats to seek the updrafts of the dry land and the rock escarpment.

Soon they circle over the eucalypt forest, a flat sea of grey-green. Some of the trees are in flower, creating islands of orange or yellow. Flocks of brilliant green lorikeets dash from one to another. Antelope kangaroos, the males reddish in colour, the females silver-grey, rest in the shade. Many of the grasses are already turning golden-yellow. Flocks of finches, some crimson, some chestnut, are feeding on the seeds. Not far away a frilled lizard catches insects in the shade of a tall termite mound.

Sailing across a wide stretch of this woodland, Marrawuti reaches the sheer walls of the rock escarpment. His sudden appearance alarms a black wallaroo who had been slumbering

Previous pages
Marrawuti, the white-breasted sea-eagle, soars over his kingdom.

Flying foxes leave their camp at dusk and set out for their nightly feeding.

in the shade of a large boulder and he dashes recklessly across the rocks to hide in a cave. A large python takes no chances either and slithers deeper into a rock crevice. Gliding close to the escarpment Marrawuti glimpses vivid ochre images; paintings of men and animals.

Finally catching the updraft the eagle rises rapidly. Without effort the bird is now lifted high above the edge of the plateau and he looks down at the criss-cross patterns on the deeply faulted and weathered rocks. The midday sun winks off streams and waterholes lying deep in narrow clefts. These sandstone rocks were laid down in an ancient sea or lake about 1.5 billion years ago. Since that time they have been lifted, fractured and eroded. Erosion has reduced much of the rock to its original components and outwashes of sand fan out from the escarpment like white skirts.

By late afternoon Marrawuti flies off in a northerly direction. Leaving the forests and rock country behind he crosses the floodplain, and rising high he follows a river meandering northwards. The setting sun strikes a golden path over the distant sea. The wide, black-soil plains below him, waterlogged for more than six months of the year, are as young a landform as the escarpment is old. The silt that formed them was carried here no more than 1500 to 1000 years ago. Kakadu's most vibrant and prolific habitats are also its youngest.

Marrawuti rides the air currents till he is barely visible from the rocks below. For hours he circles, rarely if ever beating his wings. His kingdom lies spread out, a patchwork of glittering wetlands, diverse forests and secretive stone country.

As the sun touches the horizon Marrawuti turns back to his own territory. In a playful

show of strength he dives steeply down towards the flying fox colony before levelling off and gliding to his perch in the dead paperbark. As the last light drains from the sky Marrawuti fluffs out his feathers, hunches his shoulders, pulls one loosely clenched foot under him and settles down for the night.

Kakadu Remains Unspoilt

Marrawuti's kingdom, a 20,000 sq km mosaic of floodplains, billabongs, woodlands and rock plateau in the Northern Territory's top end, is now known as Kakadu National Park.

Until recently this remote corner of Australia was only sporadically visited by Europeans. Its natural riches were protected by the difficulties of the terrain and the floods of the wet season. Since the 1920s Europeans have tried to make a living here by shooting feral water buffalo for their hides and meat or by raising cattle. But in the long run all these ventures were abandoned and made little impact on the wild plants and animals. Only the crocodile shooters of the 1950s and 1960s made inroads into native species, but their activities were stopped before the crocodiles became extinct.

So while the rest of the continent felt the scourge of development — the disappearance of

Left
Paperbark woodlands grow on seasonally inundated plains.

Above left
A lotusbird walks to his floating nest among the lily pads.

Above
Millions of years of erosion have sculptured the sandstone of the Arnhem Land Plateau into an infinite variety of fantastic shapes, including this natural arch.

Above right
The large goanna, Varanus panoptes, *was not described by scientists until 1980. Very little was known about Kakadu's plants and animals by non-Aborigines until recent times.*

whole ecosystems, vast tracts of country trampled and uprooted by feral rabbits, goats, pigs, horses, donkeys, camels and cattle, native mammals and birds driven to the brink of extinction by introduced predators such as cats and foxes and introduced plants making aggressive forays into almost every corner of the continent — Kakadu remained relatively untainted.

Despite the fact that feral water buffaloes and pigs continue to despoil some corners of Kakadu, it remains a place where the real Australia, in its full vigour and diversity and in a setting of unsurpassed grandeur, survives. For that alone its value is immeasurable.

But this is no ordinary corner of Australia. In the years since 1972 when the plants, animals and landforms began to be studied systematically for the first time, it soon became apparent that Kakadu was a place of unusual richness. There are fifty-one species of mammals in Kakadu, which is a greater number of species, found in greater abundance, than in any other area its size in Australia. About 275 species of birds have been recorded, about one-third of the total for Australia. Amongst them are all but two of the raptors. There are seventy-five species of reptiles in Kakadu which is only a few less than for the whole State of Victoria. Twenty-five kinds of frogs have been recorded, which is more than for the whole

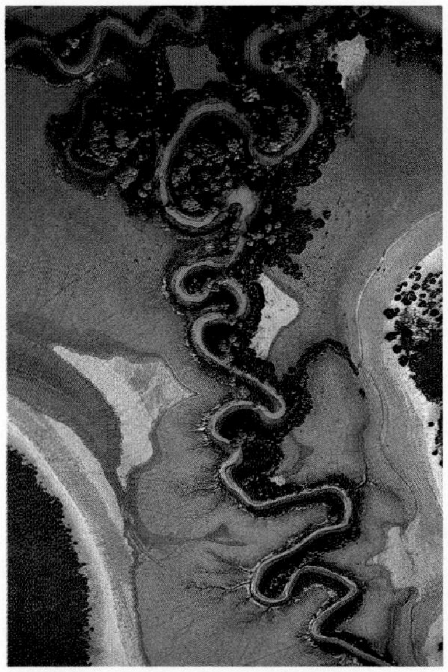

A stream meanders across tidal mudflats along the coastline of Kakadu National Park.

State of South Australia which is sixty times as large as Kakadu. Freshwater fish are also well represented with more than fifty species, which is nearly double that for the entire Murray-Darling river system, the most extensive on the continent. Insects are especially numerous and the least known. About 4000 of the estimated 10,000 species are as yet undescribed. Among the butterflies and moths alone there are 1500 species.

Before 1972 Kakadu was botanically one of the least known areas of the world. The variety of species can best be appreciated when it is realised that 38 per cent of the plants of the Northern Territory's top end occur in Kakadu, while it comprises only 4 per cent of the area. As with the insects, many, many species are yet to be described.

Mangrove tree roots, exposed at low tide, form an inpenetrable thicket.

The great diversity of life is mostly the result of a tropical climate combined with good rainfall; species sensitive to drought and frost are not eliminated. Another factor is the variety of habitats ranging from tidal mudflats and mangroves through freshwater wetlands, sparse woodlands and rainforests to the rocky gorges and the austere sandstone plateau. To date the inroads made by feral plants and animals have not altered the character and species composition beyond recognition, although this could still happen. In the meantime Kakadu is still the nearest there is to a pristine Australia.

Uneasy Compromise

As late as 1973 Kakadu had kept its secrets. Not because of some far-sighted policy, not because of the necessity to keep one last piece of quintessential Australia intact, but solely because Europeans had not yet found a 'use' for it.

Before 1974 it was still possible to make trackless journeys into the escarpment; to walk up a clear stream through a steep-sided ravine and think with some justification that you were one of the first European people to walk there. Many usually shy animals were unafraid. Wallaroos, pigeons and goannas would come towards a person, filled with curiosity. Marrawuti might catch a fish practically at your feet. Animals bathed, ate, drank and displayed to each other, ignoring the alien intruders.

It was Australia's great good fortune that the minerals, principally uranium, were discovered in an era when people had awakened to Kakadu's incalculable value as a wild and natural area and not merely as a mine. Compounding the good fortune was the fact that the Aboriginal people demanded, and were granted, land rights. After a long struggle, which is not yet over, the Gagudju people, the region's original inhabitants, were given title to their land. They in turn leased it, for a nominal fee, to the Australian National Parks and Wildlife Service, to be managed as a National Park. Other areas were added and the whole place was called Kakadu. Mining interests were also accommodated. It is still an uneasy compromise with constant frictions between the miners, Aborigines, various governments and the great throng of adventure seekers.

Marrawuti as he soars loftily over his domain is unaware of the conflicts but he can see their effects — roads with hundreds of cars stirring up dust, a great hole in the earth where uranium ore is excavated, a busy town, the tumult of hotels. Planes and helicopters invade his air space and powerboats his hunting territories. Other fishermen compete for his prey.

The scene that unfolded below Marrawuti has been described from a European point of view. The alien elements were brought by Europeans. But to another group of people, called the Gagudju, whose forebears first came to Kakadu 50,000 or more years ago, the place has a deeper, more personal meaning. To them Marrawuti is not merely an eagle but also a special force in their lives, their spiritual brother. To the Gagudju all living things, including the people, as well as the rocks and the land are all part of a single life force — a continuing force they call the Dreamtime.*

* Dreaming and the Dreamtime are literal translations of Aboriginal words. Inexplicably, however, they have little or nothing to do with dreams or dreaming in the conventional European sense.

2 ~ THE DREAMTIME

According to the Gagudju people the world always existed. But long, long ago before the Dreamtime, before time could be counted, it had no shape. The land was featureless without rivers or mountains and in neither the sea nor the land was there any life. There were no fish, grasses or singing birds. But below the surface, lying dormant, were the creator spirits. Potential life was always there.

Then, at the beginning of the Dreamtime, the time of genesis, a creator being, a woman called Warramurrungundji, came out of the sea. She carried a digging stick and a dilly bag with yams, waterlilies and other important plants. Once ashore she gave birth to the first people and bestowed on them their languages. She then planted the yams and other foods. Here and there she plunged her digging stick into the ground and created waterholes. Other creator beings appeared.

Indjuwanydjuwa and his family came across the northern plains and taught the people how and where to hunt. Ngalyod, also known as Almudj, the Rainbow Serpent, came and smote passages through the rocks and made further waterholes. Riding the storm clouds Namarrkun, the lightning man, came out of the sky with lightning arcing across his shoulders and stone axes tied to his head, elbows and knees with which he struck the clouds to make thunder. Whenever he saw men and women disobey the laws his voice would hiss and crackle in warning. If he was not heeded he would hurl fiery spears at the wrongdoers.

Some of the ancestral spirits came in the form of animals who brought order to human society and shape to the land. Gurri, the blue-tongue lizard, told the people what moiety they belonged to and what skin names they should have. In his travels he slipped and fell on his face among the rocks and that is why he has a blue tongue to this day. Djuwe, the great bowerbird, showed the people how to build the special shelter for initiation ceremonies and how to perform the accompanying dances. The catching of fish and their preparation was first told to the people by Garrkanj the brown falcon. And when a person dies, it is Marrawuti, the white-breasted sea-eagle, who carries off his or her spirit in his claws. Gundamen, the frilled lizard, is an example to all who may not want to submit to tribal discipline. When he was a man he was smooth and sleek. Once, during an important ceremony his attention wandered, he performed the wrong rituals and sang the wrong songs. The elders punished him by turning him into a rough-scaled lizard with funny-looking skinny arms and legs and a ruff of loose skin around his neck.

Other ancestral animals made parts of the landscape. Ginga the giant crocodile forced a passage through the rocks to reach the East Alligator River. Garndagitj the antelope kangaroo formed rock outcrops and hollowed out depressions as he moved about the land.

The time of creation was also a time when men and women could change into animals, and when the animals assumed their present shapes.

In the beginning Gowarrang, the echidna, was a woman, and Al-mangeyi, the long-necked turtle, a man. They went hunting together. They came upon a delicacy, a large snail. Soon they quarrelled about who should eat it. Finally, in a rage, the man hurled the bundle of light spears he was carrying at the woman. The spears stuck in her back and remain there to this day as quills. But she quickly retaliated and threw a flat stone at the man, which stuck to his back to become his shell.

In the remoteness of the creative period Ginga was also a man. One day, while asleep in some dry grass near a billabong, he accidentally caught fire. Waking up with his back on fire he rushed into the water, where he turned himself into a crocodile. But even now his back is covered in blister-like lumps and bumps.

When the spirit ancestors had completed their creative acts, they did not simply disappear. They put themselves into the landscape as rock formations, as a spontaneous image in the form of a rock painting or in other ways. And there they remain for all time. Warramurrungundji and Indjuwanydjuwa turned themselves into rocks. Ngalyod the Rainbow Serpent still lives at the bottom of a dark pool below a waterfall. Ginga the giant crocodile became a rocky ridge that shows his knobbly back. Garrkanj the brown falcon lives on as a painting on a rock outcrop and Djuwe's spirit still resides in the great bowerbird who continues to build the shelters and to dance around them as if in a ceremony. Each year Namarrkun presages the wet season as he brings thunder and lightning. At this exact time Aldjurr, the electric blue and red Leichhardt grasshoppers which are Namarrkun's children on earth, appear in the rock country.

Dreaming Sites and Totems

The rocks, pools, paintings and other special places where the spirit ancestors of the Dreamtime now reside still contain their power and creative energy. At these sacred places, the Dreaming sites, the Gagudju can draw on this power through painting, song, dance or other rituals. To maintain the integrity of the life force the people must protect and stay in active contact with the Dreaming sites. These are crucial to the survival of all living things within Kakadu. An animal's Dreaming, a Flying Fox Dreaming, for example, contains the life essence of that species. By performing ceremonies at the site and by painting flying foxes on its rocks, the people energise the creative spirit so new flying foxes will always be 'created' and are there as a food source for the people. In this way the Gagudju are tied to nearly all the animals and plants around them.

Each Gagudju person has several totems which are his or her Dreamings. This means that some of the life essence of the Dreaming species resides in the person and has the potential to change him or her into the Dreaming animal or plant. A man might, for example, belong to the Wallaby Dreaming, in which case he is descended from the same spirit as the wallaby. Throughout his life he will have a close affinity with the marsupials. He will not hunt or eat them. Wallabies will always be close to him; they are his other self. They warn him of approaching danger, guide him to good hunting places and even tell him of distant events. And when a man of the Wallaby Dreaming paints his body with the wallaby design for a

Previous pages
Kakadu has been home to the Gagudju people for thousands of years. To ensure the continuity of the Dreamtime, ceremonies must be performed.

Far left, top
Ginga, the saltwater crocodile, was originally a man who grew the blister-like bumps on his back when he was burnt in a fire.

Far left
Aldjurr, the Leichhardt grasshopper, is one of Namarrkun, the lightning man's, children on earth.

Left
Gurri the blue-tongue lizard slipped and fell on his face on the rocks and so bruised his tongue. It is still blue to this day. © *National Geographic Society.*

Gowarrang was a woman who was struck by many small spears during a quarrel in the Dreamtime. She turned into an echidna and the spears became her quills.

ceremony, he *becomes* a wallaby. Each Gagudju person is related, in this way, to one or more of the ancestral creator beings.

The Dreamtime is thus the cohesive force that weaves all life and all parts of the environment together into a single fabric. Its force continues and is as palpable today as it was when time first began. And as long as the life force is not disrupted the fabric will not be torn. It should endure forever.

Part of Nature

Of necessity this is a somewhat simplistic account of complex concepts and traditions. Its central, all pervasive thesis, however, is not difficult to grasp. It was succinctly expressed by the Aboriginal leader Silas Roberts:

> Aboriginals have a special connection with everything that is natural. Aboriginals see themselves as part of nature. We see all things natural as part of us. All the things on Earth we see as part human. This is told through the idea of Dreaming. By Dreaming we mean the belief that long ago, these creatures started human society.
>
> These creatures, these great creatures are just as much alive today as they were in the beginning. They are everlasting and will never die. They are always part of the land and nature as we are. Our connection to all things natural is spiritual.

Bill Neidjie, a Gagudju elder, put it more poetically:

> Animals like family to us.
> Earth our mother,
> Eagle our cousin,
> Tree is pumping blood like us.
> We all one.

A full understanding of all the complexities of the Gagudju's spiritual life took a lifetime to acquire. In the past, the Gagudju absorbed this knowledge from a very young age, almost from the day they were born. From then on the themes were elaborated and reinforced throughout their lives; first in play then through song, dance, hunting and a series of initiation ceremonies. Because the beliefs and traditions are so closely tied to the land, the knowledge about the Dreamtime could only be gained in Kakadu itself. Nothing was written down so it could not and cannot be studied in books. You had to live it, feel it and be one with the earth. Only then could you understand your environment through the perceptions of the Dreamtime. This living experience of the world all around differed sharply from anything that might be learned within the confines of a classroom.

An Unbroken Tradition

For the traditional Gagudju people the bush provided all of their material and spiritual needs — from the food they gathered to the smallest brushes used in their paintings and from the spirits which guided them in their hunts to the power which maintained life on earth.

The Gagudju's depth of knowledge of their environment and their physical skills were such that they needed only a few hours each day to gather their food. And they lived well. Their standard of living in terms of food and shelter was until 100 years ago higher than those for the ordinary people of Europe. Like all Aborigines they did not spend their so-

The exact meaning of these stone arrangements has been lost over the centuries.

called leisure time in pursuing an ever more elaborate material culture. Instead they pursued matters of the human spirit, guided by the power of the Dreamtime.

This is a very ancient power that may have begun shaping human society more than 50,000 years ago. Yet the most remarkable aspect of the Gagudju's culture, and that of the Aborigines in general, is not its age, even though it is the oldest culture known to man, but its continuity. It pre-dates and outlasts all the known ancient cultures. The Dreamtime had been alive for 40,000 years by the time other cultures first settled in villages and planted their first crops. Another 5000 years elapsed before the Egyptians built their first pyramids. And while the glories of the Greek, Roman, Aztec and Inca empires remain only as broken remnants, the Dreamtime endures. Any cultures surviving into the present have a history so brief that that of the Aborigines is almost incomprehensibly ancient by comparison.

The Aborigines, including the Gagudju, are heirs to the longest unbroken culture the world has ever known. Nowhere is this ancient lineage more clearly revealed than in the Gagudju's lands; in Kakadu National Park. Though unheralded as such, Kakadu is one of the pivotal places in the prehistory of man. Kakadu's significance goes far beyond that of one of the most beautiful places on earth, or as an area that contains perhaps the most important tropical wetlands. It is the place of modern man's first beginnings.

The Gagudju's distant forebears, like Warramurrungundji, came from the sea. They are thought to have come from what is now southern China. That was more than 50,000* years ago. It was at a time of an ice age, when glaciers and great ice sheets had captured so much water that the sea level was about 150 m lower than it is today. But even at these lower sea levels Asia and Australia were never joined by a completely dry land bridge.

Several routes, island hopping through Indonesia, led to Australia. One was via New Guinea which was then joined to Australia, and the other was a more direct route from Timor to the Kimberley area of Western Australia. Whatever the route, the shortest stretch of water the new colonists would have had to cross would have been 60 km wide. This was far too long a journey to attempt casually, without any navigational skills. It was also too far for people to have landed accidentally while cast adrift clinging to a floating log. Most likely it was a deliberate journey. The early navigators, the world's first, may not even have known there was more land beyond the sea, and they certainly would not have known how far it was. The only evidence of land may have been indistinct columns of smoke from bushfires or clouds.

The first Australians are most likely to have set foot on the continent in the Kimberleys or in Arnhem Land. Whichever way they came, it would have been only a short time later that they made their first camp in Kakadu. These first landfalls are not in places visible today, as they were drowned by the subsequent rise in sea level.

If their journey from Asia had been uninterrupted by long stays in the Indonesian islands, the people, at least the older ones among them, must have come ashore full of memories of large and dangerous animals: tigers, leopards, elephants, wolves and bears. They would have recalled monkeys and deer and giant snakes and such birds as hornbills and perhaps birds of

* Archaeological findings are pushing the time of man's first entry into Australia further and further back. It may eventually be revealed that the Aborigines came to this continent 600,000 or even 100,000 years ago.

paradise. Not knowing what to expect in the new land they must have come ashore with some trepidation. But with their undoubted skills of observation and interpreting signs of life in the bush they would have been reassured very soon. Compared to mainland Asia, Australia even at the end of the Pleistocene era was a benign place. The carnivores such as the thylacine or striped marsupial wolf, Tasmanian devil and even perhaps the then still extant marsupial lion, were slow-moving and easily eluded. There may have been giant goannas that could attack people. Only the saltwater crocodile was a constant danger, as it had been in the lands they came from. The new people would have met other giant and strange animals, the diprotodon not unlike the rhinoceros they may have known, palorchestes similar to the tapir, and a host of kangaroos and wallabies of various kinds. Some of these may have stood up to 3 m tall.

The new nomads were among the earliest *Homo sapiens*, modern man. For tens of thousands of years afterwards they were also the world's most advanced people; the first navigators, inventors of the first technology and the first artists.

A History in Art

From earliest times the people of Kakadu painted on the escarpment's rock walls with red ochre. Fortunately, for us, that pigment bonded with the quartzite rock and in some cases even formed a protective skin over the paintings. They will, therefore, remain as long as the rocks do and even the very oldest images can be seen today. Their exact age is not known, but most authorities agree that the earliest paintings are at least 20,000 to 23,000 years old; some claim as much as 35,000 years old. If that is so, then Kakadu contains man's oldest art works, the records of his first artistic impulses. Even if they are not as old as 35,000 years, they are still amongst the oldest art in the world. Kakadu's paintings are unique as they are the longest unbroken succession of art in the world. They also constitute the richest, most prolific body of rock paintings anywhere.

But most remarkable of all, it is a tradition that continues into the present. No other art and no other people have such a long, clear line of succession. Only the cave art of southern France and Spain may be as old but its culture and traditions died over 10,000 years ago.

Many of Kakadu's ancient lines converge in one place. The Gagudju call it Malangangerr. In a place renowned for its grandeur Malangangerr is not imposing. It is made up of a collection of sandstone outcrops, fissured by the earth's pressures and sculpted by the wind and rain. The tallest rock is no more than 20 metres high and all of them together are about 500 metres in circumference. They are outliers from the main escarpment, a few hundred metres away. Eucalypt woodlands surround the stone blocks and irregular courtyards. Fig trees cling tenaciously to large boulders. A curtain of vines screens a cavern. On the walls are careful paintings of fish, an echidna and giant spirit ancestors. Close by are crude images of pigs, goats and a buffalo, recent animal invaders of Kakadu. In the debris on the cavern's floor are well-made stone tools, spear points and axes and the bones of animals eaten long ago. Intermingled with them are the artifacts of the technological age — beer cans, plastic bottles and corroded batteries.

In the 1960s archaeologists dug a trench through the floor of the cavern. They deduced

Right
A recent painting of an antelope kangaroo.

Far right
Antelope kangaroos are found in Kakadu's woodlands and were an important food source for the traditional Gagudju.

Left
This female figure, holding a 'magic' string between her hands, was painted to invoke powerful sorcery to influence events or perhaps a person's life.

Left
Malangangerr, the oldest continuously inhabited place on earth.

from their painstaking digging, sifting and analysing that people first occupied the cavern about 23,000 years ago. In the course of their work the archaeologists found an edge-ground stone axe 18,000 years old. The tool was also grooved to accommodate a haft. No older tools that were edge ground, rather than chipped and knapped, have been found. The oldest pigments used in paintings were also recovered from the debris. The Gagudju lived in this same cavern until the 1970s.

Malangangerr in Kakadu, must therefore be one of the most remarkable places on earth. It is the longest continuously inhabited place, and contains both the oldest technology and if not the oldest paintings, the oldest pigment used in art.

In the 1970s the Gagudju left Malangangerr and will probably not return. But their spirit is still palpably present. The ashes of their last fire still look fresh and it is not difficult to imagine the ring of their laughter, the drone of the didgeridoo and the stamping of feet in a ceremony.

The people and their view of the world also live on in countless other paintings on Kakadu's rock walls, and in its shelters and caves. More than 5000 rock art sites have so far been listed and it is expected that double that number may eventually be recorded for the whole of Kakadu, making it the richest as well as the oldest storehouse of human creativity. Hidden deep in the bush, far away from musty museum corridors, glass cases and electric lights, lies one of the artistic wonders of the world. It is one of special importance to Australia, for as the distinguished archaeologist Josephine Flood says: 'In the Aboriginal art of Kakadu, Australians have their most important artistic heritage, in terms of both aesthetic quality and relevance to the universal history of art and the human race.'

The Work of Chaloupka

The paintings are almost an embarrassment of riches for anyone trying to establish their chronology and to unravel what they tell about the people who made them. The story was pieced together, ingeniously and patiently, by George Chaloupka, curator of rock art at the Northern Territory Museum of Arts and Sciences. The fact that he himself is an artist with a long held passion for Kakadu, is perhaps the essential ingredient in his success.

For more than ten years, on innumerable field trips, Chaloupka criss-crossed the escarpment country of Kakadu and the neighbouring parts of Arnhem Land. Accompanied by an elder of the Gagudju, he recorded in detail and analysed rock paintings at 1420 sites. Chaloupka paid particular attention as to how the paintings were superimposed one upon the other, and this is how he was able to establish a chronology. The following is a summary of the story so imaginatively assembled by Chaloupka.

The earliest paintings, estimated to be about 35,000 years old, were simple prints. Prints of hands dipped in pigment and then pressed against the smooth quartzite rocks. These 'hands' were grouped in recognisable patterns. Other objects such as seeding grasses were similarly printed. These were so accurate that they can be identified as the same species of wild sorghum that now grows in Kakadu.

Some 15,000 years elapsed before the first true paintings appeared. These were large naturalistic figures of men and animals crafted with great assurance and artistry. Strangely there is no sequence of crude, stick-like figures slowly evolving into these masterful larger

Dynamic Figure Style Painting of a woman with a dilly bag. This style showed the finest detail and most imaginative treatment of subjects.

Top
Hand prints, thought to be the oldest 'art' in the world, were often arranged in patterns.

than life-size images. They were confidently executed with strong flowing lines right from the beginning. A frieze of kangaroos or a freshwater crocodile painted in this style evokes a sense of awe at the artist's skill and accuracy. There is nothing crude or primitive here.

Animals which are now no longer in Kakadu were also painted in this style. They include the thylacine and the Tasmanian devil. Both species are extinct on the Australian mainland and the thylacine may be extinct altogether. There are also paintings of animals from the Pleistocene era that have been extinct for a much longer time; Zaglossus the long-beaked echidna (which still lives in the highlands of Papua New Guinea), the strange one-toed giant kangaroo Sthenurus and perhaps the marsupial tapir, Palorchestes. Human figures were sometimes shown hunting the animals with single-pronged or triple-pronged, barbed spears.

These kinds of Large Naturalistic Figures, as Chaloupka calls them, were succeeded by four separate and distinct styles of painting. Though the styles are identifiable, there are no clues as to their ages. They appeared between the end of the Large Naturalistic Figures and the beginning of the modern style, about 7000 or 6000 years ago.

The oldest of these four styles is perhaps the most elegant and expressive of all those found in Kakadu. The small finely-drawn ochre paintings of people and animals show the subjects in vigorous action — hunting, running, leaping, dancing. Animal-headed human figures reveal the presence of a mythology involving animals. Dotted lines coming out of the mouths of animals or following the line of a thrown spear were used as indications of the non-visual aspects of the story depicted. It may show sound, force or even tension or anxiety. One of the most elegant paintings, a small composition high on a quartzite wall, tells a story. It depicts three couples who have laid down their spears, boomerangs and dilly bags and have come together in a dance. The men wear elaborate headdresses and hair belts. In other paintings the men are also seen wearing small skirts, necklaces, armlets and tassles around their legs. Most notable is the fact that the people used boomerangs, which the present-day Gagudju do not. These are all things that can never be discovered about the people from archaeological evidence alone.

Chaloupka calls this the Dynamic Figure style and says that because of its accomplished draughtsmanship and innovative story-telling conventions, it is perhaps unequalled in rock art anywhere.

The succeeding two styles, which Chaloupka called the Post Dynamic Figures and Simple Figures with Boomerangs, are of increasingly simple, stylised human figures. The decline in artistic skill and imagination may be associated with the movements or even displacement of people.

Other changes or displacements may have caused the next major change in art style — the appearance of the Yam Figures. In this style, the knobbed yam tuber, its vines and leaves, are a dominant theme. Figures of men, flying foxes, turtles and birds are all shown with yam heads. The significance of the yam symbol can, of course, now only be guessed at. Perhaps, at this time, the yam was introduced from another place, such as New Guinea, which was still connected to Australia. It is also possible that this style first appeared when sea levels began to rise and the people, having to leave their old hunting grounds, came to rely more on the yam as a food.

Paintings of Ngalyod, the Rainbow Serpent, appear for the first time during this Yam

A freshwater crocodile in the Large Naturalistic Style of painting.

Figure period. She is sometimes depicted in a simple snake form and at other times as an elaborate being having a yam-like body and a snake's head. The emergence of Ngalyod may also have coincided with the rising of the sea level.

Interestingly, of all the paintings of this style and the ones before it, those of the Rainbow Serpent are about the only ones that Aborigines of today relate to. To them Ngalyod is one of the major creator beings. She made waterholes, split rocks and fashioned ranges of hills. But unlike the other great spirit heroes she became neither a rock nor a spontaneous rock painting. She still lives in Kakadu in her original form deep within a pool and each year she brings the wet season and all the renewal of life associated with that. She also punishes people who have broken the law by drowning them in floods or swallowing them.

The Rainbow Serpent and associated paintings are the last ones before the next change in style. This change can be assigned a rough date as it coincided with a drastic change in the environment, the rising of the sea to its present level, the approximate age of which is

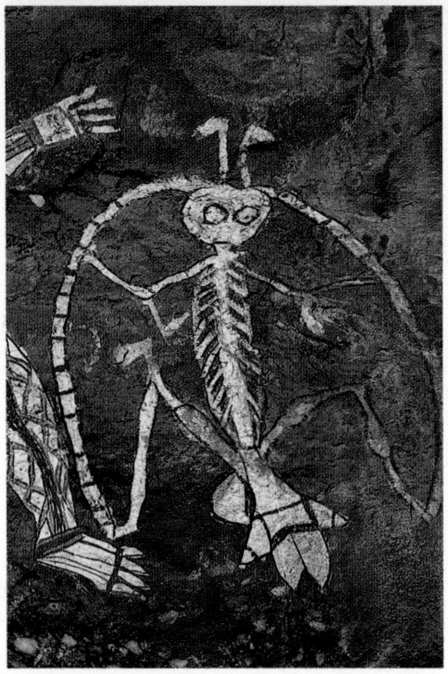

Namarrkun, the lightning man, who carries the lightning across his shoulders and strikes thunder off the clouds with stone axes attached to his knees, elbows and head.

known. Drawing on this information, Chaloupka estimates that the earliest depictions of Ngalyod were painted between 10,000 and 9000 years ago. For the traditional Gagudju of today she is still central to their rituals and beliefs, which makes the Rainbow Serpent the symbol for the longest held religious belief in the world.

Of all the other older-style paintings only those of the thylacine strike a special chord with the Gagudju. They think it was the mythical dog of the Rainbow Serpent. The remainder, from the early hand prints to the yam-headed figures, they say, were painted by the Mimi spirits. To the Gagudju these fragile rock-living beings are their spiritual progenitors, associated with the first people, who taught them how to hunt and how to paint.

Between 7000 and 6000 years ago the ice caps had melted and sea levels had risen to their present levels. In places the sea reached right to the escarpment and the people's rock shelters. Rivers meandered through the salt marshes. Kangaroos, emus, echidnas, blue-tongue lizards and other nonestuarine species had to retreat. Fish and saltwater crocodiles became more important food for the Aborigines. The climate also changed and probably became much as it is today. A most important and spectacular component of this climate is the violent thunderstorms that herald the wet season. Perhaps in response to this vivid element the Aborigines of the time painted a new spirit on the rocks — Namarrkun, who carries the lightning across his shoulders and strikes thunder off the clouds with stone axes.

The change was also reflected in the new style and subject matter of the rock paintings. The giant perch or barramundi was first painted at this time and remains a dominant subject. Mullet, catfish and saltwater crocodiles became increasingly common themes. Outstanding galleries of fish paintings in this style can be seen at Ubirr. A change of weapons was also

Left
A circular waterhole created by the Rainbow Serpent, a major creator-being, who still lives in Kakadu.

An older-style painting of the extinct thylacine (marsupial tiger or wolf) with young.

evident. The boomerang disappeared from the art and presumably was no longer in use. The spear thrower, the accessory that greatly enhanced the efficiency of their main weapon, the spear, is now evident for the first time. The spear itself changed and now was often shown as having a stone point, instead of a barbed wooden point.

More drastic even than the change in subject matter, was the change in style. Once more it was naturalistic and large, in complete contrast to the small, often tiny, stylised figures of the previous three styles. There was great artistry and fine brush work. The main innovation was that artists showed the bones and many of the internal organs of the animals and people they painted. They had created the X-ray style and from then until the present it is the dominant one. It is also unique to Kakadu and its immediate environs.

The new style was accompanied by a new technique. Instead of painting with liquid ochre in lines and dots, the figures were now first laid down in white clay, which was applied as a thin paste. Then the details were painted in, in red, yellow or even black patterns that included extremely fine cross-hatchings. But unlike the red ochre the clay paste does not penetrate the rock nor does it bond with it. In time it will flake off.

The next and last change in the environment began as recently as 1500 years ago when the clayey salt marshes slowly changed to freshwater habitats: paperbark swamps, shallow floodplains and billabongs. Waterlilies and lotuses, pied geese and whistle ducks and a whole host of other plants and animals multiplied in vast numbers in these new habitats. They created the most productive environment during Kakadu's entire human occupation. The new wealth is painted in the form of geese and ducks and lithe hunters carrying goose-wing fans and bundles of light spears especially made to bring down waterfowl. Other paintings

A large goanna, almost life size, with below it a line of storks with fish in their beaks.

X-ray paintings at Ubirr.

A gallery with paintings of pregnant women.

show women setting out on log rafts to collect the eggs of geese on the marshes. For the first time didgeridoos appear in paintings.

The Art of Change

The subject matter of the paintings changed one more time, and it is the most disturbing change as it may well foreshadow the last days of the world's oldest culture. Pictures, the earliest dating back to about 150 years, were painted of an alien, more aggressive culture — sailing ships, people on horseback, a railroad and latterly even an aeroplane. New weapons were recorded — guns, rifles, steel daggers and tomahawks; also new animals — buffaloes, pigs, goats and horses. One of the last paintings of the new invaders is of a man in western dress standing at ease. The Gagudju elders, who have witnessed most of the changes that have overtaken their culture, say of this painting, 'and soon these white Europeans, standing with hands in pockets, told us what to do'. It was, and still is, inexplicable to these traditional Gagudju that the Dreamtime, the life force, the rock art, the land itself meant less than nothing to these invaders. Their astonishment was similar to that of the native Americans at their invaders, who only wanted gold and spurned the important things — the flowers, the fruits and the animal life.

The last major rock art was painted in 1964 by a man called Najombolmi of the Badmardi clan. For a large part of his life he worked for white people on cattle stations. In a last effort to draw on the power of the Dreamtime he returned to his country, to a place called

Above
A freshwater crayfish.

Anbangbang at Nourlangie Rock. There he repainted a traditional frieze on an outcrop of conglomerate sandstone. The main figure is a large painting of the dangerous spirit Namandjolg. Beside him is Nammarkun the lightning man. Below them is Nammarkun's wife and a procession of men and women going to a ceremony. It is the finest known work of one of the last great rock artists.

His attempt to invoke the Dreamtime was to no avail. Najombolmi died a year later. No more major works were painted on rocks and nowadays painting is restricted to bark.

Perhaps the greatest of Kakadu's galleries is Yuwenjgayay. The gallery is like a single gigantic 'canvas' 70 m long and is crowded with images of men, animals and spirits. This grand sweep of paintings is protected from the elements by the slight overhang of a 180 m high cliff. At one end is a side panel that juts out at right angles to the gallery. Where the two join, water seeps out of a crack in the rock and collects in a tiny pool. The water nourishes a growth of green ferns and a bushy rainforest tree. Honeyeaters and greenwing pigeons come to drink here. Out of the ferns facing the main gallery rises the most imposing painting of all — the mythological bird Djawok whose spirit resides in the koel. The main gallery is smooth rock covered to a height of more than 2 m with layer upon layer of paintings. Some of Najombolmi's work is here also, a perfect barramundi and female figures with dilly bags. A school of small freshwater fish in an undulating composition may also be his. Another artist painted an antelope kangaroo, larger than life-size, being speared with a stone-tipped weapon. Beside it, is one of the first pictures of a white man. Above this is a procession of three echidnas, a man playing a didgeridoo, and staring over the back of a kangaroo is Namarrkun. Cranes dance, kangaroos leap, goannas slither, fish swim, and people prance in what appears to be just one gigantic painting. The power of the Dreamtime seems almost tangible.

Above left
With the coming of Balanda, the subject matter of the rock paintings changed, as is shown in this stencil of a steel tomahawk.

Above
The Balanda invaded the Gagudju lands on horseback.

Above right
This frieze of spirit figures and men and women painted in 1964, was the last major rock painting in Kakadu.

Right
The gallery at Yuwenjgayay.

Above
A school of archer fish at Yuwenjgayay.

Right
Bluey Ilkirr painting a wallaroo.

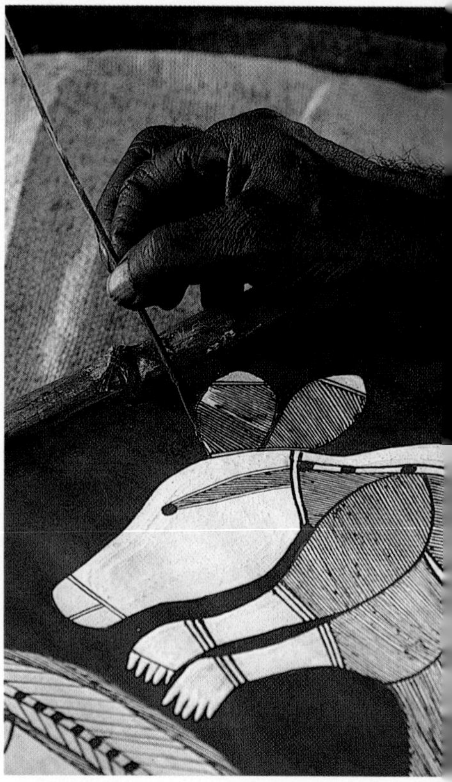

Details from the gallery at Yuwenjgayay. Female figures and fish. Above the women is a painting of a man playing the didgeridoo.

Above right
The painting tradition continues in Kakadu. Now painting is only done on bark. Bluey Ilkirr, who lives in Kakadu, with one of his paintings.

George Chaloupka sums up the immense historical importance of the extensive rock paintings as follows:

> . . . the rock art of Kakadu forms perhaps the oldest and the most significant expressions of human creativity . . . The rock paintings represent the world's longest continuing tradition of this art form, and consisting from its very beginning of naturalistic and narrative images, it forms the longest historical record of any group of people. It is a record of an encyclopaedic magnitude . . .

The paintings also have great spiritual significance which culminates in the perceptions of the Dreamtime, by the tenets of which humans can live in harmony with the world around them for all time.

The knowledge about the rock paintings and other aspects of the prehistory and history of Kakadu described here, were arrived at through European man's ingenuity, diligence and insights. To the Gagudju and their Aboriginal neighbours there is another, a mystical, truth here, one based on age-old beliefs, laws, symbolism and a different perception of life. The two are not entirely incompatible.

Many of the Aborigines' insights are inaccessible to non-Aborigines, or more accurately to non-initiates, which increasingly includes many Aboriginal people as well. These are the ceremonies, stories and knowledge that is secret and can be revealed to initiated persons only. As we shall see later there is a real possibility that the Gagudju's wisdom cannot be passed on and may be lost forever, as it has already been for many other Aboriginal groups. But before we meet the Gagudju, heirs to the longest unbroken culture, let us look at Kakadu's living environment, the plants, the animals, the land and the seasons.

3 ~ SEASONS

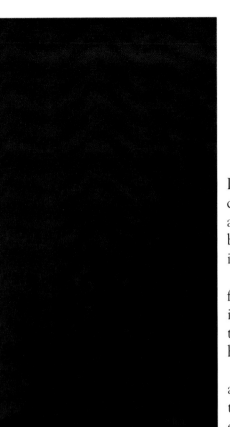

In Kakadu's seasonal cycle there are two periods when the elements seem to pause, to catch their breath before rushing on again. One occurs in May when the rains have ended and the dry season has not yet enforced its austerity. The other is in late September just before nature's forces slowly rouse themselves for the onslaught of the wet season. These interludes separate Kakadu's two distinct faces.

May's interlude is the more pleasant. It is during a time of profusion and plenty. Apart from the tall grasses, whose lives have run their course and have turned brown, the country is still lush. Flowers and fruits are plentiful. Marshes and other wetlands have not yet begun to dry and life there is teeming. Nights are cool and the days no longer stingingly hot and humid.

The dry season now sets in. The pattern of lower temperatures continues through June and July. The maximum may still rise to 30°C, but only for a short period. At night the temperature often goes down to 17°C and sometimes, in places close to the escarpment, even to 10°C.

August and September see a gradual rise in temperature to 35°C in the day and 21°C at night. These five months, from May to September, are virtually rainless. There may be occasional showers at the beginning and end of the period but during June, July and August there are very few records of any rain. The sun shines day after day and with the increasing temperatures, steadily robs Kakadu of its moisture.

By the end of September it is bleak. In the escarpment only a few springs still run and nearly all streams have ceased to flow. Water remains only in the deepest pools and larger rivers. Plants growing on exposed rocks die back. Only those trees and shrubs whose roots reach the moisture deep in the escarpment's crevices, are still green. The plateau shimmers with heat. Rocks crack. The animals retreat to narrow shady ravines where it remains cool.

The woodlands lie parched under the relentless sun. The grasses that escaped the fires have collapsed into tinder dry mats. The annuals have shrivelled. Many trees have shed their leaves and are dormant. There is little shade. Birds sit panting. Wallabies and wallaroos rest in what shade they can find along water courses where the tree cover is denser.

Great cracks open up in the soil of the drying floodplains. What little water remains in shallow depressions becomes too hot to sustain life. Only the deeper water of the billabongs remains as a refuge for fish, crocodiles, waterbirds and all the other aquatic species.

Life has retreated and holds its breath. October is hotter still and becomes ever more uncomfortable as the humidity begins to rise. In the woodlands certain trees seem to sense the approaching change. In all this heat the syzygium trees, the wild plums and apples, and

Previous pages
Lightning flashes over the floodplains during the season of thunder storms, in late October and November.

Huge monsoon clouds build up between January and March.

the ironwoods put out new leaves and begin to flower, the tender new shoots incongruous in the dry harshness. The trees anticipate that the build up of heat, the increased atmospheric moisture and the local breezes will soon conspire to end the drought.

One afternoon in mid-October giant clouds build up over the plains and along the escarpment, burgeoning and billowing as they mushroom 10,000 m over Kakadu. At first the clouds are pure, radiant white but as they blot out the setting sun they turn a purple-black. In the near-darkness lightning dances across the cloud tops, snakes from one formation to another and spears straight down to the earth. The whole system hisses, crackles and rumbles, unleashing unimaginable forces. Trees are shattered, rocks split. Finally, after a short eerie quiet, a gale-force wind springs up followed by heavy rain. The turbulence is soon over and the sun reappears briefly to sparkle on wet leaves and grass. The land was so parched that there is little or no runoff; the first rain disappears as if soaked up by a gigantic sponge. But the wonderful smell of rain and the promise of new life permeates the bush.

For a month or more spectacular storms stalk Kakadu almost daily. This part of Australia has one of the highest levels of thunderstorm activity in the world.

The storms break the drought; the land is green again. Frogs rejoice and their calls carry far and wide. But the rain, while heavy, is erratic and usually brief. Streams do not yet flow.

November and December are the most trying months. The temperature rises to 37°C, on some days even to 42°C, and the humidity becomes increasingly oppressive. Storms become less frequent. They are only the dramatic overture to the main wet season, the monsoon.

North Australia's monsoon is part of a gigantic weather system, perhaps the largest and most influential in the world. The monsoon, from the Arabic *mausim* meaning 'a season', is an immense heat transfer machine whose winds and currents distribute moisture as well as heat over huge areas of the globe. Without it, vast areas, particularly in Asia, would become either too hot or too cold for life to exist. Monsoon winds blow over parts of Africa and Mexico and may even reach the Arctic. But its main forces flow back and forth between India and the Far East and northern Australia, moving heat and moisture between the oceans and the landmasses.

During the hot season, the 'summer', the land in the monsoon regions heats up quickly, far more rapidly than the seas where currents and upwellings constantly bring cooling influences. The difference in temperature over land and sea creates differences in air pressures, and this sets winds in motion. Moisture-laden air from the sea blows over the hot landmass where the heat forces it to rise. As it rises, the air cools and drops its moisture. Steady rain falls. The rising air makes room for a further inrush of moist winds from the sea and so a cycle is begun that brings soaking rain for days on end.

In Kakadu, monsoon rains, borne on north-west winds, alternate with periods of steamy sunshine from late December or early January until the end of March. The rains set the streams flowing, encourage almost reckless growth in the plants, bring hordes of breeding insects and make the frogs sing. Rain is sometimes so heavy that rivers cannot contain the runoff, they spill over their banks and create solid sheets of water out on the floodplains.

Floods, however, are more often brought by the most violent element in this time of violent weather — the tropical cyclone. These fierce, massive storms are the most powerful of all the climatic forces. In Kakadu they may occur any time between November and May

Paperbark swamp flooded by monsoon rain.

but they are totally unpredictable. Some years two or even three invade the National Park and in other years there may be none.

Cyclones are born in warm tropical seas when moist air rises and causes water vapour to change to water droplets. The change generates immense amounts of energy in rotating, twisting winds of frightful strength. There are records of winds reaching speeds close to 400 km per hour, though in Australia the highest recorded cyclonic wind was 205 km per hour. As soon as they reach the land, however, cyclones lose much of their fury and degenerate into tropical depressions. Kakadu is rarely exposed to the full force of cyclonic winds (unlike the nearby city of Darwin which in December 1974 was virtually destroyed by cyclone Tracy) but is often lashed by their full measure of rain: even 300 mm in twenty-four hours.

April sees the winds turn back to the south-east. The monsoon loses its strength and travels north again across the equator. Plant growth tapers off. Grasses have seeded and die back. Their dead stems collapse or are blown down by the last storms of the season appropriately called the 'knock-em-downs'.

Storms, monsoons, cyclones — all are highly variable in their intensities and rainfall

As Kakadu dries out in September, trees in the paperbark swamps are left stranded on their pedestals.

fluctuates greatly from year to year. It may be as much as 2500 mm or as little as 900 mm, but on average Kakadu receives 1500 mm of rain annually. Most of it falls in January, February and March and virtually none at all between May and October.

The wet and dry seasons give Kakadu two distinct aspects. One is steamy and full of energy in a landscape of brimming marshes, strongly flowing rivers and green forests. The other is dry, brown and austere with dusty plains, water courses reduced to a series of pools, and forests of stark, often leafless, trees. It is the long dry season which limits the animal and especially the plant life. It is the dry, for example, which determines that Kakadu is clothed in eucalypt woodland and not rainforest.

How the plants and animals have adapted to the climate, the land and each other is the subject of the following chapters.

The Gagudju people perceive greater subtleties in the seasonal cycle than are described here. They recognise six distinct seasons. Their view and how their lives are influenced by the seasons are examined in Chapter 7.

4 ~ FLOODPLAINS AND BILLABONGS

RAIN DRUMS ON THE ESCARPMENT'S ROCKS, splatters on the leaves of forest trees, hisses into the waters of rivers and billabongs, and whispers on the grasses of the floodplain. Birds huddle quietly in sheltered places, mammals, snakes and lizards hide in tree hollows or caverns, but the frogs sing.

Low grey clouds roll slowly in from the north-west and swathe the escarpment's higher ramparts. Detached swirls of mist drift over the tree tops. It is a wet monochrome brought by a rain depression spawned by a spent cyclone. For three days and nights the rain pours vertically down. It is early March and the already saturated ground and sodden sandstone plateau have long since absorbed all the rainfall they can hold. Water cascades down the escarpment's smallest runnels, themselves gouged by aeons of rain, and gathers into wider gullies which rush into deeper streams. Roaring and thrashing through ravines, creeks join creeks which eventually become a river that races towards the sea. Here and there streams hurl themselves over the edge of the plateau in spuming waterfalls.

When the East Alligator River spouts out of the escarpment, it suddenly broadens, flooding the weeping paperbarks on its bank. It no longer roars but courses silently on. Giant trees, undermined and then toppled by the constant rain, speed along on the current. On the fringes, near the banks, there is little force in the river but the water inches visibly up the paperbarks. Downstream the monsoon forests are flooded. Rainbow pittas and scrubfowl must perch in the trees until the water recedes.

Beyond the monsoon forest, the East Alligator hastens onto the floodplain. For two days the levees manage the growing volume of runoff. But the relentless rain eventually defeats the raised banks. On the third day, low-lying parts of the levees, about a metre above the level of the floodplain, are breached. Water pours out on the broad, green expanse. Grasshoppers, ants, spiders, beetles and myriads of other insects, already driven from the black soil itself, climb up the grasses and sedges. Dusky rats, planigales (Kakadu's tiniest mammals), goannas, skinks, king brown snakes, slatey-grey snakes climb the higher tussocks. But the water continues to rise, drowning first the smaller plants. The animals swim, stumble or slither towards higher ground. The lucky ones find floating debris and cling to these rafts. Even the crakes and rails, marsh birds that revel in the dampness and dense grasses, must evacuate to higher ground.

After the Rain

At the end of the third day of rain, when the skies are lighter and the rain eases to a drizzle, all terrestrial life has left the floodplain. The branches of the small trees and shrubs

Right
A praying mantis seeks refuge from the floodwaters.

Far right
The escarpment is shrouded by monsoon rain and cloud.

on the levee banks are crowded with insects and spiders, lizards and snakes, birds and mammals. Dusky rats sit beside their mortal enemies, the king brown snakes; tree frogs squat immobile beside goannas. Only the water pythons, who are perfectly at ease in the flooded environment, do not observe the truce; they gobble up as many rats and planigales as they can get hold of.

When the evening slowly dissolves into darkness, the floodplains are filled; the bed of the East Alligator discernible only by the line of trees on the levee banks and the strong flow of water. Where a day ago there had been a green marsh, now there is a featureless, silent sheet of water. But where the brown floodwaters lap the edges of the woodland, in a grassy transitional area between the two habitats, male frogs call with an ardour that rends the evening air.

All night the flooded forest edge pulsates with the voices of the frogs; rocket frogs quack excitedly in several keys, dwarf tree frogs wheeze like squeaky gates, putty-coloured tree frogs give forth a rapid-fire 'eck, eck, eck', tiny red tree frogs croak in measured tones while the northern water-holding frogs call in melodious honks. Other species join in with bleating, squeaking, plonking, hooting and rasping voices. Each species has its own specific call and its own particular calling place relative to the water. Some give voice from floating vegetation, some from muddy shelters beneath grass tussocks, while others sit on leaves overhanging a pond or prefer to float out in the open. This is an essential strategy to ensure that females will approach only males of their own species. Unerringly the females find their mates. How they can find them in this incessant, ear-shattering chorus is an amazing feat of discernment.

As soon as the female reaches a male of her own species, he stops his song. He embraces her and stays tightly clasped to her back till egg-laying is complete. More than one male may attempt to clasp the same female. A kicking, pushing and shoving duel will then determine the winner of her favours. Occasionally females are in short supply, then so many males may cling to a single individual that she becomes overwhelmed and may drown.

Previous pages
The middle reaches of the East Alligator River during a flood.

The females, depending on the species, deposit their eggs in strings attached to grass

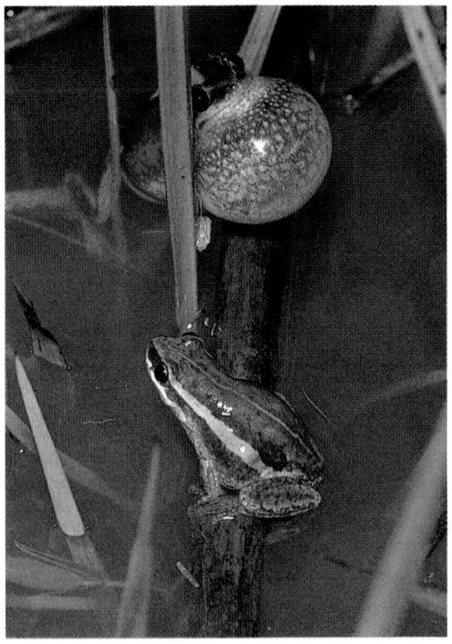

Above
A red tree frog calls from a grass blade projecting from the floodwaters. The male's ballooning vocal sac at his throat acts as an ampliflier for his voice. © National Geographic Society.

Above right
Out on the floodplain only the tops of the trees remain above water and are the sole refuges for the terrestrial animals. A water python takes the opportunity to seize a planigale, a tiny marsupial mouse.

blades, in masses of froth they whip up, or in jelly-like clumps. As the eggs are laid, the male fertilises them. Mosquitoes, seeking food so that they can lay their own eggs, suck the frogs' blood, but they are mere irritations and easily swept away. Their real enemies are the freshwater and slatey-grey snakes. Wherever these slide through the grasses or swim sinuously in open water, frogs fall silent and leap away. But such is their frenzy for song, that as soon as the snake hides silently in a grass tussock, frogs reappear almost immediately to resume their concert. They are easy prey and the snakes are bulging.

One of their own kind, the large northern water-holding frog, is also a major predator. It tracks down smaller species by their calls then engulfs them with its huge mouth and swallows them whole. Sometimes it attacks larger frogs and a desperate struggle ensues with the victim crying out pitiously.

At first light, the sky still grey and glowering, but without rain, the chorus trails off into a few desultory honks and croaks. Even these soon stop as the birds burst into song on their first rainless morning after the deluge. Aerial hunters fly out over the sheet of floodwater that stretches from Ubirr to the sea. Kites harass stranded animals hiding under leaves and branches, trying to frighten them into careless moves. They catch their share of grasshoppers, lizards and small mammals. White-breasted sea-eagles circle overhead in slow spirals, on the alert for anything that the floodwaters may have exposed for them.

Pairs of whistling ducks and Burdekin ducks, who had led their young onto the grassy plains, are now swimming in vulnerable and anxious flotillas in the open water. They swim towards the protection of the fringing woodlands. Saltwater crocodiles, which have left the river channel, cruise the brown waters, trailing the families of ducks. Time and again, in a swirl of water, they take a duckling. Whole families of young are wiped out.

The trials of the refugees of the floodplain do not last long. The day after the rain stops, the levee banks emerge from the water, and the East Alligator is once more contained in its meandering channel. For another day the floodplain's water level continues to drop until an equilibrium is reached. Once more the plains are an intense green. Displaced animals rush back to their homes.

The flood brought problems to a group of birds nesting in a mangrove forest near the river's mouth. Until then the birds had easy pickings in the limitless marshes. They caught the abundant fingerling fish, frogs and grasshoppers and fed them to their young. Their pure white forms could be seen standing all over the plains. These are the egrets — the cattle, the little, the plumed and the great, now nesting in colonies on Kakadu's major rivers.

Rain and flood had not threatened their nests, for they are built five or more metres up in the trees. There were no hard winds to blow any nests down and the adults' waterproof plumage kept the eggs and young warm and dry. But the constant rain had made hunting difficult and drowned most of their feeding grounds. However, enough insects and frogs could be snatched from the floodwaters to keep the young alive.

Now that the sedges and grasses have re-emerged and the sun is out once more, the colony is bustling with energy. Young beg noisily for food, adults returning to their nests greet their partners, pairs court and individuals fight over nest materials.

Out on the floodplain a plumed egret spears one last frog, filling her gullet almost to bursting. She now rises into the air and on slow wing beats follows the river to a dark green forest near its estuary. At a place where the foliage is speckled with white birds she descends. With long legs dangling, toes spread, the egret parachutes down to the colony. She lands gently in the top of a tall tree and shakes her feathers. Although courtship took place about a month ago, she still has the full complement of nuptial plumes on her chest and back. But the blue-green and red courting colours of her beak and face have faded to pale yellow.

Her nest, an untidy platform of sticks, is hidden from view lower in the trees. To reach it she must clamber through the branches and run the gauntlet of thrusting beaks and guttural threats of the birds whose nesting territories she must cross. As long as she does not pause she is threatened but not attacked.

She reaches her nest in a flurry of white feathers. The male, on the nest guarding the four young, forgets his offspring as he sees his mate approaching. With eyes only for each other, they touch beaks, their crown feathers raised. Briefly they intertwine their long slender necks, then spread their lacy plumes.

In this rush of emotion the young are forgotten, but they soon make their presence felt. Stabbing at their mother's beak they try to induce her to regurgitate the food she has brought. The spell is broken and the pair fold their veils. They make quiet gurgling sounds to each other, adjust a few sticks in the nest and then the male departs. Soon the female lowers her beak and with a few convulsive movements deposits a mass of fish and frogs onto the nest. Jostling one another with their puny wingstubs the hungry young soon gobble up everything. Within minutes all is devoured and the young collapse in a sleepy pyramid. Dapples of sunlight reach the nest and the female, panting with open beak, spreads her wings to protect the chicks from the heat. Intermittently she preens. Her finery is beginning to moult and a few feathers float down and land gently on the mud.

The large colony, which includes many pairs of three other species of egret as well as pied herons and cormorants, is a busy place and a ceaseless discord of throaty cackles, hoarse grunts, rumbling gurgles and guttural croaks; an unworthy accompaniment to so much elegance and immaculate plumage.

Twice a day the nesting colony's debris of empty eggshells, fallen feathers and droppings is

A pair of plumed egrets greet each other at their nest in a mangrove tree. © *National Geographic Society.*

swept away by the tide. Every new low tide brings a pristine carpet of soft grey mud. Slipping and sliding through the sticky mire, a large mangrove goanna enters the colony; he is the resident predator and one the birds are helpless to deter. As the black reptile, finely spotted with yellow, moves about, the birds raise their feathers and call in alarm and outrage. The 120 cm long reptile ignores them. Climbing a small mangrove tree he robs several nests of their eggs. He breaks them in his mouth, the yolks and eggwhite dripping down his jaws.

A muddy channel drains through the colony. In it lies a large crocodile, left stranded by the tide. She too feeds on the breeding colony, but as a scavenger picking up birds that fall out of the nests and inexperienced youngsters unwise enough to walk about on the mud.

Life on the Floodplain

Saltwater crocodiles have been nesting along the East Alligator since last November's storms. Some clutches have hatched, the young now dispersed by the flood. Nests built more recently have drowned, spoiling the eggs. A considerable number of females have not yet

Turkey Dreaming, on the East Alligator River, where saltwater crocodiles nest.

nested, but are ready to do so now that the floodwaters are receding. If there are no further floods, which is not at all certain, they will have the best chance of seeing their eggs hatch successfully.

Well out on the floodplain, on the East Alligator's eastern bank, is a place the Gagudju people call Imagirrk or Turkey Dreaming. It is the place of the life essence of the plains turkey or bustard. A lone sandstone outcrop left stranded far out on the plain, it rises sheer to a height of about sixty metres. The rock is an island roughly oval in shape and about six kilometres in circumference. Flooded ravines and bays facing the river are overgrown with mangroves. On higher ground dark monsoon forest draped with vines, hugs the rock wall. Through accidents of soil and terrain the canopy is broken here and there allowing the sun to penetrate to a ground cover of grasses and herbs. These sunny, marshy places close to the rock are sought out by the gravid crocodiles.

About a week after the flood has receded several female crocodiles make their way to the base of the cliff on the high tide. For several days each female scrapes and pushes at the grass and other ground vegetation until she has constructed a mound about a metre in height. In her digging she excavates a moat around the mound and a small pool to one side. Before long she will lay between fifty and sixty eggs in a depression on top of her nest. She then covers them, building her mound up into a cone.

Lying in the pool beside the nest, she will guard her eggs until they hatch in about three months' time. The exact time depends on the temperature inside the nest. The crocodiles do not regulate the nest temperature at all. It is done entirely by the sun and the heat generated

Pied geese feed and nest on the floodplains.

by the decaying vegetation in their nests. The optimum incubation temperature is probably about 30°C; if it goes much above or below that many hatchlings will be deformed; their jaws may be misaligned, their tails twisted or they may have spinal deformities.

The nests at Turkey Dreaming, of which a dozen are eventually constructed, are all within 50 m of the river. Each female has a clear and direct channel to the deep water as an escape route, but also simply as an easy access to her feeding place. Most of the time, however, the females spend lying beside or even on top of their nests. Should a marauding goanna or feral pig be so bold as to approach a nest, the crocodile will attack with great force and determination. Very, very few saltwater crocodile eggs are taken from the nest. The greatest destruction of eggs is caused by flooding; as many as three-quarters of the eggs laid are drowned.

Yet if floods do not eventuate, as happens in some years, the early eggs have a distinct advantage for they incubate during the warmer time of year. The eggs laid now, after the March floods, have an incubation period that includes the cool season. Cooler temperature may extend the incubation time by a month and result in many deformities among the hatchlings. Also the sex of the hatchlings is determined by temperature and temperature fluctuation, so the more varied the incubation conditions, the more likely it is that there will be a balanced number of males and females.

The young announce their readiness to hatch some days before they actually break through the shells by surprisingly loud quacking sounds. It is the signal for the female to open the nest and let the young out. One by one they hatch and then slither into the moat and the pool made by their mother. For two months she will stay with the hatchlings before leaving them to their own devices.

But that is looking five to six months ahead. Now, still only a short time after the flood, the riverplains from the East Alligator to the Wildman Rivers are inundated to a depth of 1–3 m. The spikerush and the wild rice are putting on prodigious growth. They are flowering and will soon set seed. They have attracted hundreds of thousands of pied geese to their vast nesting colonies. The largest colonies are on the South Alligator River floodplain, which with the virtual elimination of the water buffalo and the subsequent resurgence of the wild rice, is now once again the greatest stronghold of this strange and primitive goose. Years ago the largest nesting colonies were to the west of Kakadu along the Finniss and Daly Rivers. One of them, on the Daly River, covered a 42 sq km area. But closer settlement and hunting pressures have reduced the numbers there.

Before the flood the geese fed out in the swamps and flew to the surrounding paperbarks in the evening to roost in the trees' crowns. The huge, closely packed feeding groups now split up into their component families. Loose flocks of twenty to fifty birds, instead of flying to their roosts, wing their way from the East Alligator and other floodplains to Goose Camp on the South Alligator. They land out in the marsh where they build small mounds by bending over and trampling the sedges. At nightfall each goose is asleep on its own small mound.

Pied geese mate for life. Each male has either one or two females. At Goose Camp each pair or trio, with last year's young still in attendance, sets up its own territory. The male defends this space forcefully. Whenever another goose approaches he raises himself to his full height, neck stretched, and sleeks down his feathers. He stares directly at the intruder to discourage him from coming any nearer. If this warning is not heeded, the defending male walks purposefully at his adversary — who usually retreats at this point. If not, there is no alternative but to fight. Powerful wings flailing, strong claws gouging, the battle rages back and forth. Feathers fly. But territorial possession is nine parts of the law and residents are rarely ousted.

As time goes on the male geese become more and more aggressive, even towards their own offspring which they eventually drive away.

Every evening, the birds make new roosting platforms. These become increasingly more substantial and soon resemble nests. But still they are only used once. Then one morning the female goose will lay an egg on her platform. It is now rapidly built up into a large and solid nest with a cup-shaped depression at its centre. The nest is made entirely of sedges, no downy lining is added.

If there are two females at a nest each will lay a large glossy, whitish egg on alternate days until there are about ten in the nest. Both males and females take part in caring for the eggs. Actual incubation is necessary only in the cool of the night and mornings and evenings. During the day there are periods when the eggs must actually be cooled. The temperature, out on the plain, in the full sun, may reach 50°C. Even a short exposure to such fierce heat would kill the embryo.

Within weeks of the birds' first arrival, the plain is dotted with the black and white geese standing on their nest mounds. Nests are about three to five metres apart. The hundreds of thousands of eggs now lying out on the plains are irresistible to a whole host of nest robbers.

Male geese, particularly, are valiant in the defence of their nests, lashing out at kites and eagles, pythons and goannas, and even crocodiles. But the marauders are too persistent, too cunning and too numerous to keep at bay. While a goose tries to drive off one kite hovering centimetres above its head, another has quickly stolen an egg. Large sand goannas, half slithering over the vegetation, half swimming, boldly confront the birds on the nest, even whipping them with their long tails. The reptiles wear the geese down to exhaustion and then almost pushing them off the nest devour the eggs. Thick, heavy water pythons up to 4 m long also intimidate the adults and then steal their eggs. About two-thirds of the colony's eggs are taken by predators.

What eggs remain hatch after about twenty-four days into cinnamon and brown puff balls with wine red legs and beaks. Goslings are as attractive to the nest robbers as eggs, and they also need the adults' active protection. But the young are very quick and hide amongst the grasses. They are not such easy targets. Their parents guide the goslings solicitously to the wild rice plants and bend the stems down for them so they can eat the seeds. The young birds soon discover that grasshoppers are also good to eat and chase helter skelter after them.

The food is rich and plentiful after the flood and the goslings grow rapidly. In years when there is no flooding and little wet season rain, many young perish as they exhaust the marsh's food supply before they can fly to greener pastures.

Floodplain and Paperbark

Magela Creek, during the wet season, captures vast quantities of runoff in the escarpment and carries it northwards almost parallel to the East Alligator River. But unlike the East Alligator its waters are not contained in a well-defined channel, especially in its lower reaches. Soon after leaving the higher ground of the eucalypt woodlands, the creek becomes a series of billabongs joined by paperbark swamps. Beyond that its waters diffuse onto a wide floodplain which eventually joins the East Alligator. Quite early in the dry season, Magela Creek ceases to flow, but its billabongs never dry up.

Where the Magela's waters emerge out of the paperbark swamps and spread out over the floodplains is a very special place the Aborigines call Djarrdjarr. On three sides the plain is bordered by tall, straight paperbark trees with dark green, weeping foliage. To the north is the spaciousness of the open plain and close by, to the east, standing tall and benevolent is Djawumbu, an 8 km long outlier of the escarpment. Central to Djarrdjarr is a long narrow billabong sparsely fringed on one side by freshwater mangroves and by a grove of tall paperbarks at its northern tip. Standing here and there in the floodplain are other isolated paperbarks. In the tallest, most solid of these is the bulky stick nest of a pair of white-breasted sea-eagles. They preside over these wetlands.

Late May, when the first families of pied geese come from their nesting grounds to feed here, and the sea-eagles begin to renovate their nest, is the time when Djarrdjarr is at its most splendid.

Early one morning when the sun slants low over the escarpment, the male eagle takes off from his roosting perch and flying low over the crown of a paperbark, breaks off a green twig with his talons which he then carries to the female on the nest. She takes it from him in her beak and places it in the depression in the centre of the huge pile of sticks. She is in a state

A white-breasted sea-eagle brings fresh green leaves to the nest in a paperbark tree.

Top
On the floodplain, only the tops of the trees remain above water when the East Alligator River bursts its banks.

of some excitement and calls loudly. The male joins in a strident duet that carries far over the plain. She crouches low over the nest, her sharp talons folded in, and takes great care not to damage the white egg she has just laid; the first of the clutch of two.

Below their eyrie the floodplain sparkles in the fresh new day. The pale blue, almost white, waterlilies open to the sun and spread their sweet scent on the breeze. Large solitary bees hurry from flower to flower, stumbling awkwardly amongst the yellow stamens as they gather the nectar. Small groups of sleek green pygmy geese strip the seeds from aquatic plants. Turtles clamber onto the bole of an upturned tree to bask and keep a wary eye on a crocodile slowly swimming past. Cormorants and a darter diving after fish, however, are oblivious of the crocodile's approach. The 3 m long reptile slowly submerges and comes to rest at the periphery of the fishing pool, for all the world another immobile log in a marsh full of them. Fish like to hide in the tangles of logs and the birds to chase them there. The submerged, motionless crocodile is invisible and goes unnoticed by the darter twisting and turning in pursuit of a school of eel-tailed catfish. The fish dash past the crocodile, but their pursuer is trapped in his ambush. In a lightning quick snap of the jaws the crocodile seizes the bird. Rising to the surface the victim struggles briefly, sending sprays of water in all directions with its frantically beating wings, but soon it is crushed.

'Peep, peep, peep', with piercing cries a male lotusbird rises from his floating nest only a few metres away. In wild agitation he hovers over the crocodile's head, but the reptile soon takes his victim underwater. The lotusbird is not immediately reassured and flies to a patch of waterlilies still voicing his alarm. His outsize toes allow him to spread his weight over a large area; even the least amount of vegetation supports him and stops him from sinking. Judging the threat to have passed the bird walks back to his nest in long strides, at times appearing to walk on the water. The fleshy comb on his head is brilliant scarlet, an indication that his agitation has not completely subsided.

The four exquisitely marked eggs, as though written on by a master calligrapher, are

Left
A male lotusbird guards the eggs in his floating nest. The eggs are thought to be the most beautiful of any Australian bird.

Right
A darter calls from his perch in a billabong.

Far right
Flocks of plumed whistling ducks gather on the floodplain.

pipping. Perhaps calmed, or wishing to be less conspicuous to predators, the colour drains from the male's comb, as he lowers himself onto the eggs. He scoops them under his body with his wings, lifting the eggs from the cool damp surface of the nest. For more than three weeks the male has guarded and incubated the eggs, sitting beneath waterlily flowers towering over him on long stems. Earlier the slightly larger female had courted him. Not long after mating she had laid an egg in his nest on four consecutive mornings. She then moved on to court another male in an adjoining territory. The female takes no part in the care of eggs or young.

In the space of a few hours the young lotusbirds hatch. To begin with, the male pulls the empty egg shells under himself, still wanting to incubate them. But when the second chick hatches, he seems to accept the new situation. He carries the shells away and dumps them. The sun and slight breeze soon dry the chicks into tiny scraps of down with giant feet. After only a few hours they are able to walk on the floating plants, chase barely visible insects and peck at lily stems. Their father talks to them constantly in what must be a reassuring undertone. But as soon as he suspects any danger, he peeps loudly and the young squat down and freeze immediately.

The male is anxious to move his brood to a less open place. With soft cheeps he calls the young to him, bends down low and half opens his wings. The tiny chicks unhesitatingly push their heads and bodies under his wings, two on each side, and stand still. Closing his wings, the male stands up and carries the young to a safer place. Four pairs of legs dangle from under his wings.

While the young lotusbirds are hatching, flock upon flock of wandering whistling ducks land on a nearby expanse of water. Twenty, thirty at a time they come, calling in high-pitched whistles. With black legs dangling, their webbed feet looking like heavy boots, they drop into the middle of the growing raft. Now the twittering, diving, splashing, jostling and quarrelling melee is about 5000 strong, as they dive for stems and roots of aquatic plants.

A white-breasted sea-eagle has dragged a barramundi out of the water and tears it open with her powerful beak.

Far right
A kite watches and waits for an opportunity to snatch some of the fish.

The pair of sea-eagles watch the wild scramble of ducks from their perch beside their nest. They are poised, ready to pounce on any careless or ailing bird or a fish fleeing the diving mob. But it is another movement that attracts the female eagle's attention: a barramundi swimming along a shallow gutter close to the water's edge. She takes off with strong wing beats then glides in a semicircle out over the marsh, across the raft of ducks who fly up on a froth of panic, and approaches the large fish from behind. The barramundi sees her, just as she launches herself, air hissing through her wings, talons extended forward, into her final attack. The fish speeds through the water, but in the wrong direction, into shallows. The eagle's talons sink into his back. She tries to continue her flight, to carry her catch to the trees, but the fish is too heavy. Beating her wings, her body half submerged, she struggles to hold onto the barramundi. Her needle sharp claws soon find their way between the fish's scales and reach his backbone. There is no escape now. With all the strength at her command the eagle drags her catch onto the trunk of a fallen paperbark tree sticking out of the water. Panting, with wings spread, she stands over the dying fish.

The male eagle lands in a tree a few metres away. Four inquisitive opportunists, whistling kites, also land close by, ready to make off with anything they can scavenge or steal. The kites' own beaks and talons are not big enough to penetrate the scales of such a large fish. They wait impatiently for the eagle to do that.

The female eagle has soon opened the barramundi with her heavy, hooked beak and tears off large chunks of flesh. There is still a great deal left when she walks down the log, wipes her beak clean and bending down to her reflection, takes several sips of water. Her crop is bulging. As soon as she moves away to drink, two of the kites land near the fish and cautiously pull off a few beakfulls. But the male eagle is hungry and is not about to forgo his share. In a whoosh of wings and giving a loud clanging call he lands on the fish and scatters the kites. The female takes off to fly back to her nest. The kites immediately chase after her, perhaps to defend their territory which the larger bird is about to cross, or perhaps in

A black flying fox, clasping her small young, hangs upside down from a branch.

frustration in not being able to feed on the barramundi.

The kites are quicker and more manoeuvrable on the wing and rise above the eagle, then one after the other they dive at her. She is a match for them. Turning completely upside down in the air, she confronts the kites with her formidable claws just as they are about to strike her. The kites soon give up and return to try their luck with the slightly smaller male eagle. One of the kites lands on the log beside him as he tears a long strip of meat off the barramundi. For only a split second he juggles it in his beak, to get a better hold for swallowing. It is long enough for the kite to rush in and snatch it from him. Another kite sneaks slowly up behind the eagle and then pulls at his wing feathers. He ignores the lesser birds completely.

Eventually he too has had sufficient and flies off. As soon as he leaves the log the kites descend and begin to devour the remains. But another player even larger than the eagle has been observing the drama. She now strides in on long, vivid pink legs, stares the kites down with bright yellow eyes and threatens them with her heavy, black, pickaxe beak. Whistling in protest the kites reluctantly relinquish what they had waited for so long. Jabbing and hammering at the barramundi, the black-necked stork breaks it up into manageable pieces. Only a few scales and scraps of skin are left for the kites.

Midday is hot and calm on the floodplain, the water like a mirror. Deep in the paperbark swamps bordering the plain, it is cooler. The still, dark water, the shaggy trees with contorted limbs, the greenish light filtering through the leaves all impart an eeriness. In a dense corner of the forest where row upon row of large animals hang upside down from the branches this air of mystery is reinforced. The animals fan themselves with broad black wings often giving vent to long shrieks and screams. Tens of thousands of flying foxes roost and squabble.

Daytime is roosting time for the big bats, a time of rest before flying off to feed at night. If undisturbed there are long periods of quiet. Sooner or later, however, one of the bats will feel compelled to fly to another place and set off a chain reaction of discord as he lands to establish a new roosting space. If one goes too close to another, he or she is challenged with loud screams and thrusts from sharp, hooked claws on the animals' thumbs.

At this time of year, late May, most females have young clasped to their breasts. Slightly older young hang beside their mothers. The females spend long hours grooming themselves and their offspring. The wings are given special attention, licked thoroughly clean and then rubbed over oily glands at the back of the neck to keep them soft and supple.

It is also mating time, occasion for the loudest, most drawn-out shrieks. Males have staked out small territories along the branches. They noisily and vigorously defend them from other males. Females, of which there are usually several in close proximity, are approached most gently, however. If a male is not immediately rebuffed by a prospective female's hooked claw, he slowly moves closer and sniffs her. He then tries a few gentle prods with his wing claws. Suddenly the two spar furiously, lashing out with their hooks and shrieking loudly into each other's faces. The male tries to seize the female with his wings from behind. If he succeeds, the two will mate.

Flying fox camps are nearly always over water, perhaps for the extra coolness and humidity, and in Kakadu paperbark swamps are their favoured places. Paperbark is the collective name for a group of trees belonging to the genus *Melaleuca* which is in the myrtle family. The bark of the trees is soft and up to 25 mm thick, and is composed of layer upon layer of the thinnest tissue 'paper' imaginable. When fresh, the bark is pale pinky-brown in colour, or in some species white, which weathers to a dirty brown. As the trees grow their bark stretches, splits and peels off in ragged strips. Paperbark trunks are shaggy. This bark is used in 101 different ways by the Aboriginal people.

There are many kinds of paperbarks in Kakadu and nearly all of them have a liking for moist habitats. There are hundreds of square kilometres of paperbark swamp forests and from the air they look like vast stretches composed of but a single species. But this is not the case, the swamps are a mosaic of many different kinds, each adapted to a particular combination of soil and waterlogging. The most imposing paperbark at Djarrdjarr is the weeping paperbark which grows to an immense size.

In the heat of the day the flying foxes seem to be the only animal life in these mysterious forests, where the undergrowth is not composed of grasses and shrubs, but of waterlilies and bladderworts. But as the day cools, full-scale activity returns. In the deeper water whirligig beetles zip over the water surface like drops of animated quicksilver and waterstriders walk on the water. A freshwater snake undulates across a patch of open water, interrupting two slender waterdragons in head-bobbing display. A pair of bar-breasted honeyeaters resume their nest building. Orioles sing and peaceful doves coo to each other.

Out on the floodplain where the trees are widely spaced, the bushbirds, ignoring the marsh and the waterbirds beneath them, treat their environment as a woodland. At dusk, as the sea-eagle settles on her nest to brood her egg during the night, they are in full chorus. Flycatchers and honeyeaters sing, lorikeets screech and blue-winged kookaburras laugh raucously. A little falcon races in pursuit of a dove. Corellas that came to drink, now converse in harsh voices in the tops of paperbarks. Soon the sun has set and the orange sky is brilliantly reflected in the mirror of the floodplain's waters. Bush curlews' wailing calls come from the edge of the plain as the flying foxes, etched black against the sky, fly off to distant flowering trees.

The next day the sea-eagle lays her second egg. For about six weeks the pair incubate them. All the time they add more sticks to the nest and daily they bring fresh leafy twigs.

The floodplain slowly dries; the lilies become fewer and fewer and aquatic grasses invade the open water. The two eaglets, when they hatch, are tiny, helpless and covered in white down. Their parents must exercise great care when they feed them so as not to inflict any injuries with their sharp claws and massive, hooked beaks. The female offers the young their first meal, the flesh of a saratoga that the male caught close to the nest tree. Gripping the fish in her talons, she rips it to pieces with her beak. She eats the first large chunks herself. With a delicacy and precision unexpected from such a huge beak, she then pulls tiny pieces from the fish and holds them near the young. Still somewhat uncoordinated, the chicks peck at the morsels. Their first meal is slow but the female shows great patience and forbearance.

There is no shortage of food for the eagles on the floodplain and the young grow rapidly. After three weeks they sit boldly upright on their nest. Their brown plumage is already pushing through the white down. The adults no longer brood the young and only come to the nest to feed them. The male catches the bulk of the food. Most of it is fish, but he also

Above
Pelicans take off from a billabong.

Above right
The billabongs provide food for a wide variety of animals. A black-necked stork has caught a file snake.

catches flying foxes, whistling ducks, file snakes and turtles. He too now feeds the young, but he does not have the female's patience.

Both young, in this land of plenty, are well fed. In less favoured habitats, where food is scarcer, one chick usually receives the major share. As it grows it becomes increasingly aggressive towards its smaller sibling, eventually killing it.

Life in the Billabongs

When the chicks of the Djarrdjarr eagles are six weeks old, at the end of August, much of the floodplain has dried up, its marshes have changed to fields of green grass. Many thousands of pied geese gather here, grazing across the damp meadows like an advancing army. The fish and file snakes that had dispersed over the plain during the wet season have retreated to the billabongs and deeper gutters. Many of these channels, some hundreds of metres long and a score wide, are cut off from the deep water. Their immense load of fish, large and small, is trapped.

Pelicans are most adept at dredging these narrow ponds. Sweeping all before them hundreds of the large birds swim from one end to the other, dipping their scoopnet beaks in unison. Many catch fish so large that they can barely hold them in the bags of their lower mandibles. To swallow them takes concentration, and these lucky fishermen leave the team and waddle up the bank.

As well as the pelicans, there is a solid mass of white birds in and around the water. Great egrets stand at the water's edge spearing one fish after another. Little egrets run along beside the moving flotilla of pelicans and catch anything that leaps into the shallows. A tight phalanx of white bodies walks rapidly along the edges swishing their black spatulate beaks back and forth through the mud. These royal spoonbills, more used to dredging up crustaceans, now hunt for fish. White ibis, usually careful mud probers, also take advantage of the changed circumstances. Above them all hovers a cloud of small white birds, whiskered

Sunset at Djarrdjarr.

terns, who dive in amongst this multitude to catch the tiniest fish. Dotted here and there head and shoulders above the rest, are the black-necked storks, about half a dozen of them, stabbing at the largest fish and chasing any birds that get in their way. And always there are the whistling kites, the opportunists. Any of the fishing birds, be it pelican, egret or stork, that is the slightest bit hesitant about swallowing its catch, will find it confiscated, quick as a flash, by the kites. They steal their fish without getting their feet wet.

This wild melee of birds strips the pool of its fish in little more than a day, leaving it lifeless with white feathers floating on the turbid water and trampled into the mud.

The sea-eagles disdain these undignified scrambles. By mid-September there is still a small sheet of water around their nest tree where they catch barramundi, catfish, long toms and an occasional mullet. Their principal prey is the surface swimming long tom, of which they may catch as many as five in a single day.

The young birds have lost their down and in its place have grown the brown plumage of the immature sea-eagle. Their parents still feed them but for increasingly shorter periods, they have to feed themselves on prey left on the nest. Restlessly the young exercise their wings, beating them forcefully as they jump up and down. Sometimes the wind catches them and they float in the air for just a few seconds.

Then one day at the end of September, as an early storm rumbles in the distance, the young beat their wings so vigorously that they become truly airborne under their own power. Flailing their wings, they rise higher and higher and lose contact with their nest and must make their first flight. It is a wild, unsure sortie, dipping and rising with little control, till they crashland in the top of a paperbark. From then on their skill and confidence develop rapidly and before long they are able aerialists. For a few weeks they are still given food by their parents, but by mid-October they have to make their own catches. That is still easy. Fish trapped in the last pools on the drying floodplain are ready targets. They provide essential training for the days when life will be harder.

A few pied geese are still at Djarrdjarr but the vast majority of the about one million geese in Kakadu have again moved to the South Alligator River plains, not to Goose Camp but in one vast cacophonous gathering on the Mamukala Swamp.

The heat from the constant unrelenting sunshine contracts the swamps and eventually banishes the multitudinous life. The animals concentrate in the stable environment of the deep water. Just south of Mamukala is a chain of billabongs along Jim Jim Creek just upstream of its junction with the South Alligator.

In late October the long, narrow lagoons are all that remain of the stream. Water flows only during the wet season.

Trees crowd closely along the shores of the more remote billabongs. Tall weeping paperbarks lean out over clumps of dark pandanus to hang the tips of their trailing branches in the water. Gnarled silver-leafed paperbarks hunch low in the shallow water, their branches covered with greenish-yellow bottlebrush flowers. Small bays are filled with freshwater mangrove bushes, their red flowers hanging in strings among the dark foliage. Thick clumps of bamboo stand like islands higher on the banks. In the water a crocodile's eye glints below a pandanus, then sinks from view. A water python swims across the billabong making small fish jump out of his way. From concealment in the bamboos come the hoarse roaring calls of the skulking great-billed heron.

Here too the dry season is felt. The waters are warm and murky. The leaves and other vegetation that constantly drop into the billabong are rotting and rob the water of oxygen. Fish, quite large barramundi among them, lie gasping in the shallows. Many have died already. The too sweet scent of the paperbark flowers and the rank odour of those of the freshwater mangroves mingle with the smells of rotting vegetation and decaying fish.

A large barramundi has come aground on the bank. Its stench attracts a terrestrial scavenger. A lizard more than one and a half metres long, his greenish-black body dotted with yellow, ambles slowly out of the undergrowth, his belly barely clearing the ground. Briefly he pauses, testing the air with a long pink tongue forked at its tip, then continues on to the stranded fish. But the barramundi is armoured with large overlapping scales. Biting where it can, pulling hard with curved claws, the floodplain goanna cannot breach the fish's skin. Even when he forces its huge mouth open and pushes himself inside up to his back legs he cannot make an impression. Finally using both front feet and his teeth, he manages to penetrate the scales and skin at a weak spot behind the gills.

Despite the rank odours, the dead fish and the scavengers, these tree-shrouded billabongs are never sombre places. The air is always filled with songs of woodland birds. Their colours, the luminous blue shoulder patches of pittas, the scarlet finches, the yellow figbirds, the orange and green lorikeets, the intense blue little kingfishers, the metallic iridescence of shining flycatchers, flash through the green.

The end of one billabong curves out onto the floodplain. The banks are devoid of trees except for the occasional, lone paperbark. The grass-lined shores and the water are thronged with birds. But it is also the favoured place for a number of saltwater crocodiles. This species, growing to about seven metres in length, is the largest of all the world's twenty-one different kinds of crocodiles. It is also the most aggressive, fastest moving and most territorial. At this time of year, the time of mating, the male saltwater crocodiles are at their most pugnacious and irritable.

This particular stretch of water is the domain of a large male nearly five metres long. He has just heaved himself onto the bank to rest in the shade of a single paperbark tree; spreadeagled on land he looks broad and massive and seems ponderous and slow. He lies facing the water, mouth agape showing the yellow insides of his wide jaws. Now and again he raises his head and yawns prodigiously, impressively. His eyes blink shut in sleep yet very little escapes his attention. When another male, only his nostrils, eyes and the serrations on the top of his tail visible, slowly swims within his territory, the big fellow is immediately aware of it. For the moment his only reaction is to close his mouth and dig his feet firmly into the ground.

The newcomer is smaller, about three metres long, but continues his intrusion, perhaps to test the other's resolve. Slowly, hardly making a ripple, the big male enters the water and sinks from view. Several minutes later he surfaces directly behind his rival about twenty metres away. So slowly he barely seems to move, he closes the gap. The smaller male remains motionless. When the two are about eight metres apart the big male explodes into action. Slightly raising himself out of the water he attacks with unbelievable speed. With split-second reflexes the smaller crocodile rushes back to the main billabong, not slowing down till he reaches safety. The water boils and froths with the big male's anger. Birds from hundreds of metres around rise in the air, twittering and honking in agitation.

The male courts the two females in his territory at dusk and at night. He lies on the water surface, his rough textured back showing, as the sun's last colours hang vivid in the sky. Ibis and herons, dark silhouettes, hurry to their roosting places. Flying foxes skim low over the water, taking a drink on the wing. The male crocodile bellows his readiness to mate and the females slowly drift towards him. He raises his head high out of the water, jaws agape, white teeth gleaming in the last light. Male and female rub each other's chins, then the male mounts the smaller female and the two submerge.

The underwater world they enter is as full of life and as predatory as the one above water. The details are more easily observed after next morning's sunrise.

Life Under Water

In the furthest reaches of the billabong, undisturbed by birds and large crocodiles, the water is clear and warm. Green stems of waterlilies snake up to the surface. Bladderworts grow in

A barramundi is quickly devoured by a saltwater crocodile. Of all the species of crocodilians in the world, the 'saltie' is the largest and most aggressive. © National Geographic Society.

floating rafts; their yellow flowers reach above the water while their stems, equipped with bladder-like traps, catch microscopic animal life beneath it. These same minute organisms are the staple food of an array of aquatic insects and their larvae. Beetles, bugs, caddisflies, damselflies and dragonflies, trap, poison or filter this rich and prolific life. The insects are one of the main food sources for another link in the food chain — the fishes. The number of fish in an undisturbed billabong defies comprehension; there are many more fish in the water than birds in the air.

Schools of spangled grunters, silvery with sparkling flecks of red-brown, swim slowly through the fallen branches and other debris along the shoreline. With their noses they turn over leaves sunk to the bottom and snap up insects and crustaceans hiding beneath. With them are striped grunters, of a golden colour with broad, black vertical stripes.

In deeper water, swimming close to the surface, are schools of checkered rainbow fish, nibbling fallen flowers and leaves and eating any insects that might be clinging to them.

Schools of rainbow fish swim in the deeper water of the billabongs.

Horizontally striped in gold and silvery-blue and with their shiny yellow-green fins and tails, these are the most colourful of the fishes. They are the very antithesis of the solitary freshwater sole, a tiny fish no more than 75 mm long. It is so well camouflaged that it is only noticed when it moves. Its shape, colour and pattern are those of the fallen, waterlogged brown leaves. And even when it swims, it does so in the same zigzagging movement of a leaf slowly sinking to the bottom.

Sail-fin perchlets swim slowly amongst the stems of waterlilies. Their transparent bodies are almost invisible in the water. Below them, among the lily roots, eel-tail catfish in large schools sweep in tight formation over the mud bottom, probing the ooze with their sensitive 'whiskers' for insect larvae and shrimps. So tight are the formations that each seems to be a single being constantly changing shape.

The fish swim in unhurried, fluid and elegant movements. But when the shadow of a large bird passes overhead, or a predatory fish looms in the deep, they dash as one into the green depths, disappearing in the twinkling of an eye. The main enemies of these small fish, here in the deeper water of the billabongs, are not the birds but the large fish lurking in snags, under banks, or in deep holes.

The permanent home of a saratoga is amongst the roots of a pandanus thicket growing in the water. The fish's head is just discernible amongst the criss-crossing roots, but its body is hidden in the depths. An archer fish looking for insects to shoot off the overhanging vegetation recognises the danger zone and shoots past. Less alert, a spangled grunter dawdles under the pandanus. With one swish of its tail, the saratoga surges forward and swallows the

The pig-nosed turtle is a rare species and in Australia is found only in the rivers of the Northern Territory's top end.

grunter, whole. As the big fish turns to go back to its lair, the sun briefly glints on the bright red spots on its fins and tail.

Only a little way out from the bank, the billabong's bottom drops steeply to a dark place where no water plants grow. During the day the silver barramundi, or giant perch, cruise in this twilight world. Their huge orange-yellow eyes appear luminescent. Most of the barramundi, swimming in schools, are less than 50 cm long and weigh between 4 and 5 kg. But every now and again the dim outline of a giant passes by, perhaps weighing as much as 50 kg.

At dusk these fish swim closer to the surface, sometimes leaping out of the water and whacking it with their tails. They hunt the smaller species with bursts of great speed and with aggression. Another predatory species, the fork-tailed catfish, shares the billabong's deep water with the barramundi. In schools of hundreds they scour the bottom devouring all animal life before them. The tarpon and freshwater long tom shun the billabong's depths; they are fast predators hunting close to the surface. Their silvery-blue, semi-transparent forms are difficult to detect both by their prey below them and by the eagles and other birds that hunt them from above.

By the end of October and early November, frequent storms sweep across Kakadu. It is insufficient rain to fill the billabongs and floodplains, but enough to refresh the country and turn it green again, to tide it over until the resurgence of a new wet season.

The storms bring greatest relief to the stone country of the escarpment and the plateau where drought has reigned for several months.

5 ~ ESCARPMENT AND PLATEAU

THE FIRST STORMS OF NOVEMBER, the pre-monsoon season, have little effect on the stone country. Rain is brief and erratic; striking here, missing there. Often there are spectacular displays of lightning and thunder and no rain at all. What little rain that might fall disappears almost immediately, soaked up by the dry rocks, running into crevices or rising as steam from the hot stone.

Since April, when the last rain of any consequence fell, the sun has been merciless on these exposed surfaces. Mosses, herbs and grasses have died back leaving their spores and seeds in tiny cracks. The plants themselves have long since shrivelled to dust. Hardy perennials like the spinifex are dry and yellow. Small trees and shrubs are dormant and have shed their leaves. Some, like the turkey bush, have become brittle. Their twisted stems, tortured over many dry seasons, lie like ropes over the rocks. They appear to have died, but their roots, groping deeply into cracks, cling to a precarious life. Only the fig trees whose roots reach many metres down into cool and moist chasms, remain green all year.

Every day in this most trying month the temperature rises a little higher. The rocks are too hot to touch a few hours after sunrise, and each night they take a little longer to cool. There is little or no animal life on the exposed sandstone.

But there are many hidden places where it has remained cool and damp and that is where the animals have retreated. The plateau is not the solid block of stone it may at first appear to be; fissures hundreds of metres deep criss-cross it from end to end. Some of these gorges are a kilometre or more wide while others are so narrow a man can barely squeeze into them. During the wet season water streams along all the valleys and ravines, large and small, but now only pools remain and hidden in narrow corridors where the sun never shines are a few small springs. The rock massif gives up its water reserves slowly in a parsimonious trickle but it is enough to keep the stone country alive during the long dry season.

A Hidden Spring

Where the escarpment is most miserly in releasing its water it drips slowly into depressions in the rocks no larger than saucers. These 'springs' are in caverns at the deeply undercut bases of tall sheer cliffs. They are further hidden from view by bushy trees whose roots are nourished by the soak's water. Concealed such a water source may be, but animals know exactly where to find it. Should it be well away from large permanent pools and at a place where stone country and parched eucalypt woodland meet, it is a very busy place with a constant procession of animals from both habitats coming and going.

One such soak seeps out at the base of the escarpment not far from Lightning Dreaming.

The Arnhem Land escarpment dominates the Kakadu landscape.

Top
The roots of a fig tree grip the rock and reach deeply into cracks for moisture.

Previous pages
The escarpment at Lightning Dreaming.

At dawn a pair of barking owls bark a gruff 'wook-wook' at each other before retiring to the dense foliage of the tree that screens the soak's cavern. They will remain there for the day. Small bats flit in and out of the cave, only landing briefly among the mosses and damp boulders for a sip of water before returning to their roosts. Sandstone frogs who had been feeding on thirsty insects during the night squeeze into tiny cracks. Rock wallabies shuffle along narrow ledges then steal a quick drink before leaping off again, ever fearful of a large python lying in wait.

The first birds appear with the rising sun. Honeyeaters, like nearly all the animals, approach the water carefully for it is deep in a confined, rocky place. Many predators can hide there. Also it is dark and claustrophobic, an oppressive place for animals from the open spaces. White-lined honey-eaters, sandstone shrike-thrushes and sandstone friarbirds are first to arrive. These are birds of the rock country. After a hurried drink they burst into song as if relieved at having survived.

Soon mobs of pushing and shoving forest birds besiege the spring, mostly seed-eaters who must drink at least once a day. They seem to think there is safety in numbers for they mill around the cave entrance and only when enough of them have congregated do they rush in.

Yellow and black mud wasps fly in and out through the throng of birds and a cloud of tiny native bees flies up as a pair of peaceful doves comes to drink, then settle all over the birds. Five chestnut-quilled rock pigeons come dribbling along the same ledge as the rock wallabies. They hold their wings drooped low like skirts and their feathers rustle against the stone. They coo softly to each other as they gently nudge and push between the smaller birds to find a place to drink.

The looking-over-the-shoulder unease of the drinking birds is well founded. A large Oenpelli python slowly emerges from a vertical crack that ends at the water. A pair of white-gaped honeyeaters spots her immediately and flutters agitatedly around the snake's head, shrieking a warning. Panicking, getting in each other's way, the birds flee, leaving the snake with the wasps and bees. But she is intent only on drinking. She does so leisurely

Above left
Mud wasps build their nests in the escarpment's rocky recesses.

Above
A rock pigeon drinks at a small soak.

Above right
The Arnhem Land Plateau's sandstone has been fractured and eroded over millions of years.

while the birds wait patiently outside the cavern.

The python returns to her rock crevice and soon the birds return to drink.

The escarpment, the rock wall that dominates Kakadu, contains many such small and intimate formations where life is concentrated. In other places the scenery is built on a colossal scale where stone columns, spacious valleys, and deep pools with sandy beaches create uncommon grandeur. From saucers of water in caverns to exalted towers of stone, all are part of the rugged, fractured Arnhem Land Plateau.

The Plateau

The plateau lies like a roughly carved island in a sea of eucalypt forests and woodlands. Only in its northernmost parts, along the East Alligator River, does it break out of the enveloping trees and meet the floodplain. This sandstone massif stretches about two hundred and thirty kilometres in a north-south direction and is about one hundred and sixty kilometres wide. The western face forms an almost continuous rock wall, 100–250 m tall and rising to over 300 m in a few places. Only a narrow band along this scarp is within Kakadu. Most of the plateau itself is in the Arnhem Land Aboriginal Reserve.

The sandstones, quartzites and conglomerates, collectively called the Kombolgie formation, that constitute the plateau, are of a great age. They are among the oldest sedimentary rocks. They were laid down 1800 to 1400 million years ago in the middle Proterozoic era. It was a time when life was restricted to microscopic, single-celled organisms living only in the sea. The land was barren and lifeless. In places the formations are 450 m thick, but on average only 200–250 m of it outcrops above the plain.

Since the original layers of sandstone were laid down, they have been subjected to massive tensions, pressures and upheavals. Gigantic uplifts raised them above the plains. Internal pressures metamorphosed much of the coarse-grained sandstone into smooth quartzite. This rock, almost impervious to weathering, makes up the tallest, sheerest cliffs. Mighty folding movements twisted and buckled the strata. But these pressures were localised and in most

The East Alligator River flowing north along a faultline in the plateau.

places the horizontal bedding of the rocks remains much as it was at the time they were laid down. Ripples made by wave actions all those millions of years ago can still be seen on some exposed slabs. Fault lines criss-cross the plateau and have carved it into neat geometric patterns. Vertical displacement along these faults and subsequent weathering have broadened and deepened the fractures, giving the massif its fissured, dissected face.

Vertical erosion also maintains the steep western scarp. Huge square-cornered blocks and slabs have split from it and have collected in piles and heaps along its base. Some sandstone strata are softer, more readily weathered, than others and the differential erosion creates honeycomb patterns where the harder layers stand out in bas relief. Textures vary. Quartzite is smooth, sandstone sometimes fine-grained and sometimes coarse-grained. Conglomerate, made up of pebbles set in a cement of sandstone, is rough and knobbly. The leaching of iron and other minerals colours the rocks with streaks, bands and daubs of warm tones. From escarpment wall to river pebble the rocks are sculptured and pigmented in an infinite variety of combinations.

The entire plateau is slowly breaking up. Rivers carve wide valleys scores of kilometres long. Creeks cut narrow ravines with sheer-sided walls hundreds of metres deep. Less organised weathering, following faultlines, slices wildly irregular networks of narrow chasms and leaves towers and blocks of stone hewn into singular and exotic shapes. Rock walls are undercut by wind and rain creating airy caverns, retreats for bats and geckoes and places where humans executed their earliest paintings.

Weathering is a never-ending force that implacably eats away at the rocks, reducing the massif to giant blocks, the boulders to pebbles and the pebbles to grains of sand — a white sand that, washed down by the streams, fans out from the entire plateau. The main weathering agent is water, from the pounding rush of waterfalls to the accumulated impact of millions of years of rain.

Every square centimetre of exposed rock has felt the effects of aeons of erosion. The stone is shaped as though by a master sculptor fashioning abstract forms ranging from small cornices to giant stairways, from towers to mammoth castles. The whole plateau and especially the escarpment, is one harmonious sculpture, perfect to the finest detail in shape and colour.

Life in the Stone Country

Despite the harshness of the dry season and the inhospitable nature of the rocks, the sandstone's wildlife is most diverse, especially among the plants. Two factors have brought this about. Firstly the rock formations harbour a great many different habitats, from Kakadu's harshest to its most benevolent. The exposed, often unbearably hot, rocks are almost devoid of life, only an occasional lichen is able to establish a foothold. But down at the base of the sheltering ramparts where springs release a steady, year-round supply of water, thrive dynamic wildlife communities. Between these two extremes lies a host of varying circumstances of available moisture, soil fertility and protection from the desiccating sun. The second factor is the adaptations of many plant species to long dry seasons and low soil nutrients. Sandstone does not break down into fertile soil; it becomes sand. Many plants are dry season deciduous. They simply shed their leaves and remain dormant till the rains return. Another

Sandstone myrtles are the largest trees found within the escarpment.

Top
The secretive rock possum is a species of ringtail completely adapted to the sandstone country.

Top right
The short-eared rock wallaby, soft-furred and dainty, makes its home in the most rugged parts of the escarpment.

adaptation is to shoot up quickly from seed at the onset of the wet season, grow rapidly to maturity and then disperse the new crop of seeds before dying back at the onset of the dry. Other species conserve their energies in underground bulbs.

The animals, being mobile, cope more easily. During the wet they scatter and multiply. During the dry they migrate to the protection of the escarpment's cool, moist recesses.

Besides its dramatic appearance and structure, there is one other thing that distinguishes the rock country from the other habitats: the large number of plants and animals that are found nowhere else. This endemism relates to both the diversity of rocky habitats and the plateau's long isolation. Plants and animals have become so adapted to particular sandstone environments that they cannot live outside them; they cannot colonise the surrounding swamps and woodlands. Also, species survived here that became extinct in other parts of Australia. The result is a self-contained, compact island of stone markedly different from any other place.

About a hundred species of plants, many of them not yet scientifically described, have been recorded only from this massif: hibiscuses, grevilleas, goodenias, bladderworts, wattles, grasses and others. One escarpment endemic, the tree *Allosyncarpia ternata*, was not described by botanists until 1976. This giant evergreen, growing to over thirty metres in height, belongs to the myrtle family, to which the eucalypts, paperbarks and the myrtle of Europe also belong. The spreading *Allosyncarpia*, which could be called the sandstone myrtle, dominates moist, soil-rich habitats throughout the rock country. *Allosyncarpias* are the largest trees within the escarpment, and where they grow in forests give rise to an endemic habitat, very different from those dominated by eucalypts or paperbarks.

Among the animals too there are many endemics. Each major group of insects has representatives found only in this stone country. There are sandstone grasshoppers, dragonflies, beetles, flies, mosquitoes, termites, ants and so on. The most spectacular of Kakadu's insects, the rare blue and red Leichhardt grasshopper, is one of these endemics. As many as twenty frogs and reptiles are confined to the sandstone. The sandstone antechinus and the black

Tiny flowers, such as these of the delicate bladderworts, grow on damp rock ledges.

Top
Nourlangie Rock with a flowering Dryander's grevillea bush in the foreground.

wallaroo are endemics among the mammals. The short-eared rock wallaby, the rock possum and the large rock rat, and among the birds, the white-lined honeyeater and the sandstone shrike-thrush, were believed to be escarpment endemics, but have since also been found in the Kimberley region of Western Australia. The white-throated grass wren, the chestnut-quilled rock pigeon and the banded pigeon, however, are found only in the escarpment area. There are about thirty other kinds of birds whose representatives living in the Arnhem Land massif are deemed to be sufficiently different from their ilk elsewhere, to be recognised as separate, sandstone races.

Endemic species seen nowhere else, plants and animals adapted to unique habitats, sandy pools, waterfalls, but above all ancient, sculptured rocks, have given rise to a different world; one more stimulating, more stirring than almost any other. Add to this man's oldest paintings with a clear lineage to the present, and it can truly be said that the stone country is the soul of Kakadu.

Wet Season

As November progresses, storms become more frequent and slowly the escarpment's harsh exterior is softened by green.

Perhaps the season's most violent storm begins to build up in mid-afternoon. From the summit of Jabiru Dreaming, an isolated outcrop beside the East Alligator River, it can be seen rolling in over the escarpment's ramparts. Soon the entire eastern and southern sky is pitch black. White cockatoos, screaming raucously, stand out starkly as they fly over the tree tops below. Darkness falls as if it were dusk. A gale advances and whips the spinifex clumps. Black clouds surround the outcrop. Lightning bolts hit the rock, the air hisses and crackles with electricity. Other bolts jag down to the forest while long fingers of it claw from one cloud to another. The sound is earsplitting, terrifying. The lightning, almost continuous, illuminates the forest with a white light almost as bright as the sun's. Then a different thunder approaches, a steady, ominous thrumming, growing louder and louder — it is the rain, almost a solid sheet of water, advancing. As the icy cold rain hits Jabiru Dreaming, cascading down its rocks glistening in the now intermittent lightning, it is virtually dark, though it is still hours from sunset.

The storms and later the wet season saturate the sandstone and fill every crack and fissure. The water supply is recharged. Plants awaken from their quiescence to send down new roots, put on new leaves and to flower. The animals, especially the insects and the frogs, respond with an explosion of breeding activity.

On a sunny day in February, the middle of the wet season, Nourlangie Rock's sandstone washed by recent rain looks fresh and clear. Bands of black and orange, the stains left by countless wet seasons, weep down its southern face and stand out vividly in the early light. This outlier from the main plateau looks like a solid, sheer-sided monolith squatting on the plain. In truth it is honeycombed with fissures and chasms and riddled with caves. Nourlangie Rock is hollow. Despite this the summit is difficult to reach. The network of narrow ravines have sheer, smooth sides a hundred or more metres high. Only a few of the numerous fissures in this maze have a path that leads to the very top. One such secretive passageway begins as a cleft so narrow, that a man spreading his arms wide can touch both sides. Underfoot is

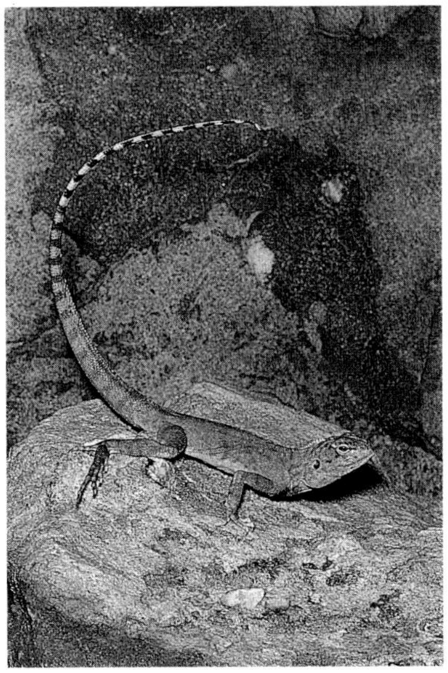

Above
A ring-tailed rock dragon is one of the fastest moving animals of the escarpment and one of the few to be seen on the inhospitable summit of the plateau.

Top
The large, carnivorous ghost bat lives in the caverns deep inside Nourlangie Rock.

Top right
A huge thunderstorm rolls in over the escarpment and approaches Jabiru Dreaming.

white sand with clear water running over it. Rough conglomerate rock rises vertical and unclimbable. Only a little light comes through the slit at the top. After several hundred metres, the fissure suddenly widens into a huge chamber. On one side it has collapsed into a tumble of enormous rocks and is open to the sky. Vines coil over the stones. Between them, in shaded places, dark green mosses and ferns cling to rock surfaces. A fig tree and flowering shrubs frame the entrance to a cavern on whose high, domed ceiling hang hundreds of large bats. A forest of faces closely packed together watch everything with black eyes and listen with huge ears. These ghost bats twitter and bicker. Some fly off on large pale wings, deeper into the cave, when harassed by their neighbours. Though belonging to the same group as the tiny insect-eating bats so numerous in the escarpment, the ghost bats are quite large and carnivorous. The reason for the quarrelling is that one still has part of a rock rat, last night's catch, clamped in his jaws and others are trying to take it from him.

Beyond the cave and the amphitheatre of rocks the passage continues, moving upwards. Not far along, water trickles over dark stone. Small indentations have trapped a little organic matter, enough for masses of tiny plants to have taken root and to flower. The blue bladderwort flowers tremble on their thin stems on the breeze that sighs constantly along the passage.

The same wind, generated within the mountain, blows gently through a cave further up the passage. At the top it is open to the sky through a narrow fissure, where water drips and trickles down, splashing onto the cave's floor. The updraft slows the falling drips creating a slow motion shower. Briefly the sun passes across the fissure, turning the rock a rich ochre

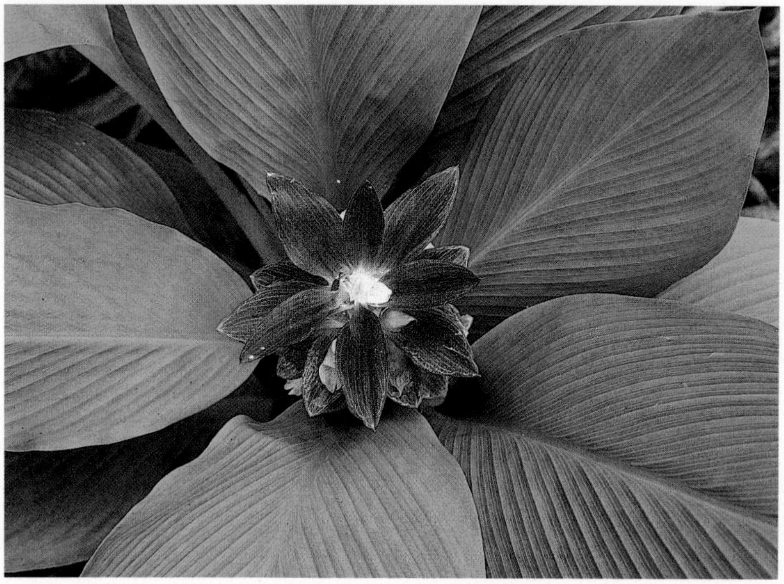

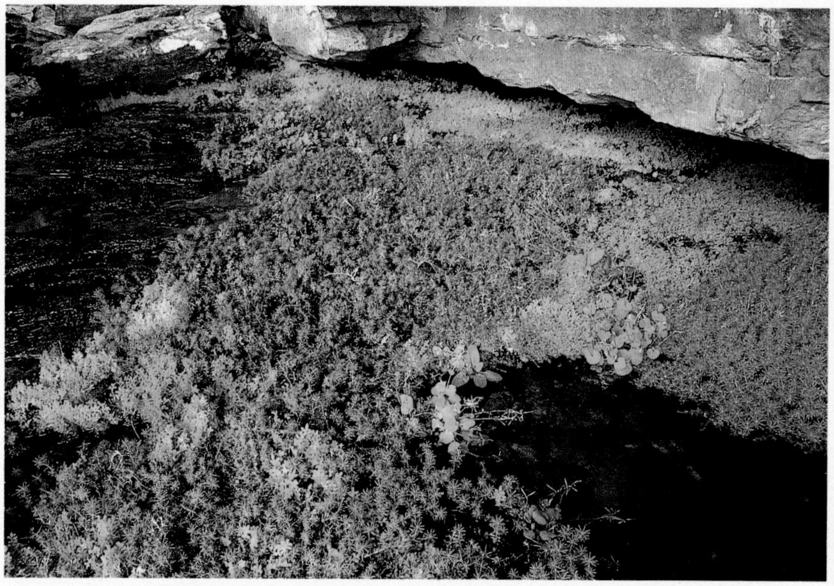

Curcuma australasica, *a native tumeric, flowers in the monsoon forest during the wet season.*

Above right
Where water seeps out from a rock ledge during the wet season, an apron of green mosses and flowers flourishes. These same plants shrivel almost to dust during the dry season.

and sparkling on the falling drops. The narrow alleyway winds on. Roots of fig trees stretch down the rock walls like taut cables and disappear into the ground. Their trunks and foliage are out of sight above.

Finally, around one last bend, the passage emerges in the blinding light on a wide shelf more than halfway up the rock. The shelf's edge drops 150 m straight down. Water runs out of the passage over green mosses and trickles down onto a carpet of pink triggerplant flowers. On the cliff edge a row of sandstone pandanus stand perched on their aerial roots. Turkey bushes flower in pink starbursts close to the rocks. A pair of white-lined honeyeaters has built its nest in one of them and the female patiently incubates the two eggs.

The ledge leads into another dark chasm. Several short-eared rock wallabies rest in the entrance. In a dark corner behind a boulder a giant cave gecko waits for nightfall. After a short distance, the chasm reaches yet a higher level of the rock. From this ledge a dozen wider clefts, undercut by water, run deeply into the rock. Water courses through them. Being wider and not so deep, the sun reaches here for several hours, illuminating the orange rock. There is enough light and soil for a large *Allosyncarpia* tree to grow. On the outermost twigs of the tree's largest branch a pair of banded pigeons has put half a dozen small sticks together. On this sketchily built nest the female has laid a single white egg which she now incubates. Every breath of wind makes her and her nest dip and sway.

At the end of the chasm is a rockfall; it is the staircase that leads to the summit, to open space and a cooling breeze. From the distance the domed summit appeared like solid, smooth rock, but again the appearance is deceptive. The entire surface is broken up; in some places into horizontal steplike furrows, in others into forests of stone pillars that tilt down into yet more chasms.

From the summit there is a steep descent, down a loose scree, where constant seepage from the rock and the protection from the dry season, have given rise to an *Allosyncarpia* forest. The tall trees' crowns intertwine into a closed canopy which shuts out much of the

Brightly coloured fungi grow in the dark monsoon forest.

light. Even now in the hothouse season of dampness and heat not many plants grow beneath the trees. This monsoon forest is too dark. But as always there are a few specialists that can cope. Broad-leafed green ground plants that sprang up after the last rain now bear fleshy pink and yellow flower spikes.

Because fires do not penetrate here, the leaflitter builds up. A pair of scrub fowl scratches for earthworms, ground beetles and other organisms in the deep layer of fallen leaves and twigs. Building on the efforts of many generations before them, the birds heap decaying vegetation onto the top of an 8 m tall mound. Here the female will lay her eggs in small chambers dug out of the leaf mould; the heat of the decaying vegetable matter will incubate them. The chicks, on hatching, have to fend for themselves.

Along Djuwarr Creek

It is during early May that the ravine above Djuwarr Rock looks its freshest. Water channelled along cracks and crevices on top of the plateau runs through a series of pools before cascading into the ravine down a bare dark rock face. The circular plunge pool at its base is surrounded by vertical cliffs on three sides and it too is dark. It is said to be very deep. According to Gagudju legend, Almudj the Rainbow Serpent lives in this pool.

The stream issuing out of the pool burbles among rounded boulders and pebbles for a few metres before making a sharp right-angled turn to the north. The ravine is narrow here, its floor bare shelving rock. A few river box trees have taken root in the lee of some large boulders. But it is an uncomfortable compromise, the trees leaning precariously in the direction of the strong wet season current. But now the clear water runs gently from one pool to another. Sunfish swim lazily against the cool flow and in a deeper, green pool a freshwater crocodile floats motionless on the surface. A pair of barn owls returns to its roost in a cave high on the cliff. The rising sun's warmth will not reach here for some hours.

But a few hundred metres downstream the ravine's eastern wall has fallen back in a series of giant terraces littered with rocks of all shapes and sizes. The sun has just risen over this lower rim and effects an instant transformation. The western rampart, as steep and as high as before, changes from dull grey to a lively earthy orange in colour. Pebbles in the stream also take on colour — mauve, dark red, yellowish. Deep pools reflect the straight white trunks of weeping paperbarks. Where a snapping turtle surfaces to breathe, the sun sparkles on the ripples. Rainbow bee-eaters flashing green over the water catch dragonflies on the wing. The dawn chorus of the birds begins with the haunting whistle of the white-lined honeyeater, the voice of the sandstone. Soon the entire canyon resounds with song.

The sun picks out the brilliant colours of the flowering shrubs on the terraced slope. Grevilleas with scarlet flowers stand beside wattles decked in yellow. Pea bushes and small grevilleas spill orange flowers over the prickly spinifex. A male lavender flanked wren, a tiny enamel blue jewel, flits in and out of the spinifex and sings with trembling ardour; throat vibrating, feathers fluffed, he pours out his high-pitched rolling song. The song defines the bird's territory, keeping away other males and attracting a female. A pair does not claim a large holding; a few boulders for shade, a clump of spinifex to build a nest and a damp gully to hunt insects.

The dip in the eastern rock face flanks the creek for about a kilometre before rising again.

In its upper reaches, Djuwarr Creek flows through a narrow ravine.

Top
Freshwater crocodiles nest in the sandy banks below Djuwarr Rock. Here one rests on a submerged rock shelf.

At its lowest point a tiny rivulet trickles down the terraces. The rivulet's pools are full of tadpoles, the last broods of the several species unique to the stone country. They feed on the algae growing on rocks and on the vegetable matter that falls in the water. Should their ponds become critically small before they have completed their life cycle, many tadpoles will forsake their vegetarian diet and become cannibals. That way at least some will reach maturity instead of all perishing.

Continuing downstream, the creek once again flows through a steep-sided chasm. Numerous small tributaries issuing from the porous rock have swollen its volume. The creek is wider here and after a few hundred metres flows into a long, narrow waterhole. The sun is higher now and shines down on the pool, warming a Mitchell's water goanna basking on a rock. A belt of monsoon forest grows on the sand on the waterhole's western side. The trees screen the entrances to the fissures. One is a little wider than the others, its entrance hidden by a robust beauty leaf tree, its shiny variegated leaves contrasting with its sombre furrowed trunk. With pale yellow eyes half shut, a rufous owl sits in a low branch with the remains of a black flying fox clasped in its powerful talons. The tree is the bird's roost. Other flying fox remains hang from various branches. Pellets of indigestible animal remains, regurgitated by the owl over the months, litter the ground. They contain the skull of a sugar glider, leg bones and jaws of rodents, craniums and ribs of marsupial mice and the bright green wing cases of large beetles.

The sun, almost directly overhead, sends shafts of light to the floor of the monsoon forest. A beam falls on a moss-covered rock and hundreds of brown butterflies spotted with white take flight in a blizzard of soft wings. For a few moments the insects flutter in the light then settle in a shady spot. Above them a score of rufous night herons roosts in the dense foliage. Mostly they sleep with their dark-capped heads drawn down into hunched shoulders. Their white headplumes lie over their warm-brown coloured backs. Occasionally one scratches itself with a large yellow foot. But mostly they are silent, watchful and inconspicuous.

Where the waterhole ends, the stream babbles quietly over a bed of waterworn pebbles and enters a completely different world, a world strangely pale after the dark green of the monsoon forest. This forest is made up of thick-trunked, enormously tall paperbarks. Their whitish, peeling bark hangs down in long tatters. White sand covers the ground. Over and through the sand the trees' exposed roots, equally pale, coil and writhe in long snake-like ropes. The silvery streams flow through the forest splashing and gurgling through the root systems. Pale yellow bladderwort flowers stand crowded in patches of damp ground. Red and orange mistletoe flowers, fallen from plants high in the paperbarks, are strewn over the sand. Brown spiders marked with yellow have built miniature webs between grass blades and dwarf tree frogs squat among green sedges. A fire-tailed skink, shiny black with an orange tail, scampers after tiny grasshoppers. Minute black ants hasten along well-marked trails and harvest the paperbark seeds that rain down constantly. High in the tallest paperbark a pair of sea-eagles is busy at its bulky nest.

As it drains out of the paperbark forest, the creek broadens and leaves the escarpment behind. At this exit it flows into another large waterhole, wider and deeper than the others. Dominating this pool and guarding the creek's entrance is the rough-hewn face of Djuwarr Rock. A broad sandy beach stretches below it and across the pool stand widely spaced, tall

The rainbow pitta nests during the wet season in the monsoon forests. © *National Geographic Society.*

paperbarks. Beneath is soft green grass. A little upstream from the trees a huge flat rock shelves towards the water's edge. Water pandanus flank it on both sides. The pool itself is alive with fish of all sizes from tiny perchlets among the pandanus roots to big barramundi smacking the water with their tails. Six mature freshwater crocodiles cruise the waters.

These crocodiles, with narrower snouts and sharper teeth than the saltwater species, grow to only about three metres in length. During the wet season the freshwater crocodiles caught fish, frogs and crustaceans. Insects were the principal diet for the young and growing crocodiles. Now that the dry season is approaching the adults will feed less and less and for a few months may not feed at all.

In the middle of August the females will crawl onto the sandy banks along the creek, such as the one beneath Djuwarr Rock, excavate their nest holes and lay their clutches of ten to sixteen eggs. Unlike the saltwater crocodiles, the females do not tend and protect their nests, though they remain nearby in the waterhole. But when the hatchlings begin to make their strange quacking sounds, indicating that they are ready to emerge, the females dig out their nests and carry their young to the water in their jaws.

A Mertens' water goanna basks on a rock in Djuwarr Creek.

The nocturnal brown treesnake is as much at home in the maze of caverns and crevices of the escarpment as it is in the trees.

The northern quoll or native cat is a fearless and audacious nocturnal hunter.

Because the females do not protect their nests, predators, especially goannas, destroy a lot of eggs. Young that hatch from the surviving eggs fare even worse and only about two out of every hundred make it through their first year.

The setting sun catches Djuwarr's face and paints it in its brightest colours. Its perfect reflection is mirrored in the pool. Occasionally the image trembles and wobbles as a crocodile surfaces and ripples the water. A pair of sea-eagles perches in an ancient paperbark overlooking the water, intent on the possibility of one last catch. Along the rock's upper slopes little wood swallows skim and dive after flying insects. The sun drops out of sight behind the escarpment and the colour drains from Djuwarr. Immediately it is cooler.

A black kangaroo-like animal bounds fearlessly from ledge to ledge, boulder to boulder then down the scree slope sending loose rocks clattering. The male black wallaroo pauses to groom himself. In the subdued light he appears jet black, but in the sun chestnut trimmings on legs and underside would become apparent. He scratches his small ears and washes his face with his paws. Slowly he hops to the water's edge and drinks, but he is not at ease away from the rocks and soon he leaps back up the cliff.

Darkness comes swiftly. The wood swallows fly to a small cave and, clinging to the wall, sleep closely pressed together. The day animals fall silent. Bush curlews slink from their hiding place beneath a leafy shrub and in their mournful voices call a drawn out 'gurrwerlu, gurrwerlu'. Dark shapes outlined against the sky's last remnants of light move in and out of the ravine; night herons move out to fish and black flying foxes fly upstream to feed on fruits. Small bats skim low over the water and drink on the wing. The rufous owl flies silently off to hunt in the ravine.

A sandstone antechinus devours a large grasshopper. This tiny marsupial is found only in Kakadu's stone country.

By the light of the stars and a crescent moon animals come out from caves and crevices. First out of hiding are the irrepressible, athletic northern quolls. A male emerges from his lair calmly enough and for some minutes grooms himself. Then displaying his carnivorous teeth in a huge yawn, he stretches himself and in an instant dashes away. Leaping and running he streaks down the rock face and into the monsoon forest. It is dark here and even the quoll's large eyes can detect little; his sensitive nose leads him to the crickets, beetles and centipedes in the leaflitter. His white-spotted form is hyperactive. Tail bristling and long whiskers trembling, he squirms into caverns after spiders, geckoes and rats, digs in the sand for burrowing frogs and races up trees to catch grasshoppers and rob birds' nests.

A tiny hollow between shelving rocks only a few centimetres apart is enough space for the diminutive sandstone antechinus to have made his nest. He looks, and acts, like a miniature replica of the quoll, only without the spots. Like the quoll, he is never still, flitting from rock to rock in quick, darting leaps. He is rarely in the open long enough to be a target for an owl or a ghost bat. This pocket-sized predator is game to tackle anything. He rushes fearlessly at a grasshopper as large as himself and bites at the strong armour plating on its neck. The insect tries to defend itself by lashing out with its spiny legs at the same time leaping among the ground plants. But to no avail, the antechinus holds on tightly, eyes closed, till the insect dies of a hundred tiny bites.

A large-eyed, brown-and-white-banded snake eases its long slender form from a narrow crevice high up on the cliff. The nocturnal brown treesnake, feeling its way with its flicking tongue, glides effortlessly up the sheer rocks. The slightest surface irregularities on the rocks

Little wood swallows roost clinging closely together.

Right
The view from Jabiru Dreaming looking east. In the foreground is a marsh and beyond that the East Alligator River.

are sufficient for the snake's belly scales to get a hold.

On the terraced rock slopes below, the black-headed python moves smoothly and quickly. With his ever-moving tongue he detects the scent of a rock-living goanna. Before the sleeping lizard senses danger, it is seized by the python and wrapped in its constricting coils.

An echidna, confident of the protection of her coat of sharp spines, waddles along sniffing for termites among the spinifex. The tiny insects have built covered passageways from their mounds to the prickly grasses. The echidna sweeps the termites' structures aside with her strong claws and inserting her long sticky tongue into the passages, licks up the insects.

Last to come out of hiding is the woolly-furred rock possum, a placid and unhurried eater of leaves and flowers. A female, carrying her half-grown young on her back, climbs out of the cool depths of a gigantic pile of boulders. Walking, but rarely leaping, she makes her way to the topmost rock and then transfers smoothly to the branches of a flowering eucalypt tree. Her nails, though sharp, are worn short on the rocks, but it does not affect her tree-climbing skills. In the tree's branches, while its mother feeds on leaves and flowers, the young sets off on exploratory trips of its own. The animals' fur, grey tinged with a hint of drab green, blends well with both the rocks and the tree's foliage. Only the dabs of white around their eyes and ears stand out in the dim light.

Out beyond the entrance to Djuwarr's ravine stretches a sea of woodlands and forests dominated by eucalypts. They make up the largest areas of Kakadu. During this night in May animal life among the gum trees is perhaps even more varied than it is among the rocks.

6 ~ WOODLANDS AND FORESTS

AS THE CRESCENT MOON SETS on the May night at Djuwarr Rock the calls of bush curlews, magnified by the cliff, carry far along Deaf Adder Creek. Further along the valley, past where wallabies graze and flying foxes feed on paperbark flowers, far beyond the limits of the escarpment, out in the seemingly limitless eucalypt forests lies a place where a small spring percolates from the base of a low ridge. A tall tree with flaky brown bark on its trunk but whose upper branches shine a glossy white, rises above the small pool. The Darwin woollybutt, a kind of eucalypt, is in full flower. The bright orange colour, however, is not evident now. Scores of black flying foxes clamber over the blossoms, licking the copious supply of nectar. Among the black shapes, often squabbling in loud shrieks over feeding territories, skips and dashes a smaller more elegant animal: the pale grey sugar glider moving delicately from flower to flower.

Now and again stopping to clean her soft fur, to sniff the air with a pink nose or to look around with her huge black eyes, the marsupial has an air of vulnerable innocence about her. But her appearance belies an, at times, ferocious nature.

The glider has seen a large katydid moving among the gum leaves. With a speed too fast for the eye to follow she pounces on the insect with her sharp claws and bites its head off. Sitting on the branch she eats her catch fastidiously, pulling off the grasshopper's wings and dropping them to the ground.

The patch of forest around the spring is alive with even more night animals than the escarpment country. During the day most slept or dozed in the hollows so numerous in the eucalypts. The animals are now busy foraging. Northern quolls rush about here too, catching grasshoppers and chasing mice. But the possum is of a different kind; it is a brush-tail, brash and agile, who is busy in the tree tops. The forest antechinus is different also — a browner, larger species but possessed of the same quicksilver speed and ferocity as its sandstone cousin. Another small marsupial hunter, however, is quite different. The red-cheeked dunnart does not climb trees or squeeze into cracks in the rock, it lives strictly among the grasses. The same place where the delicate mouse — Australia's smallest rodent — is eating grass seeds, and the grassland melomys builds its nest in a thick clump of wild sorghum.

Another animal with a silky black brush, the brush-tailed rabbit rat, has come down from its tree hollow to sift the soil for spear grass seeds. Tawny frogmouths have discarded their daytime disguises of motionless eyes-closed postures in which they resemble dry branches, and are now fluffed out, bright yellow eyes wide as they look and listen for large insects on which to pounce. A pair of spotted nightjars skims low over the tree tops and intercepts moths and beetles on their way to sip from the woollybutt flowers. Small insectivorous bats, of

Above
The red-cheeked dunnart lives among the grasses of the forest floor.

Top
One of the first voices of the dawn chorus is that of the raucous blue-winged kookaburra.

Previous pages
A sugar glider licks nectar from woollybutt flowers.

Left
The barn owl hunts small mammals in the forests at night.

Above
An agile wallaby with large pouch young.

Right
A male antelope kangaroo bounds across a grassy clearing.

which about twenty different kinds come to these forests, are also hunting on the wing. Down on the ground a huge olive python faintly rustles the dry grass as he searches for prey — a brindled bandicoot snorts and leaps out of his way at the last moment, a wallaby thumps the ground in alarm at his approach.

Towards dawn a heavy dew falls, making a large green tree frog croak before returning to its hollow. Yet another brush-tailed animal, the phascogale, a marsupial hunter, leaps through the leaves and bathes in the shower of drops, then sitting at the entrance to her nest hollow cleans herself thoroughly.

As the first faint light seeps into the eastern sky, the flying foxes return to their roosts, frogmouths and nightjars resume their disguises and all the small mammals go back to their tree hollows. Only the wallabies and kangaroos continue to feed; their faces and undersides becoming saturated with dew. It is cool and the small young stay warm and dry in their mothers' pouches.

When the sun rises there is instant warmth. The agile wallabies and their taller relatives, the antelope kangaroos, stop grazing and stand facing the sun with eyes half-closed. Offspring that are big enough climb out of their mothers' pouches, the younger ones stick their heads out and blink in the bright light.

The sun reveals the intense colour of the orange woollybutt flowers and of the lorikeets that come to feed on them; the orange, green and blue of the red-collared lorikeets and the

The jumping spider, Mopsus mormon, *lies in wait for insects among the foliage of shrubs and small trees.*

scarlet caps and rosy breasts of the varieds. Woollybutt trees are scattered all over the gentle slope and along the ridge. Closer to the spring grow the taller, straighter Darwin stringybarks, so called for the thick, fibrous and dark grey covering of their trunks. Grass grows taller and more uniform under the stringybarks. The spring itself is really only a small soak feeding a sheltered pool of water. It does not give rise to a stream, but on the other hand it never dries up. Life is rich and varied within a radius of several hundred metres.

When the sun has dried the dew, the wallabies and kangaroos lie down in the shade and doze. Now the great concourse of birds animates the forests. Honeyeaters, pardalotes and warblers glean tiny insects from the eucalypts' drooping leaves, while treecreepers prise spiders from cracks in their bark. Rosellas, pigeons and quail search the ground for fallen seeds while finches dangle from grass stems to pick seeds that are still green. Flycatchers pursue insects. Untidy red-tailed black cockatoos chisel open hard woollybutt fruits and extract the seeds. A forest kingfisher dives on a ground beetle in a streak of intense blue as a cuckoo picks a hairy caterpillar off a shrub. A troop of a dozen red-breasted babblers, yahooing in exuberant voices, turns over the leaflitter looking for insects. One of them is the first to spot the silent arrival of a grey goshawk. Chattering anxiously the whole flock flies to the cover of a small leafy tree and scolds the intruder.

Another raptor, the handsome crested hawk, its underside neatly banded in rufous and pale grey, is busy hunting in the foliage of a stringybark. It spreads no alarm for it is mainly a hunter of insects. At this time of year grasshoppers are its main food and among the leaves

An azure kingfisher, nesting in the bank of a woodland stream, brings a carp gudgeon for its young.

the hawk catches one katydid after another. In the forest's lower strata the smoky grey and white little cuckoo-shrike catches smaller grasshoppers. The ground litter grasshoppers try to elude glossy skinks by imitating the dry leaves in colour and shape.

It is a rich harvest for grasshoppers are exceptionally numerous; they, not the wallabies and kangaroos, are the chief herbivores in Kakadu. In fact, of all the animal groups, insects are the most numerous and exert the greatest influence in shaping the forests and woodlands. Most visible are the ubiquitous grasshoppers. But there is another group even more numerous, a group that actually determines how tall the trees grow and how many have hollows in them. These are the termites, or white ants as they are sometimes erroneously called. Termites are not closely related to ants; their nearest relatives are the cockroaches. But before looking into the lives of the insects let us closely examine the forests and woodlands.

The Woodlands

Considerably more than half of Kakadu is covered with eucalypt dominated forests and woodlands. At first these might appear as flat, uniform habitats that go on and on, unchanging. But this is deceptive. In reality they form a mosaic of subtly different environments. Two broad divisions, however, are easily distinguished, the forests and the woodlands.

Woodlands are the most extensive of all Kakadu's habitats. They grow on the poorer, harder soils. Their trees are low, never growing over 13 m in height and often considerably less. They are widely spaced and lose their leaves in the dry season. Their crowns, if

The white gum sheds its old greyish-white bark each year. The colour of the fresh bark underneath fades in a matter of months.

Right
Flowers of the Darwin woollybutt.

projected onto the ground, would take up no more than 10—30 per cent of the area. The woodlands' dominant plant species are not trees at all, but grasses. Botanically the woodlands are the most complex, as well as the least known of all of Kakadu's habitats.

Forests have tall trees over 13 m in height which grow closely together. Their crowns when projected onto the ground would cover 30—70 per cent of the area. Only the monsoon forests of river flats and the escarpment have completely closed canopies. Forests grow on deeper, better soils and have year-round ground moisture available to them. The trees are therefore evergreen. Two species dominate, *Eucalyptus tetrodonta*, the Darwin stringybark, and *Eucalyptus miniata*, the Darwin woollybutt. Stringybarks grow on the better soils and encourage an understorey of grass while the woollybutts are on the poorer, sandy soils with mostly shrubs growing beneath them.

Both woodlands and forests have a wide array of plants growing in them, including many beautiful wildflowers, and have the most diverse flora of all Kakadu's environments. The vast majority of fruits, seeds and tubers gathered as food by the Aboriginal people, come from the woodlands and forests.

These places also support a wider variety of animal species than the others. This is not always apparent on a casual visit, especially during the dry season when the animals congregate around small springs. The apparent lack of wildlife has given the wooded places, the places occupying the greater part of Kakadu, the undeserved reputation among white

The flowers of the swamp bloodwood to which lorikeets are attracted.

Right
Flowers of the bridal tree, a common medium-sized species.

people of being dull, useless, uninteresting and unimportant. But this is a superficial assessment and not borne out by a careful and sensitive examination. For example, there are more species of mammals in Kakadu's eucalypt wooded areas than in any other area of Australia except one, and that is the tropical rainforest of north-east Queensland. Even within Kakadu there is a greater variety of birds in the wooded areas than in the billabongs and floodplains, more mammal species than in the stone country and a greater number of plant species than almost all other habitats combined. The woodlands and forests may not have the grandeur of the escarpment nor the vast flocks of birds of the wetlands, but biologically they are the most important and exciting. Nothing is more fascinating, for example, than the close association between eucalypts and termites.

Termites

All termite activity is centred around the nest which is built and maintained so that it is independent from the outside world except for food. This is the key to the termites' overwhelming success; they thrive because their society is insulated from the physical environment whose vagaries of temperature and humidity make it impossible for unprotected individuals to live in.

Most nests are maintained at a steady 30°C–35°C and close to 100 per cent relative humidity, no matter what the outside conditions are. This is made possible through a

Right
The queen of a Coptotermes acinaciformis *colony. An immobile egglaying machine, her every need is catered for by the workers. This termite species is perhaps the most numerous in Kakadu.*

Far right
Kakadu's woodlands and forests are riddled with countless termite mounds. Those of the spinifex termite, shown here, are the tallest.

Below right
Spinifex termite workers, protected by soldiers, repair a hole in their mound.

complex system of tunnels and passages with only minimal openings to the outside world. So well-organised is a termite nest that it can be considered as a kind of super organism in its own right; the different kinds of cells being represented by the individuals within the nest. Termite nests are everywhere, deep underground, in fallen wood, in hollow tree trunks, as round balls high in trees and as huge independent structures five or more metres tall made of hard clay. If these ever-present nests, most containing millions of individuals, are considered collectively, then indeed it is more readily realised what a great power they exert on the forests and woodlands.

The termites' great strength is that they can digest, and so live on, what is indigestible to virtually all other animals. Their food is cellulose, the basic material that wood and dry grasses are made of. In the wooded habitats with their grassy understoreys there is a super abundance of this material. Because termites can eat the inedible and live in closed colonies in which they create their own optimum living conditions, they thrive where no other animals can. They are most numerous in Kakadu's least hospitable woodlands, places where the trees are sparsest and the soils the poorest. Thirty-six of Kakadu's sixty or so species of termites live in these places. Monsoon forests, paperbark forests and the stone country have few termites in them and the wetlands virtually none at all.

Every conceivable corner of Kakadu's woodlands and forests are riddled with termite nests and their radiating networks of covered tunnels and passageways. They reach everywhere, through the soils and up the tree trunks. Only marshland and solid rock thwart them. Endless processions of the insects, sometimes more than 20 million per hectare, are constantly gnawing at the plants; they tunnel the dry heartwood of trees, eat away living bark, digest the branches and leaves fallen to the ground, harvest the grasses and turn over the soil for minute particles of vegetable matter. Between them they gather 300 kg of dry plant matter per hectare each year. They are possibly the most efficient animals in converting their food into their own kind, certainly in the drier areas of poor soil. In Queensland, in an area somewhat like Kakadu, it was discovered that termites were up to ten times more efficient than cattle in using the plant resources.

All these millions of insects go about their ceaseless activities almost totally unseen and unheard.

Not all Kakadu's termite species are equally numerous nor do they affect the woodlands and forests in the same way. By far the most influential, largely shaping the wooded places, is a single species: *Coptotermes acinaciformis*, copto for short.

In a typical woodland grass grows tall among glistening woollybutts and sombre stringybarks. Dotted among them, partially hidden, are domes of yellow-brown clay and earth. These humps vary in height from 30 cm to almost two metres. Many are built at the bases of trees or engulf an old stump. They have no openings, no outward signs of life. These are the nests of coptos. Deep inside each mound is a central system of narrow passages and small chambers; the nerve centre for a radiating network of tunnels to nearby living trees. In the larger mounds live more than a million individuals.

Each mound's outer layer is built of countless tiny blocks the size of grains of rice which the workers fashion out of a mixture of clay and their own saliva and droppings. It is a hard, waterproof shell that insulates and protects the central core of galleries. This complex is a nursery producing stupendous numbers of individuals. At the very centre is a chamber a little larger than the others; the royal cell where the colony's queen lives. She is continuously tended by workers and guarded at all times by platoons of soldiers. Occasionally the king comes and mates with her. The queen and king are the sole functioning reproductives. All the others, all one million of them, are their offspring. These are either workers, soldiers or immature reproductives which will develop wings and fly out of the nest at the beginning of the wet season.

A nest's king and queen begin their adult lives as such winged individuals, called alates. Over the years, the king grows very little. But the queen's abdomen distends grotesquely, until she is four times as long and four times as wide as when she emerged as an alate. She becomes an egglaying machine. Unable to walk, she is taken care of by the workers.

Workers take away the thousands of eggs the queen lays and place them in the nursery galleries. Others feed the nymphs from the time they hatch to the day they are fully fledged members of society — the bulk of them workers. Workers can live up to two years of age.

It is the queen's fecundity together with the workers' longevity, that allows for the enormous build-up of numbers in the colony. This build-up could go on forever, for when a king or queen dies, it is immediately replaced by reproductives already in the nest. Theoretically the colony is immortal. But for unknown reasons copto nests rarely survive for longer than forty years.

A colony's non-reproductive activity is far-flung. Long lines of workers bring pellets of moist soil from deep underground to expand and maintain the mound's outer layer. Extensive underground tunnels fan out to surrounding trees which are then gradually hollowed out. Armies of workers mine the heartwood with their jaws. Each worker is no more than five millimetres long, yet such are their numbers and is their industry, that in time they will hollow out entire trees. Out in the woodland 85 per cent of mature trees are hollowed out. In some particular woodlands *all* the trees are piped. Coptos from a single nest may hollow out twelve trees and tunnel towards another four.

The termites' main enemies are ants. Against them the soldiers are most effective, cutting and slicing them with their pincers and enmeshing them with a white sticky substance they exude from glands in their jaws. There is constant warfare between the two kinds of insects.

The ants usually attack at the termite colony's weakest point: the thinly covered feeding tunnels. Soldiers usually repel the invaders but only after a deadly skirmish that takes many casualties. The ants may win and wipe out an entire nest, leaving it an empty fortress.

By the end of October some forty thousand new reproductives mill around the upper passages of a mature copto nest. These alates are a little larger and darker than the workers and each has four long, transparent wings. Alates are ready to leave the nest should the right weather prevail. It is not till one damp, overcast afternoon in mid-December that conditions are right. The workers open up concealed passages on top of the mound. Soldiers rush out first and stand guard at the entrances, then the alates stream out to face the first daylight of their lives. For nearly half an hour the winged termites stream out, looking like a plume of smoke. Those that escape the lizards and birds that have quickly gathered, fly high into the air, then drifting on the breeze glide slowly back to earth. They may land several kilometres away or fall beside the nest. On landing, they shed their wings with quick twists of their

A woodland scene with Darwin woollybutts as the dominant trees. There is a remarkable association between the eucalypt trees and termites.

bodies. Pairs will team up and search for suitable places to establish new colonies. Only very few will succeed.

During its forty-year life span, a coptos' nest will send some 1.5 million alates swarming through the woodland, that is 750,000 pairs. But to maintain their numbers, only one pair need replace them.

While many species of termites attack the trees, especially the eucalypts, by far the greatest excavators of tree hollows are coptos. Eucalypt and copto are closely linked throughout wooded Australia, but especially so in Kakadu. The partnership is of great benefit to many animals. The tree hollows they jointly provide are essential to a surprisingly large number of them, more than in almost any other part of the world. Possums, gliders and other mammals live in tree hollows by day and use them as safe havens to raise their young. Many different kinds of birds — parrots, cockatoos, owls, tree creepers, ducks, kingfishers, rollers and others — cannot nest in any other place than a tree hollow. Snakes, goannas, frilled lizards and even frogs retreat to the cavities excavated by termites to escape the sun, rain, fire, predators and even the cold of night. About a quarter of Australia's land vertebrates use tree hollows for one purpose or another. And, except for one or two species of parrot that chew nest hollows out of rotten wood, not one of them chips out its own niche.

It would seem that the constant, remorseless onslaught of termites in such overwhelming numbers would in the end destroy the susceptible eucalypts and eliminate them from the forests and woodlands. Certainly the termites weaken the trees. Even though trees need only about half of the wood they produce to support themselves, the termites often take more,

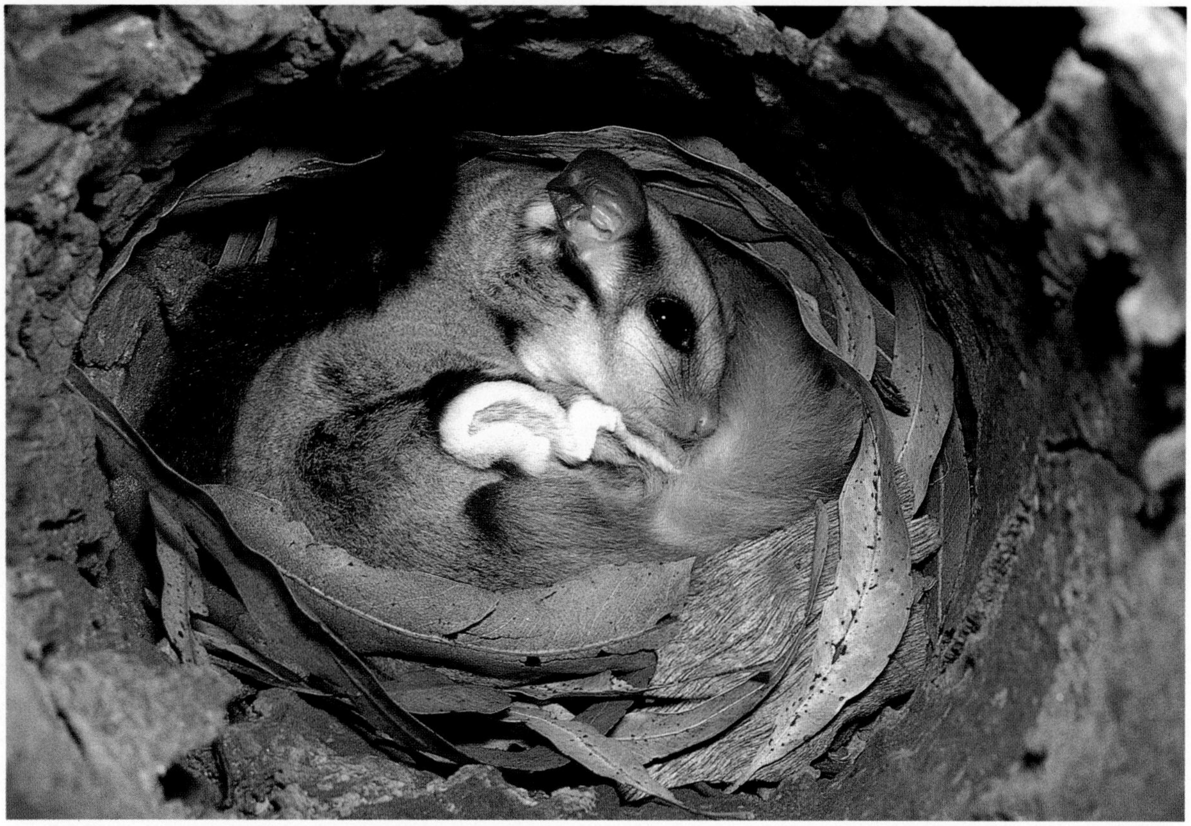

A sugar glider sleeps in a tree branch hollowed out by termites. Termites hollow out more than 80 per cent, and in some cases 100 per cent, of the trees in eucalypt forests and woodlands, and so provide shelter for an unusually large variety of animals.

with the result that the eucalypts blow down in storms or are undermined by fire long before they have reached their maximum possible size. There are no ancient and giant gum trees in Kakadu, something that is determined almost solely by the coptos. But there is now some evidence, gathered by scientists of the Commonwealth Scientific and Industrial Research Organisation working in Kakadu, that the eucalypts may actually benefit from the termite attack. The scientists postulate that termites and eucalypts together can live better in areas of poor soil and with a long dry season, than either could separately.

The fundamental factor is that the trees are hollow. By 'allowing' the coptos to hollow them out, through weak chemical defences and not too dense a heartwood, the eucalypts provide homes for many, many different kinds of animals. These animals, including the coptos and other species of termite, deposit significant amounts of organic matter, mostly in the form of droppings, in the pipes and hollows. Eventually this material finds its way back into the soil where it acts as a fertiliser. The termite mounds themselves, compared to the soil around them, are also rich in nutrients. When a colony dies, the decaying mound enriches the soil further. But it is a slow process. It may take as many as thirty years for a mound to disintegrate completely. Even so, in an area where termites are numerous, decaying mounds may add between 300 and 400 kg of this fertiliser per hectare each year. As well as that, the termites' many tunnels and galleries aerate the so often rock-hard soil and make tree growth easier. The result is that more and healthier trees can grow in the woodlands providing more food for termites and refuges for a host of other animals.

A woodland grasshopper. Grasshoppers are among the most abundant insects in Kakadu, especially during the wet season.

Above right
A male great bowerbird displays at his playground.

Grasshoppers

The wooded environment must also carry the burden of another insect force: the vast number of grasshoppers. But with a few exceptions, they do not attack the trees; the grasses, herbs and shrubs are their victims. Unlike the termites, the grasshoppers must live out in the open, exposed to all the elements of a turbulent environment. During the dry season, when most of their food is dry and unnutritious or burnt to ashes, the vast majority of grasshoppers perish. The next generation passes the inhospitable seasons as eggs in the soil. With the onset of the rains and the regeneration of the plants, the eggs hatch and the nymphs soon eat their way back to prolificness. The total mass of grasshoppers in Kakadu is four to five times as great in the wet season than in the dry. So numerous are Kakadu's 151 species of grasshoppers and crickets that their combined mass represents about half that of all insects living there.

The Great Bowerbird

In the woodlands and forests, the season has advanced from May to late August. It is dry and already hot. Grasses have died back to straw and much has been burnt. Woodland trees are beginning to shed their leaves. But strangely this is the time of courtship and breeding activity for a number of birds. One of them is the great bowerbird. The males are now busy renovating their playgrounds which have lain untended during the wet and early dry seasons. The bower is a sturdily made structure, placed on the ground, consisting of two parallel rows

The ferocious-looking frilled lizard spreads his neck ruff in threat. Very little is known about the life history of this most spectacular lizard.

of dry twigs placed upright in a platform of the same material. The twigs meet at the top like a miniature archway. At either end and in the centre of the avenue the bird has put piles of ornaments gathered from near and far; bleached bones, snail shells and white stones. Neither the bower nor the ornaments have deteriorated greatly during the months of the male's absence but still he spends several hours each day improving and repairing his arena. He brings new snail shells, some wallaby bones and also fresh display items: green berries, small leafy twigs and a few large brown seeds. But mostly he works on the avenue, bringing new twigs and inserting them carefully.

The purpose of this amazing structure is first of all to attract a female and then to entrance her to such a degree that she will come back again and again until the pair mate. It is not till September that the male begins his rituals in earnest. At dawn he advertises his presence by singing from a perch above his bower. It is a strange song in which he mimics the calls of

Crimson finch. Many species of finches live on grass seeds in the late monsoon.

other birds and weaves them together with his own hissing and churring notes. After some time he flies off to collect a stem of a small green plant with pink flowers. He breaks a few centimetres off this stem, mashes it in his beak, and hops inside the avenue. With broad strokes of the pulped stem, still held in his beak, he paints the sticks. From time to time he discards his paintbrush, hops over to the plant stem and breaks off a new piece. He may spend an hour patiently painting the inside of the avenue. The reason is difficult to fathom for there is no discernible difference after the sticks are painted. Perhaps the juices of the plant act as a kind of preservative and insect repellent so the sticks will not rot or be eaten by termites. The bowers are certainly durable.

Painting finished for the day, the bowerbird rearranges his ornaments. All the while he watches keenly for a female. Suddenly in the middle of picking up a snail shell he stiffens. A female has arrived in the tree above. He drops the shell which lands with a clatter among the others. Straightening himself to his full height, drooping his wings till they almost touch the ground, he prances stiff-leggedly around the bower, all the while uttering churring and choofing sounds. The female flies down to the bower and lands by the pile of ornaments at one end of the avenue. The male rushes to the other end, churring and hissing like a locomotive, picks up a green berry and holding it in his beak, bends forward so that the female at the other end of the bower can clearly see the back of his head. Then he spreads the covering feathers at his nape and reveals the brilliant lilac-pink plumage hidden beneath. The female appears unimpressed. She fiddles with a few twigs, picks up a bone and drops it. The indifference seems to inflame the male, his voice sounds more urgent, he picks up and drops his ornaments with quick jerky movements, he displays his colourful feathers, he bows and weaves. Suddenly he picks up a large brown seed and with it clamped in his beak rushes around to the female. She flies away.

Over the days and weeks the female becomes less skittish and in due course the pair mates in the bower's avenue. The female then builds a nest in a small tree nearby, lays her two handsomely marked eggs and rears the young without any assistance from the male. His energies are entirely focused on his bower.

Rain Comes to the Forest

Inevitably, reliably, the rains return and in early November the forests are drenched by almost daily downpours. The transformation is immediate and soon the country has taken on a veneer of green. The first storms bring that most spectacular of reptiles, the enigmatic frilled lizard, out of hiding. The lizards have spent the entire dry season hidden in tree hollows. But now they are everywhere. They sit in open spaces among the grasses, noses in the air, their frills loosely arranged around themselves. Periodically they totter off on their hindlegs to snap up some insect. Every time they open their mouths to grab their prey, their frills spread like scaly discs around their heads. Ants are a favoured food and many of the lizards sit on tree trunks and pick up the insects as they come down their trails. Life is easy after the rain.

Growth among the multitude of grasses that have sprouted from seed or from perennial rootstocks is intermittent. But when the monsoon breaks the grasses shoot up to establish a tall, lush cover. Some species of spear grass will grow 4 m tall in a matter of three months.

Rain brings abundant grass growth to the forest. Spear grass is named after the shape of its seeds which resemble miniature spears complete with barbed points and shafts.

In March when the grasses have reached their maximum size, when many are flowering, the forests are at their most beautiful. When high cloud softens the light the solid dark trunks of the stringybarks brood over the tall jungles of grass, among whose stems glow a profusion of pink, yellow, red, blue and white flowers.

By April the annual grasses, dominated by *Sorghum intrans*, the spear grass, have grown to maturity. The seeds are ripe and drop to the ground.

Once the seeds have been shed, the annual grasses have run their course. The water pressure within the tall stems, which kept them green and upright, dries up. The stems yellow to straw and collapse. This process often coincides with the last fierce storms of April which are consequently known as the knock-em-downs. The spear grass will not germinate till November, no matter how much rain falls in the intervening period.

April's knock-em-down storms have flattened the already withering spear grass.

Fire

As the season becomes hotter and less humid, the grasses compact into a tinder-dry mat. Together with the fallen litter from the eucalypts, Kakadu's forests and woodlands become one of the most flammable habitats in the world. Each year 85 per cent of the woodlands are burnt while the forests are burnt two out of every three years. Such frequent, extensive fires are an artifice of man. Before Aboriginal people came to these parts the only fires were set by lightning. Their effect on the vegetation was minimal.

Aborigines, using fire, profoundly affected the drier forested areas throughout Australia. Over the millennia the Aboriginal people lived on the continent this is the only major way in which they influenced the natural environment — they *changed* it but did not *destroy* it. Over the generations the Aborigines used this 'fire-stick farming' to great effect to create a mosaic of varying habitats that provided a great diversity of plants and animals. They developed great skills as fire managers.

Fire favours species of plants which can tolerate heat, scorching and even being partly burnt. Eucalypts are the most resilient of the trees. After fire has completely defoliated them, they shoot again from dormant buds on their trunks and main branches which had been protected by thick bark of low flammability. Even if their trunks are destroyed, many species regrow from their root boles. Ground plants also survive as underground rootstock or as seeds either in the soil or protected in fire-proof capsules. Fire sensitive species, the ones which are killed when defoliated or whose seeds and rootstocks die when scorched, are eliminated. Most rainforest plants fall in this category. The hardy, vigorous species survive and make up the forests and woodlands.

The same characteristics that make plants fire resistant are also adaptations to long dry spells and low soil fertility. So in Kakadu, as in much of Australia's tropical north, with its long, hot dry season and its gravelly, sandy soils, frequent fires reinforce adaptations that already existed. As a consequence fires as a rule do no permanent damage to the woodlands and forests. Every wet season they are regenerated and the same species as before the fire grow vigorously again. None is lost. Only in Australia are there such fire-resistant environments. Fires in conifer or hardwood forests in Europe and North America, for example, destroy them and they take centuries, not just one wet season, to regrow to their original state.

But even so fire at the wrong time at the wrong place can do great damage in Kakadu. The fire-stick farmers of old knew this. It was something they learned over 2500 generations of experience. They exercised great care in the annual burn-offs. The actual lighting of fires could only be done, or had to be strictly supervised, by the fully initiated elders.

They knew that the time to begin burning had arrived when the black kites, brown falcons, magpie larks and red-backed kingfishers returned from their wet season exile in the dry country to the south. First the Aboriginal people would burn the woodlands, which growing on moisture poor soils and being open to the sun, had dried out more quickly. Fires would be lit in the afternoon so that they would not burn during the hottest part of the day and race out of control. The evening coolness and dew would extinguish them. About a month later, in June, the open forests had also dried out and would then be burned by the Aborigines.

Effects of Fire

When the elders set their paperbark torches to the dry spear grass it catches instantly. The south-easterlies whip it into a sheet of flame and the fire soon roars through the undergrowth. It leaps from the grasses up the trunks of palms and pandanus whose dry fronds burn fiercely in an explosive hiss. Acrid smoke and ash are swept up in the hot updrafts. With the first crackle of flame and the first plume of smoke, a signal seems to move through the forests summoning the kites, falcons and other birds to a ready food supply.

But the small terrestrial animals must seek shelter: ants race into the safety of their underground nests; lizards hurry down cracks in the soil or hollows in trees; mice retreat to their deepest underground chambers; bandicoots run from their grass nests to hollow logs or empty termite mounds; snakes slither into burrows or hollow trees; cockroaches scurry away in front of the flames; grasshoppers take wing.

Sitting on shrubs just in advance of the wall of fire, are brown falcons. Every time some small animal dashes out to try to outrun the smoke and heat, the falcon strikes. Hundreds of kites soar on broad wings, keeping pace with the advancing fire. So closely do they flirt with the flames as they swoop on grasshoppers and skinks, that many are singed.

Tiny flying insects are swept up by the updrafts and rise high in the air. Wood swallows and tree martins skimming over the tree crowns scoop them up in midair. Higher still, hundreds of metres above the fire, flocks of swifts catch the insects in their beaks.

The fire advances quickly leaving a blackened landscape of smouldering logs, glowing embers and layers of ash. Finally, it runs its course. By evening there is no breeze to fan it, no hot air to create updrafts. The flames are finally extinguished by the morning's dew.

The next day, and for as long as three weeks afterwards, kites, falcons as well as other raptors such as little eagles and black-breasted buzzards, linger in the burnt areas. They are joined by butcherbirds, kookaburras and red-backed kingfishers. All of them have designs on the fire's survivors, for the small, once grass-living animals are vulnerable. They have been affected by the smoke and heat and are disorientated as their cover and their food has been stripped away. The predators take full advantage of the changed circumstances. Scavenging birds, kites and eagles among them, continue to search for larger animals, such as bandicoots and olive pythons, who may have perished.

The fire does not benefit the hunters and predators alone. The heat has opened many seed pods and freed their contents for the red-tailed black cockatoos and partridge pigeons. These birds barely wait for the ashes to cool to rush in for this food supply. Even when the plants begin to reshoot, drawing on the last remaining soil moisture, many birds who hunt or glean their food from the forest floor, prefer the burnt areas. Food is more plentiful here and they are less likely to be ambushed. Wallabies and kangaroos gather to feed on the green flush.

These fires set at the proper, that is cooler, season may appear devastating as they roar along, but they do remarkably little damage. The trees are not affected; their crowns remain green and unscorched. Because the fires are extinguished at night and also because some moist areas resist them, the forests are not burnt uniformly. They are a patchwork of burnt and unburnt country. Places unburnt this year may go up in flames the next or the one after — the mosaic is infinite in its variety. As the fires kill small saplings one to two years old, it

A late dry season fire has devastated this forest. The trees have been scorched to their crowns by the intense heat and the entire understorey has been reduced to ash.

is necessary for the regeneration of the forests to have unburnt sections where young trees can shoot up to a fire-resistant size. The greater the diversity of fire history the greater the diversity of plants and animals in the forests. Fires of the cooler season are themselves cooler, about 250°C, and this combined with some reserves of soil moisture allow the forests to recover quickly and completely from the effects of cool season fires.

But when the fires are set late in the dry when there is no soil moisture left, when the grasses and other fuels are completely dehydrated, when day temperatures reach 40°C, when winds are stronger and there is no dew, it is a very different matter.

Unstoppable walls of flame 15 m or more high then sweep through forest and woodland at a terrifying speed and with a fury of heat and a hissing, roaring sound. The wind whips the fire into an ever-widening front and while it quietens down at night, it does continue to smoulder. The next day it rages on again, consuming all before it. These fires are hotter, up to 550°C. They scorch the trees, killing all leaves, to the very tops of their crowns. Saplings several years old are destroyed. There is no patchwork of burnt and unburnt country but kilometre upon kilometre of charred forest. As no moisture reserves linger within the soil, recovery is slow. Fewer animals escape; many that escape the actual flames succumb to the smoke and the heat. Hollow logs lying on the ground are burnt to ash where earlier fires would have barely singed them, leaving them intact as animal refuges.

So wild are these late fires that they invade pockets of the fire-sensitive monsoon forests destroying parts of them, probably forever. They also leap onto the escarpment where the resinous spinifex explodes into balls of flame and black smoke.

Ever since the Aboriginal people lost control of their lands fifty to sixty years ago, fires are more frequent and too many rage in the late dry season. Kakadu is being changed. Forest and woodland are now dominated over vast uniform tracts by spear grass. To the Gagudju this is a clear indication of lamentable mismanagement of the fire regime. In certain areas several species of eucalypt are slowly disappearing as old trees collapse under frequent, severe fires which at the same time kill the young trees coming up to replace them. Pockets of the herb *Pityrodia*, the sole food plant of the rare and spectacular Leichhardt grasshopper, are burnt, killing both the plant and a generation of grasshoppers before it can reproduce. On Nourlangie Rock wet forests have been burnt and replaced by virulent fire weeds that choke the ravines where banded pigeons used to nest. At Malangangerr monsoon forest trees that shelter man's longest continuously inhabited place are undermined by fire. Each year a few topple and no new ones are growing up. Hot and destructive fires, little by little, are changing a rich and varied mosaic into uniform, degraded forests and woodlands.

Kakadu's wetlands, recognised as perhaps the most important in the world's tropics, captivate with the sheer number of birds, fish and other wildlife. The stone country is the soul of Kakadu and its grandest landscape. The forests and woodlands are a paradox, the poorest soils sustaining the most varied life and so providing one of the most intriguing chains of interconnecting relationships. The three environments together are the quintessential Australia.

In the next chapters, we see how a group of Aboriginal people, calling themselves the Gagudju, lived in close association with this extraordinary place and how they looked after it.

Previous pages
Aboriginal people burned the country strictly according to their methods of fire management. Dry season fires are now more frequent and wild, and cause great damage to Kakadu.

Black kites scavenge for victims in the wake of the fire.

Monsoon rains will eventually restore even badly burned forests. However, frequent late season fires degrade both forests and woodlands.

7 ~ THE GAGUDJU YEAR

For uncounted years the clans that together make up the Gagudju people lived as a part of nature in the Alligator Rivers region. But today no Gagudju live fully traditional lives in what is now known as Kakadu National Park. Many of them still live in the bush, on outstations, but ritual life is minimal. Large ceremonies where hundreds of people of all the necessary clans gathered together, have not been held for many decades. The shelters the Gagudju now live in are made of canvas or corrugated iron and not of bark or stone. Food is only partially gathered from the bush around them — much of what they now eat is grown, harvested and packaged in places far, far away.

To see how the Aboriginal people lived in Kakadu, undisturbed and uninfluenced by white people, we must go back a long time, at least 150 years, to 1839. Even then there already were outside influences. Macassan fishermen from the island of Sulewesi to the north came every year to gather trepang, a kind of sea-slug they considered a delicacy, turtle shells and mother-of-pearl. They came on the monsoon winds and departed with them and camped only along the beaches. There was little change. However, the sailing people from the north spoke of strange men with white skins and often of an angry disposition. The Macassans called them Balanda, for Hollander or Dutchman. The first Balanda, as all white people were, and still are, called, to come to the region were indeed Hollanders. They came in the early years of the 17th century, sailing along the northern coastline. They seldom made a landfall and they never actually entered Gagudju country. For over 200 years the Balanda made occasional and unremarkable appearances.

On 20 September 1824 all this changed. In a place the Balanda had named Port Essington on Cobourg Peninsula, they came ashore and performed an ominous ceremony. A Captain Bremer, who was British, raised a flag on a tall pole and unwitnessed by the Gagudju claimed their land and that of their neighbours for a faraway kingdom. For the next twenty-five years, on and off, these Balanda, overdressed in heavy clothes and red-faced from the sun and heat, tried to establish themselves. To help them survive they brought horses, cattle, buffaloes and pigs. Several times these animals were let loose in the bush to fend for themselves. They spread rapidly into the Gagudju's lands where the buffaloes and pigs especially, became serious pests. The settlements were finally abandoned in 1849. But the Balanda returned again and again and eventually changed the lives of the Aboriginal people forever.

But in 1839 the Gagudju still lived in a land unscarred by bulldozers. There were no cars, powerboats, aeroplanes or engine noises of any kind. No beer cans, paper or plastic littered the country. Toilet blocks, hotels, stores, concrete, wire and fences were not even imagined.

Above
The Badmardis arrive in Bunitj country, on the East Alligator River, when the floodplain pandanus fruits are ripe and falling to the ground.

Above right
Forest in monsoon rain.

In Kakadu's heartland there were no Balanda, nor tobacco, flour, sugar, tea, alcohol or money. Life for the Aboriginal people was untroubled for the most part. Food was plentiful. Violent fights within families or even clans were rare, though there was occasional devastating warfare with other tribes. Gagudju society was close-knit; no-one had an identity crisis or ulcers. There were no epidemic diseases, no poor and undernourished, no dispossessed. What little crime there was, was severely dealt with.

The Gagudju, then as now, are divided into many clans. Each clan is made up of five or six extended families. Family size and consequently the number of people per clan, varies greatly. A clan may have as many as a hundred members or as few as twenty, but on average each clan consists of forty to fifty people.

One of the clans is called the Badmardi, and it is a Badmardi family of 150 years ago who we will follow in this chapter. Their language is Mayali which they share with a small number of other clans.

While the people travel widely through the Alligator Rivers region, each clan has its own home range, its own country. They have a close spiritual connection with it and strict responsibilities for its maintenance. Each clan member identifies with this place and has a special relationship with the ancestral being that resides there. It is his or her home, the place where the spirit comes from and must return to after death. Even within each clan's estate, each family has its own special place. For this Badmardi family, their home centres around Djuwarr and Nawulabila in the headwaters of Deaf Adder Creek. It is their spiritual homeland where they feel especially good and secure. It is also one of the most beautiful places on earth.

For the greater part of the year each family lives and travels by itself, but its members mix socially with other families and other clans they meet along the way. Every so often, maybe only every four to seven years, many clans gather for really large and important ceremonies. Several hundred people may then come together.

Previous pages
Djuwarr Rock is at the centre of the Badmardi family's country and their spiritual home.

People cannot marry anyone from their own clan but must seek partners from neighbouring groups of the opposite moiety.* Through intermarriage and ceremonial contact a network of relationships extends throughout the area. During a year's travel each family group can move through their neighbours' country unmolested as long as good manners are observed.

Travel is largely determined by the seasons as they in turn dictate where foods will be most abundant. Every fully initiated Aborigine is finely attuned to the seasonal cycle. If, for example, a special kind of grasshopper calls, it is the signal that a certain yam is ready for harvest. By responding to the seasons' nuances the people always know where the most abundant foods are.

The Gagudju recognise six seasons:

GUDJEWG (January to March) North-west winds bring low monsoon clouds of the main wet season. There are long periods of heavy rain during this time of growth and renewal.

BANGGERDENG (April) To begin with light easterly winds blow, but towards the end of the season these suddenly turn to freshening south-easterlies. The change brings a few, often violent, storms — the last rain of the season. It is a busy time for the women, who must harvest the yams and other roots.

YEGGE (May and June) Steady south-easterly winds bring the long dry season. Nights are cool and the mornings misty. Seed-eating birds move south and kites become more numerous as they chase the insects in front of the first fires.

WURRGENG (June and July) The coolest season with nights especially cold in the escarpment. Many trees flower, their abundant nectar feeding sugarbag (native bees) and lorikeets. Drying winds continue from the south-east.

GURRUNG (August and September) South-east winds continue becoming ever hotter and drier. The dry air ripens the pandanus fruits, turning them orange. Pied geese gather in hundreds of thousands on the drying plains to feed on the spike-rush tubers.

GUNUMELENG (October to December) The hot weather becomes more stifling as the humidity increases. Winds are unsettled and can blow from any direction. Violent thunderstorms bring short bursts of heavy rain. Grass begins to grow, deciduous trees put on new leaf.

The imaginary Badmardi family of 150 years ago is headed by a respected and wise elder of about fifty years of age. He is a person of authority and consequence among the Gagudju. Having gone through all the five stages of initiation and travelled his lands widely, he now understands man's relationship with his environment. He is committed to pass this knowledge on to his sons and daughters and their children so that they too reach a level of understanding which enables them to assume custodianship of the Badmardi lands. Mostly he teaches with great kindness, understanding and patience, but he also uses fear and mystery especially with the uninitiated.

This senior man has three wives. The eldest is just a little younger than he is, the other two are much younger. His eldest son is about twenty-five years old and has a wife of about twenty-two. Besides these six adults there are seven children ranging in age from three to twelve years old.

* The word moiety is derived from an old French word meaning half. Aboriginal society in Kakadu is divided into two categories, that is, moieties. One is called Dhuwa the other Yirritja. Animals, plants and landforms, as well as the people, belong to one moiety or the other.

The Badmardi family camped beside Djuwarr waterhole.

An Aborigine's name is determined by a complex set of social and spiritual rules and is usually bestowed by the patrilineal grandparents. It is not something that can be guessed at or given casually. In this account each person has been given a nickname, the name of an animal as sometimes happens in real life. The senior male, for example, we have called after Wamut, the wedge-tailed eagle, because of his penetrating gaze and sharp features. His eldest son has great skill with the spear and is called Nyalgan after the straight shooting archer fish who 'spears' insects with jets of water. Nyalgan's wife is of a delicate and elegant build and is named after Lambalk the sugar glider. Their son loves the water like Yirrku the water rat. His close friend and uncle is Djati because he hops about like a frog when excited . . .

The Badmardi Way of Life

In the grey hour before sunrise Djuwarr's rock face glowers over a deep waterhole. On the far shore tall paperbark trees shelter a grassy flat. A group of pandanus trees, their jagged-edged fronds trailing in the water, crowd around a giant flat rock that slopes into the water.

Three small fires smoulder under the trees, the smoke curling lazily through the foliage. These fires are the camp of Wamut and his family.

Most of the people lie sleeping, uncovered, beside the sloping rock. As the first rays of the sun slant through the trees, Marrawuti, the white-breasted sea-eagle, flies over the waterhole calling loudly, the sound echoing off the cliffs. The people wake slowly. Wamut, the patriarch, sits up first. He is a lean wiry man of slight build, yet very strong-looking. His long hair and stubble beard are greying. There is an air of dignity and calm wisdom about him. His eldest wife, about forty-five years of age, is called Melpe because like the wallaby of that name she is tolerant and gentle with the young children. She slowly gets up and coaxes the coals into flame. One by one the others wake. Wamut's other wives, Berrep who like the masked plover is very vocal, even strident, in defence of her family and Ngaleklek, talkative like the corella, are soon helping the older woman. They reheat the remains of yesterday's food,¨ freshwater turtle cooked in its shell, a goanna's forequarters and some yams.

Three children, two girls and a boy, ranging in age between six and ten, are soon awake, sitting up and rubbing their eyes. All sit in the open around the fire on sleeping mats made of sheets of paperbark. There is no need for the shelter of a shelving rock or a bark structure in this hot dry season of Gunumeleng.

Soon the family is joined by two boys, about twelve years old. They slept by their own fire a little distance away, but now come to look for some food. The two are half-brothers — the youngest son of Wamut's elder wife and the eldest son of the second wife. They are Gabu, named after the ever-moving, rushing about green ant, and Barradja whose somewhat raucous laugh is like that of the blue-winged kookaburra. Food supplies are low this morning and Gabu is teased, for if in his impatience he had not missed the bandicoot with his throwing stick, there would have been plenty. Their laughter drifts down the waterhole, where Nyalgan and his wife Lambalk are just finishing their meal of fish and yams. The couple have two children, a seven year old boy, Yirrku, who loves the water, and a three year old daughter, Nabiwu, named after the small bee of whose honey she is so very fond.

Yirrku soon rushes over to the big camp to play with the other children; their young, shrill voices ringing off Djuwarr's stern face as they run about in the shallow water.

Nyalgan, tall, muscular and well-proportioned, selects two spears from about six leaning against a tree, inserts a small club into his belt, picks up his spear thrower and walks over to his father's camp. Lambalk is still feeding their small daughter. Wamut is also ready, carrying his spear. Both are identically 'dressed'. They wear belts, about ten centimetres wide, made up of twenty or so strands of string fashioned out of human hair. Suspended from its front is a tassle about fifteen centimetres wide made of the same material. On both arms, just above the elbows, they wear armlets woven out of split cane. Around their necks they carry small spherical bags about seven centimetres in diameter. In them they carry some red ochre and sharp slivers of quartzite they use as knives. Across their chests and down their upper arms are the welted scars of their initiation ceremonies.

Tucked into their belts are the throwing clubs; rounded pieces of hardwood bulbous on one end and with a wax covered handle on the other. The clubs are painted with the Badmardi clan designs in red, white and black. Each man has one long and one short spear. The long spear measures more than three metres and is about one and a half centimetres in diameter. Its main shaft is made of the hard and heavy wood of the ironwood tree. The bottom 30 cm of the shaft, however, is bamboo forming a kind of handle to which the hook of the spear thrower can be fitted. Projecting from the spear's tip are 4 cm of bone sharpened to a needlepoint. This piece of kangaroo shinbone is fastened into place with a cane binding covered with the resin of an ironwood tree. This spear is for hunting wallabies and wallaroos.

The men's favourite spear, however, is the shorter one, about half the length of the other and weighing only a few hundred grams. The shaft is bamboo painted in red ochre to which is fitted a sharpened splinter of ironwood toughened and hardened in fire. They wield it with deadly force and accuracy. But it is meant for smaller animals; kangaroos could easily run off with these lightweight weapons unless speared through the heart.

As the two set off, the children mill around them asking in competing voices, 'Where are you going?' 'When will you be back?' 'What will you bring?' 'Can I come?' The men laugh, briefly pat the young shoulders then walk briskly, lithely along the waterhole to its shallow end and cross it. The older boys run after them carrying toy spears. Wamut pauses and explains that they are after kangaroos and wallabies, an exacting task that requires care and concentration. Later, when the family travels to other parts of the country he will help them make proper spears and show them how to hunt. Now they must stay behind.

The Hunters

Father and son walk through the woodland of eucalypts and wattles that skirt the escarpment's tall cliffs and discuss the possibilities. Nyalgan is keen to spear Garndagitj, the antelope kangaroo. The two agree that at this time of year a mob of them probably grazes on a small open plain about an hour's walk away. It is a good place to hunt, for the animals can be approached from the cover of a narrow band of trees. Nyalgan should reach the place just when it will be too hot for the kangaroos to graze, when they move towards the shade. Storm rains have brought a new flush of green to the plain, which had been burnt earlier. Nyalgan heads off into the eucalypt forest while Wamut follows the escarpment looking for Barrk, the black wallaroo, goannas and snakes.

Nyalgan's senses and awareness of his surroundings, while acute at all times, are heightened now that he is out hunting on his own. At a glance, without breaking stride, he can tell of the movements of bandicoots, possums, cockatoos, goannas and pythons by the signs they left and the sounds they make.

The forest opens out to a low heathy scrub. Buluydjirr, the black kite, circles low then lands in a tree close by. Nyalgan speaks to the bird and asks if anyone is approaching with hostile intent, to come and quarrel with his family. The bird rises into the air without uttering a sound and so reassures the man. Had the kite called in reply as it took off, it would have meant that people were coming, probably to fight.

After walking for half an hour Nyalgan stops by a small puddle of water left in a

Buluydjirr, the black kite, warns the Badmardi if hostile people are approaching.

depression in the black soil. He digs up some of the mud and smears it over his body, especially under his armpits. He crushes some small plants and rubs their juices over his chest and so hides his scent from Garndagitj's sensitive nose. While he is busy, Djikirdi-djikirdi, the willy wagtail, lands on a branch only a few metres away. The bird pirouettes and twitters on its perch. Nyalgan smiles for he knows the tiny, friendly bird is the spirit of someone who was once close to him. He can feel it. He is confident the bird will guide him to a successful hunt.

The belt of trees now in front of Nyalgan is the last barrier between him and the small open area favoured by Garndagitj, his mate Garnday and their family. With extreme caution Nyalgan slips amongst the taller trees, placing his feet carefully so as not to break even the smallest dry twig or make the leaflitter crackle. He follows a faint trail made by the animals. Suddenly, Galawan the sand goanna, appears on the path in front of him. The reptile rises on his hind legs and lashes out with his long, forked tongue to try to sense who is following

Garndagitj, the antelope kangaroo, hunted by Nyalgan.

Galawan, the sand goanna, stands on its hind legs for a better view over the vegetation. The lizard is Nyalgan's Dreaming and helps him to hunt.

Barrk, the black wallaroo. Wamut could not kill it because it was favoured by the Mimi spirits.

him. After a few moments the goanna lowers himself to all fours and waddles off. Nyalgan feels assured of success now. Galawan is his totem, his Dreaming; his other self has come to help him. Djikirdi-djikirdi and Galawan have done their part, now it is up to him.

Slowly Nyalgan fits his long spear to his spear thrower and raises them to shoulder height. He leaves his smaller spear resting against a tree. The sun has risen over the escarpment and it is getting hot. Garndagitj may already have reached the forest edge, so Nyalgan must be at the ready. Crouching low, spear poised, he moves forward using a small pandanus as cover. He sees Garndagitj and his mob about two hundred metres in front of him, just entering the forest. Here at the edge, tree cover is sparse and there is room for Nyalgan to approach and to wield his long spear. About twelve kangaroos, mostly females and adolescents, are grazing. Towering over them is the big buck, Garndagitj himself, almost as tall as the man. Excitement rises in Nyalgan. To suppress it he clamps the small round bag he carries around his neck between his teeth.

Slowly, almost imperceptibly, Nyalgan moves forward. Whenever one of the grazing animals looks up, the hunter freezes, then moves again when all heads are down. At the time of Gunumeleng it is difficult to take advantage of the wind; it is capricious and unpredictable. But Garndagitj does not catch the man's scent. The gap between them gradually narrows. When about fifteen metres away, Nyalgan draws his throwing arm back as far as he can. Garndagitj senses something is wrong and stands up to his full height — at that instant Nyalgan hurls his spear with all his strength. The force is so great that when

Above
The Rainbow Serpent forced this passage through the rocks during the Dreamtime.

Above right
Nawaran, the giant rock or Oenpelli python.

Garndagitj is hit, just above the hip, he is knocked over. Before he can regain his feet Nyalgan is upon him and kills him with a blow from his club.

Panting with the effort and the excitement, Nyalgan squats beside his victim, strokes the soft reddish fur and looks into the large dark eyes. As always, once the hunt is complete he has a moment of sadness. But it passes. He rests for only a short time before hoisting the heavy animal onto his shoulders and walking back to camp, wishing to reach there before the heat of the day.

Wamut, in the meantime, has left the forest and climbs up the scree slope to the base of the escarpment's sheer cliff. His short spear, the best weapon in the confined spaces between the huge blocks of stone, is ready in his spear thrower. He hopes to surprise a black wallaroo, rock wallaby, goanna, snake or even a rock pigeon. Easing his way between two gigantic boulders, Wamut is suddenly face to face with Barrk the muscular male black wallaroo. The man is poised to strike — the animal is within easy range. But instead of dashing away, the wallaroo stands his ground and stares at the man, unafraid. For a moment the two look into each other's eyes, then the wallaroo hops quietly away. Because the big marsupial was so unafraid, it means that he is a special favourite of the mostly friendly, rock-dwelling Mimi spirits. They would not have wanted Barrk killed. So had Wamut speared him he would have angered the spirits. They might have come out of their hiding places, blown on the rocks to part them and then enticed Wamut in. Once inside, the rocks would have closed again and the elder would have been locked up forever. He vividly remembers that when he

Gallery of rock paintings dominated by Nawaran, Wamut's Dreaming or totem, not far from Djuwarr. © National Geographic Society.

was a young man he had been shown a cave by the men of a distant clan where people had been trapped like that. He had even heard the people call out to be released.

Although Wamut has never seen the Mimis, he feels they are watching him from caves in the cliff above. The reclusive Mimi spirits have such long and slender necks that they would break in the slightest breeze. Therefore they must remain hidden in caves. Wamut knows that Mimis live here because the paintings on the rock face before him, small delicate drawings of running and dancing figures wearing elaborate headdresses, were done by them. There are other paintings on the smooth rock, luminous in white, red and yellow ochre. These are more familiar. Leaning on his spear, the foot of one leg resting on the thigh of the other, he contemplates the gallery; a procession of echidnas, goannas, kangaroos, turtles, fish; all the animals of the country around him. But Wamut's eyes are drawn to a painting of a gigantic snake — more than five metres long, that threads through the other animals. It is Nawaran the giant python. The snake is one of his totems, his Dreaming with which he has a special affinity. This is a painting Wamut did himself. Some of the painting's white clay is flaking off. Soon, he realises, he will have to come back and repaint the snake so its spirit will retain its potency and its connection with him.

In a gallery further up the valley, beyond the cleft in the rock made by Almudj the Rainbow Serpent when she forced a passage through the cliffs, Wamut knows of another very important 'painting'. It is a manifestation of Garndagitj, not a mere painting of him. It is the ancestral kangaroo himself, where he came to rest at the end of the creative period.

The dark, mysterious paperbark forest, with a tangle of coiling tree roots underfoot which the boys, Gabu and Barradja, had to move through.

Being in their country, this image is of special significance to Wamut and his family.

Wamut descends the scree. Looking down, his sharp eyes discern a small goanna lying spreadeagled on a cool shady rock. Stealthily Wamut works his way down the slope. He puts his spears and spear thrower down and pulls the small club from his belt. A few more steps forward. The goanna raises his head and is ready to flee — but too late. The hardwood projectile hits him on the neck, killing him instantly. Tucking the lizard in his belt, Wamut retrieves his spears and leaping from rock to rock, quickly reaches the woodland.

He hears Nyalgan calling and answers him. When he sees his son approaching with the kangaroo across his shoulders, he calls out again in admiration and delight. The two smile at each other and Wamut briefly grasps his son's upper arm. Animatedly Nyalgan tells of his hunt, not forgetting the parts Djikirdi-djikirdi and Gawalan played.

Life at Camp

After the two men had left Djuwarr all the children, except three year old Nabiwu, go to the water's edge to play, all of them unencumbered by any clothing or ornaments. The women wear only hair belts with small aprons made out of paperbark.

Nyalgan's wife Lambalk feeds her small daughter and plays with her a while. Then she walks over to the main camp where the other three women are quietly talking. Melpe calls out for her granddaughter and takes her from her mother. The laughing and smiling little girl goes from one to the other. Being the only small child in the family she is the centre of their affections.

Once through the forest, the boys came upon a waterhole and speared the fish Guluybirr, the saratoga.

It is warm now. The women cool themselves with fans made out of goose wings, a legacy from their camp of a week ago when they feasted on the birds caught on the drying plains of the South Alligator River.

Melpe picks up a dilly bag filled with narrow strips of pandanus fronds and starts weaving a basket she has been working on.

The weaving is the signal for the day's activities to begin. Lambalk and the other two women pick up their digging sticks and dilly bags and walk into the forest, following the waterhole downstream. They call out to their elder daughters, Amurak, long-legged like the black-winged stilt and Mobiny called after the barn owl because she likes caves and is not afraid of the dark, to come with them. Melpe stays at Djuwarr and keeps an eye on the younger children playing near the water.

As they dig out tubers and gather bush peas from vines, the women talk and chatter about the people at their last camp, the children, what the men might be getting. Some tell teasing jokes. The girls, about nine and ten years old, are all ears and whisper to each other as they gather green plum-like fruits from small trees.

The two older boys, Gabu and Barradja, about eleven and twelve years old, set off upstream into a broad ravine. Each carries a short bamboo spear tipped with four sharp prongs made of bone. The boys are more adventurous than the other children and venture into rocky places and dark forests full of spirits. Seized by a show of bravado and an unquenchable curiosity, they dare each other on. The first part of their explorations requires the greatest courage. It takes them through a dark place with tall trees shutting out much of the daylight. While birds make strange calls among the rocks and the pandanus leaves creak and whisper in the breeze they must clamber over a tangle of thick snake-like tree roots coiling out of the sandy soil. When Marrawuti calls loudly from a tree above them, they are ready to bolt. But they hold fast and soon reach a broad pool of clear water. Both boys love the water and soon they have forgotten the dangers and become absorbed in their search for fish and turtles. They watch entranced as Nyalgan, the archer fish and their brother's namesake, shoots ants and grasshoppers, knocking them down with jets of water. They wonder if their brother's spear will be as accurate today.

Sitting quietly beside a pandanus leaning over the water, the boys watch Guluybirr, the handsome saratoga, swim slowly to the surface. Barradja, acknowledged to be the better spearsman, stands up. As he raises his spear the fish, its red spots glinting in the sun, lazily swims back into the dark green depths. But the boys remain motionless. After a few moments the saratoga cruises back towards them. Barradja holds the spear with his index finger hooked on its end, like a spear thrower, and so giving him greater leverage. Allowing for the distortions of the water, he throws his spear. It goes right through the fish. Laughing his noisy kookaburra laugh, the boy jumps into the pool and retrieves his catch. Gabu jumps about in excitement. The boys are getting hungry and decide to go back to camp and ask their favourite mother, Melpe, to cook the fish for them. They know she will praise them for their cleverness.

Barradja, with the fish dangling from his spear, walks into camp just as they hear the two men calling to each other. They can hear from their voices that the hunt has been a success. The women and girls, out along the creek, also hear the men and hurry back to camp.

When the men appear on the other side of the waterhole, the children rush out, shouting and laughing, to meet them. They run through the shallow water, then stop, awed by the size of the kangaroo. Only rarely have they seen one this large.

It is now the hottest time of day at the hottest time of year. Nyalgan's profuse perspiration streaks the mud with which he had coated himself. The mud has dried to a light grey, making the women laugh at his strange appearance. He runs into the cooling water, drinks deeply and washes off the mud. It has been a good morning.

Wamut studies the sky and the winds. Earlier, when out in the woodland, he had noticed a certain bird had returned to the area and that another had begun its courtship songs. Both are sure indications of the onset of the second half of Gunumeleng when the storms bring less lightning but more rain. The atmosphere is more humid and big clouds are building up over the escarpment. Wamut feels sure that the first of the female storms will come this afternoon.

Quickly and with authority he tells everyone to move to the shelter created by a huge slab of shelving rock, about a hundred metres upstream from their camp among the paperbarks. The new place is in dark forest and the small children are a little fearful. Wamut tells some to bring the food and others to gather fire wood, clear a space in the cavern and put down the paperbark sleeping mats. He builds the fire himself, at the entrance to the cavern, while Gabu and Barradja dig the pit and gather the special stones for the earth oven in which the kangaroo will be cooked.

The stones are already hot in the fire in the pit when the first thunder rolls over the

Monsoon rains poured down upon the escarpment and the Badmardi family sought shelter.

escarpment. Before long a huge black cloud extinguishes the sun. Big green frogs call a slow 'wark, wark, wark' from rock crevices and tree hollows. They probably felt the sudden gusts of cold air, the invariable prelude to the downpour of large cold drops. When the rain finally starts the wind drops and it pelts straight down, thrumming on leaves and ground litter. Rivulets run down the steep rock faces and disappear in the hot dry sand. The family sits huddled under the rock overhang, dry and with a fire going. Some of the smaller children giggle nervously. Then it is quiet again, except for the dripping leaves. From up high comes the lazy whistle of a white-lined honeyeater, a voice from the Dreamtime when the bird was Bindjanok calling for her lost lover.

The song is an all clear. The sun comes out again and glistens on the wet rocks and vegetation. The children run out and squeal as cold drops fall on their warm skins.

Around the Fire

Food preparations continue. The kangaroo's fur is singed off and his kidney, liver and other viscera removed to be prepared separately. The red-hot stones at the bottom of the pit are covered with green leaves. Water is splashed on the rocks to create steam. Some stones, wrapped in green leaves, are put in the kangaroo's body cavity. He is then placed in the pit, covered with paperbark and finally sand is heaped over everything. Garndagitj will be cooked and ready to eat in a few hours.

In the meantime the women have prepared the yams, bush peas, goanna and saratoga fish for the young children. They cannot eat Garndagitj as they would have bad dreams.

Dusk approaches. Nyalgan builds a fire out on the sloping rock near the waterhole. Night herons, which roosted in the ravine's dark forests, fly downstream, low over the water, to fish the smaller ponds. Black flying foxes fly higher, upstream, to feed on flowers and fruits.

Wamut, to the beat of his song-sticks, sings of the new season, of the rain and the renewal — the procreation — of the land. Nyalgan plays the didgeridoo. The sounds are made the richer by the reverberations off Djuwarr's darkening face across the water. Only little Nabiwu sleeps, secure in her mother's lap. All others are attentive, their eyes glistening in the firelight.

His song over, Wamut tells of the seasons. He says that the white-breasted wood swallows have arrived and that this morning in the place where a grassy flat meets the rocks of the escarpment he had heard the song of a bushlark. The birds told him that the female storms would arrive. He reminds everyone that these are different from the earlier, male storms, which were noisy with a great deal of thunder, and crackled with lightning but brought little rain. Sternly he says that no-one must look at the male lightning for it is part of the shame of an ancestral being. But now that the female rain has come, they could look at it. Wamut explains that storms will soon be more frequent and will bring more rain. The winds will steady, blowing from the north-west and bring cold days when the rain goes on and on. That will be the season of Gudjewg.

The rains, Wamut says, will bring profuse plant growth which will fatten the insects, snakes, lizards, birds and mammals. All this is possible, he adds, because their kinsmen and other clans are performing the right ceremonies out on the plains to ensure that the rains will come as they do every Gunumeleng and Gudjewg.

Some of the boys ask who brings the thunder and lightning. They have heard the story of Namarrkun, the lightning man, before but they thrill to its mystery and force every time. Wamut, understanding that through repetition the Dreamtime will become part of the children's lives, is glad to tell the story again.

He says that Namarrkun lives high up in the sky and carries the lightning in an arc across his body. Most of the time he lives where no-one can see him, absorbing so much of the sun's radiance that his arc of lightning shimmers with golden light. Only when Gunumeleng comes to the land does Namarrkun come down to ride the billowing clouds. He warns wrongdoers, people who do not share their food, or perhaps someone who fought his brother, by hurling his stone axes against the clouds, so creating thunder and by throwing down spears of lightning. His voice hisses and crackles in warning. Wamut opens his eyes wide, his voice too thunders and his hands make dramatic gestures as he continues. Should the wrongdoer ignore the warnings he will be struck dead by a bolt of lightning. At this dramatic finale, Wamut looks directly at everyone in turn with his piercing eyes, his face a stern mask. A delicious thrill runs through the children as they huddle closer together. Wamut's face slowly dissolves into a smile and then laughter. Everyone relaxes and soon tease and joke with one another. Wamut says that Namarrkun is always close by in this season. His children are all around in the form of Aldjurr the brilliant red and electric blue grasshoppers that are most conspicuous at this season of violent thunder and lightning.

It is dark now as the family returns to the cavern where the fire's embers still glow. The

Nawulabila Rock, home of the Badmardi family during the wet season.

children are soon asleep. The adults rekindle the fire and dig Garndagitj, succulent and cooked to perfection, from the underground oven. Their fire is a speck of yellow light in the dark immensity of towering cliffs and woodlands stretching out across the plain. A pair of barking owls calls in duet, 'wook-wook, wook-wook', as the fire dies to a red glow.

And so time passes. Almost every day there is a storm and water levels begin to rise. Wamut closely monitors the weather, the movements and sounds of birds and insects, the growth of the grasses and the ripening of fruits. It is when the spear grass is of a certain height and a green grasshopper calls, for example, that the pied geese will lay their eggs out on the floodplain.

Moving Camp

When the capricious, shifting winds steady to a strong north-westerly, Wamut knows that Gudjewg, the wet season, has arrived. During the many days of rain that are imminent, Djuwarr's stream will gather so much water that it will break its banks and flood the campsite. It is time to move to higher ground, to Nawulabila their wet season home, only a short walk westward along the base of the escarpment.

Moving camp is a simple matter. The women pick up their few dilly bags and baskets, giving some to the children to carry. The men take their full complement of spears (six each), spear throwers, stone axes, a couple of small clubs and their fire-making sticks. Everyone knows the way, so the family does not travel together. The older boys take a circuitous route hoping to catch some lizards or birds and to collect the big red fruits ripening on the syzigium trees. Melpe is the last to leave. She takes a smouldering stick from the old fire, ready to start the new one. By the time the first monsoon clouds veil the sun, Djuwarr is deserted.

Hundreds of thousands, perhaps millions, of years ago a gigantic piece of sandstone came loose from the escarpment. The stone crashed and bounced off the rock face and speared into the sand 200 m below. There the rock still stands, its strata pointing up at a 45° angle and giving perfect shelter from the sun and rain, but open to cooling breezes. The sandy ground is level and the rock is surrounded by rough-barked eucalyptus trees. Its top is shaggy with green ferns and several fig trees cling to its surface. There is a pleasant scent of spinifex resin in the air.

The women and children are the first to arrive. They spread the paperbark sleeping mats they brought. Ten year old Amurak fashions a water container, also out of paperbark, and places it where she knows it will fill with the runoff from the rock. There is no waterhole here and the small sandy streams are not yet running. The older boys bring fire wood and from the smouldering stick brought by Melpe, kindle a smoky fire to drive the mosquitoes and other insects from the shelter. The women insert sticks into cracks in the rocks and hang their dilly bags with food from them, out of the reach of rodents and native cats.

In the evening the rains come gently and unlike storm rains do not let up after a short time. It rains and rains. Around the fire that night Wamut explains that the Rainbow Serpent, called Almudj in their language, has emerged from her bottomless pool at the base of the waterfall. She will flood the land. Occasionally she can be seen as she stands on her tail and forms the rainbow. The new season will bring a time of plenty and later of adventure when they all go to the floodplain to hunt geese and collect their eggs. They will meet other clans from other places and there will be much ceremony, singing and dancing. Wamut's words are given dramatic emphasis as the firelight flickers on the ochre and white paintings on the rocks behind him. Garndagitj, Galawan, barramundi and turtles. Glowering down at them all, his aura of lightning seeming to move in the shifting light, is Namarrkun.

For five days and nights it rains. But food must be gathered. On the wet, cool days the people make small paperbark cloaks to put over their shoulders. The men spear several agile wallabies and Nyalgan kills a black wallaroo. Yams, the pods of native peas and some fruits are brought by the women and girls. The older boys knock frilled-neck lizards out of the trees with small clubs or stones. On one of their forays they have a windfall. Coiled under a dry rock ledge, digesting a bandicoot it has just caught, they find Mandjurdurrk, the olive python. The snake is so heavy that the two boys between them can hardly carry it.

On the sixth day the sun breaks through and for a few weeks there are only passing showers. Then the rains set in again. These hothouse conditions encourage rapid growth in the plants and within a month some grasses have grown as tall as Nyalgan's spear. On one of the sunny days Djatete, the green grasshopper, begins his thin song, 'dzzzt, dzzzt, dzzzt'. It is the sign that the yams are mature and ready to be dug out. Digging the tubers is easy. Then they have to be chopped, shredded and soaked in running water to leach out the poison.

The children are no great help. From the eldest to the youngest, they are absorbed in their games. Making spears out of the tall grass stems, they have competitions as to who can throw the furthest and most accurately. They stalk and ambush one another. They have war

Above
Grooves have been worn in the rocks where the Gagudju people sharpened their stone tools.

Above right
The quarry, high above Nawulabila, where the Badmardi people used to make stone (quartzite) implements.

games when they draw up into two opposing lines throwing and dodging spears. For the boys this is essential training, for in later life they may face a real war and have to dodge real spears thrown by experienced marksmen. But now it is all fun and high spirits.

One day when the weather is cloudy and cool four men approach Wamut's family camp. They call out from a distance, politely establishing their identity and friendly intent. The two older men, one of them with a long grey beard, are heads of families. The younger men are their sons. They are fellow Badmardi clansmen, their camps a brisk hour's walk away.

The four men, together with Wamut and Nyalgan, sit down beneath a spreading fig tree. At first the talk is of recent hunts and the effects of the wet season. But soon their conversation turns to the imminent travel to the wetlands, the other clans that will be there, the ceremonies and trade. They must take a number of stone implements — knives, spear points and scrapers — to the freshwater people who rarely come here. The Badmardi will exchange these for lengths of bamboo, which does not grow in their stone country, to be used as spear shafts. And this is the main purpose of the four men's visit, to go to the stone quarry above Nawulabila camp.

The six set off, carrying their spears upright, and nimbly climb the bouldery slope to the quarry, at the undercut base of a sheer quartzite cliff which rises 100 m above them. Beneath the overhang the floor is littered with discarded stone flakes, the rejects of uncounted generations of toolmakers.

Each man selects a core rock, a cube of 30 or 40 cm of quartzite, of the many that lie on the floor. Implements are struck off these cores with smaller stones. To do it just right so that a sharp knife or spear point results, requires skill. The younger men are trying to outdo each other and need many hits to get a passable implement. There is no need for competition among the elders, their long years of experience have made them great experts and soon they have an array of perfect flakes laid out in front of them. Implements wrapped in paperbark and stowed in dilly bags, the men return to their various camps.

Rain is less and less frequent now. Water levels at Djuwarr begin to fall. Wamut knows that floodwaters are also receding on the river plain and that their traditional campsite, a narrow arc of higher land in a sea of green sedges, is no longer waterlogged. He knows too, that the geese have waited for these receding waters and are now building their nests and will soon lay their first eggs. The time has come for the family to move to Gummungkuwuy, their camp on the South Alligator River floodplain.

To the Floodplain

On a sunny morning when Barradja the blue-winged kookaburra calls in noisy chorus, Wamut tells his family they must set off for the floodplain. It is not a long walk, perhaps sixty or seventy kilometres, but at this time of year when the grasses are tall and all plant life is lush, it can be arduous, especially for the smaller children. Preparations are brief. Those dilly bags, spears and other items not needed are stashed in rock crevices for their return in about a month's time. No-one will carry any embers; fire will be made with the fire sticks. Within a few minutes of the decision having been made, the cavalcade is on its way.

The two adult men walk on ahead. They are the ones to spear any wallabies or kangaroos they may encounter, a potential food source too important to be missed. So the boisterous children must stay further back with the women. Gabu and Barradja, the older boys, would like to go with the men. As a compromise Wamut tells them they can trail some distance behind him, but carefully and quietly so as not to spoil any hunt. Each boy carries a short bone-tipped bamboo spear, a spear thrower and club. Lambalk, Nyalgan's slight and graceful wife, carries Nabiwu on her hip. Sometimes she is carried by one of the other women.

Wamut leads the family along high ground below the escarpment. The valley soon widens and they enter a stringybark and woollybutt forest with an understorey of grass and fan palms. While the women pause to collect the hearts of some of the palms, the children pick the tough fibrous planchonia plums. They discover a small clump of bush currant trees and swoop with joy on the sweet black fruits.

Up ahead Wamut and Nyalgan follow a low stony ridge. Agile wallabies like to lie up here away from the mosquitoes of the valley floor. The two men walk abreast but about one hundred metres apart scanning all possible wallaby hiding places and keeping in visual contact with each other. Nyalgan's sharp eyes pick out a slight movement under a fan palm. He stops stock still. Wamut follows his example. Moving slightly to one side to get a better view, Nyalgan sees a wallaby that has stood up to scratch one of its many March fly bites. Using hand signals Nyalgan tells Wamut that he will try to get within range of the wallaby, but in such a way that should it bolt it would run within striking distance of Wamut's spear. Slowly Nyalgan begins his stalk. But the wallaby gets wind of him and bounds away. Wamut is ready, hidden behind a termite mound. The unsuspecting wallaby hops past him at such close range that he is speared easily.

Above
The Badmardi women and children gathered the sweet-tasting bush currants.

Above right
The sun sets upon the waterlily-filled billabong where the Badmardi family camped.

After walking on for a few more hours, the family passes the imposing sandstone towers, standing about two kilometres apart, that guard their own special enclave. They leave the stone country and enter the forested plain. Another hour's walk finds them at a small billabong where they camp for the night.

For three more days they travel along well-defined if somewhat overgrown paths that keep to the high ground. On the fourth day they are confronted by dense growths of paperbark trees standing in still, dark water. They seem impenetrable, but here too an intricate network of paths leads through the maze. Then, abruptly, they emerge out of the trees, onto a boomerang-shaped, treeless knoll — Gummungkuwuy. Before them, to the horizon, is a

Rock paintings of spear-throwing fights. They show the scene Wamut described, and the deadly nature of the fights between the clans when he was young. Larger figures have been superimposed on the battle scenes.

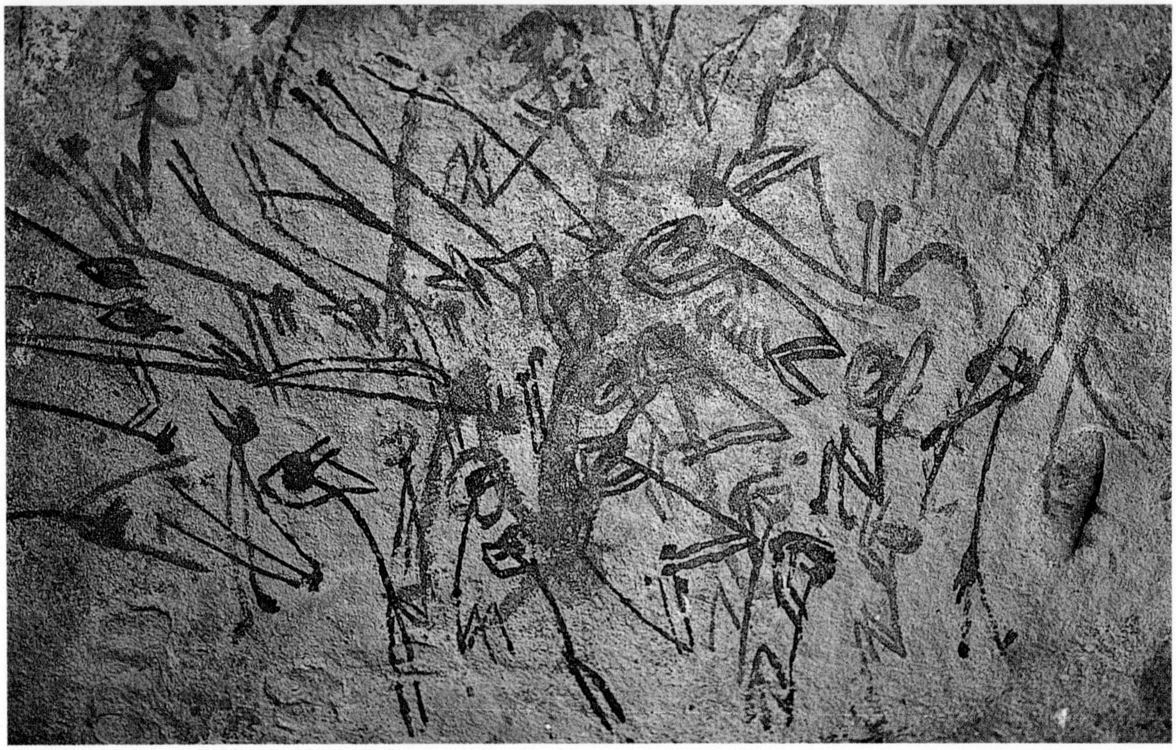

flat, deep-green marsh. The warm air is filled with the murmur of innumerable pied geese busy at their nests. Flocks of the birds fly to and fro over their heads.

Wamut looks appreciatively around the camp ground. It curls around the top of a billabong full of pale blue waterlilies and red lotuses. Further round the billabong is a thin line of umbrella-shaped trees. Several families are camped there. Wamut recognises them as members of the Murumburr clan. This is their country. Wamut calls out greetings and asks formal permission to camp and hunt on Murumburr land. Permission is readily given and the family sets up camp on a narrow strip of high ground between the forest and the billabong's northern tip.

As the sun sets in lurid colours over the marsh, the senior Murumburr man, jovial and heavy-set, and his senior wife come over to Wamut's camp. They bring food — geese and their eggs, waterlily roots and a water python. As is customary all food is shared. If this courtesy is ever overlooked, if greed and selfishness prevail over good manners, it would be considered unpardonable rudeness. Fights would break out and people could be speared and even killed. But this is very rare. Wamut has experienced it only once or twice in his life.

Tonight all is peaceful and soon after darkness, to the sounds of flying foxes squabbling in the flowering trees and frogs calling in the swamps, the family is soundly asleep.

These are the latter days of Gudjewg and rains are still frequent. So shelters are built from sheets of bark cut with stone axes from eucalypts and the ever useful paperbarks. The family sleeps in these smoky places to get away from the hordes of mosquitoes. When it is hot, on sunny days, they camp under lean-tos made of poles and covered with leafy branches or palm fronds. The women recover the oven stones and grindstones brought here over the years. The men cut lightweight saplings and lash them together to make rafts — one for the women to go out on the marshes, and another for themselves to pole along the spidery, narrow channels to spear fish. The young people make their own improvisations to paddle out onto the billabong.

Even though the Murumburr's camp is at the other side of Gummunkuwuy, the families intermix during the day. When not out gathering food, they sit around in the shade catching up with one another's lives, recounting adventures, who is moving where, who has died, what ceremonies are planned, which tribes are fighting. The Murumburr have heard rumours that a strange new people have arrived to the north — people with white skins and riding large, grotesque animals. Nyalgan, who loves to wander and see new things, listens intently but keeps his own counsel. There is talk of tribes to the north-east looking to resurrect a blood feud. The young men are stirred by such talk, half eager for the excitement and to show off their fighting prowess and half afraid of the consequences. But the elders are alarmed, they know that such skirmishes and ambushes will take a heavy toll of the young men on both sides and that it will breed fear and suspicion. Wamut recounts how, when he was a young man, so many had been killed in a war that the clan's very survival was threatened. They had walked the bush in constant fear. Finally both sides were so concerned about the bloodshed that they agreed to hold one last battle to settle the score; a fight to end all fights. Wamut recalls vividly how the two sides had got together. They had painted their bodies with sacred clan designs, danced to the drone of didgeridoos — then they faced each other, eight men on each side about twenty metres apart, holding wickedly barbed spears in

Dragonflies abound on the floodplain and the air shimmers with their wings.

their spear throwers and with the small bags from around their necks clamped between their teeth. Then they threw the spears at each other. At the first casualty, it had been agreed, the fighting would stop and peace be restored.

Wamut gets up and mimes the confrontation — how he watched his opponent and could see straight away that the spear he had thrown would miss him. So Wamut hurled his own spear with all his strength hoping to catch his man before he had recovered his balance. He succeeded and the man died with a spear through his ribcage. The war was over.

Wamut, noting the shining eyes of the young men, recalls that he was exhilarated at first. But very sad afterwards and ever since he has argued against war and the havoc it brings to the clans and the families. So far his wisdom and eloquence have prevailed.

That evening Wamut walks over to the edge of the camp and sits down alone. Under the wide sky the green treeless plain is bathed in brilliant light. The scene is dazzling, seeming to expand and grow larger than life. To the west the setting sun has edged the few low clouds with gold, a gold that catches the shimmering wings of countless dragonflies making the air wink and sparkle. The open vastness of the plain exhilarates Wamut but there is also a small touch of unease, for after all he is a Badmardi man more used to the rocky confines of the escarpment. He scans the shallow water where the tall lotus leaves sigh and rustle in the slight breeze. Here and there pandanus trees, seemingly standing on the tiptoes of their stilt roots, make vivid green patches. Is it a crocodile's head slowly sinking beneath the water close to where Amurak and Mobiny are gathering waterlily roots? Wamut takes no chances and calls the girls back to camp.

During the night a light rain drums on the roofs of the bark shelters, but the morning is clear and refreshingly cool.

Around the Billabong

The next day, before he and Nyalgan set off to spear barramundi, Wamut tells the children to be careful about Ginga, the saltwater crocodile who lives in the billabong. He can swallow small children whole, Wamut warns, or bite off an arm or leg. Over the years several people have been killed or maimed by crocodiles right here at Gummunkuwuy. If you see Ginga in the billabong, perhaps with only his eyes and nostrils showing, get out of the water straight away and make sure you warn everyone. Ginga is very dangerous.

The men pole their raft out along the grass-lined channels. Egrets and pied herons fly up in front of them and settle again behind. Cormorants and darters swim and dive in the clear water. Where two channels join, a bigger pool has formed. Here the men drag their raft onto the grass, disturbing grasshoppers and small frogs, which jump into the water. This may tempt the big carnivorous fish within range of their spears.

The women, with Amurak and Mobiny, have a more difficult time with their raft. They must travel over the sedges and grasses of the marsh itself, out to where the geese have their nests. Often the vegetation is too dense to float the raft, but not dense enough to carry the people's weight. They must wade out pushing their flimsy craft along. The water comes up to their waists and sometimes even up to their shoulders. But they wade only as a last resort for they hate the leeches.

For an hour or more the women push on before they reach the first nests. The geese fly

Ginga, the dangerous saltwater crocodile, lurks in the billabong.

up, their noisy protests rising above the general cacophony, then settle again a short distance away. Quickly the women and girls gather the warm creamy-white eggs from one nest after another. They do not take all the six or seven eggs in each nest. Some are left to hatch into goslings.

Other nest robbers take advantage of the intrusion. Kites hover overhead and descend onto untended nests to eat as many eggs as they can. Overfed goannas also feast on the eggs. When they have sufficient eggs the women wrap them in grass and put them in their dilly bags and pole back to camp.

Gabu and Barradja have made friends with three Murumburr boys about their own age. Being freshwater people they are skilled in catching animals in the billabong. In a good natured, showing-off kind of way they like to teach the rock country boys how to go about it. They have a certain disdain for Ginga, confident that they can outsmart him. But they do tell their Badmardi friends that a particular, large crocodile in the billabong is not afraid of people. Often he slowly drifts towards anyone fishing or collecting waterlily roots. Perhaps it is curiosity on the crocodile's part, but it could be more sinister.

The red lotus flowers mostly during the wet season. The plant's seeds are an important food for the Gagudju people. The large leaves were used by Gabu and Barradja to hide behind while stalking pygmy geese.

The trick Gabu and Barradja are keenest to learn is how to get close to swimming birds and then catch them by grabbing hold of their feet from under the water. Enviously they have watched the Murumburr catch pygmy geese, whistle ducks and cormorants that way.

The 'water boys' show Gabu and Barradja how to prepare the huge umbrella-like leaves of the lotus as a shield to hide behind. They must fold the leaf so that it falls over their faces. Next they must tear a single small hole to look through, not two holes, for the birds would then feel that two eyes were watching them. Once prepared like that, their friends explain, they must wade out slowly, submerged up to their noses, heads hidden by lotus leaves and patiently work their way towards their intended victims. The birds will not fly off if they are approached carefully and slowly. The most difficult part is to bring a hand up to grab the bird's feet without being detected.

There are many green pygmy geese feeding on floating vegetation at the shallower end of the billabong. Gabu sets off for one group, Barradja for another, intent, forcing themselves to be patient. The billabong's bottom is slippery and the water cold. Lily stems and other plants tug at their legs. When a fish or water snake brushes their skin they do not flinch. Leeches are ignored. They persevere, crouching low when the water is shallow and struggling not to make disturbing ripples when it is deep.

Gabu, ever active and impatient like his namesake the green ant, closes the gap first. Suppressing his natural restlessness, he is so close that he can see the barbs on the birds' iridescent wing feathers and the filter plates on their beaks. The nearest bird looks straight at him and Gabu is convinced his disguise has been detected, but soon the pygmy goose is busy filtering plant seeds from the water again. Hardly daring to breathe, Gabu takes that last step forward. He cannot believe how close he is. Cautiously he reaches for the bird. Incredulity and his natural impatience force his hand to move too quickly. He lunges for the bird's feet but it flies off with a shrill piping call.

The birds Barradja is stalking look up at the disturbance, but it is far enough away not to put them to flight. In fact the unsettled birds fly over, circle once and land close to Barradja. So close that he can grab the feet and legs of one of them before it knows what happened. The boy's laughter skips across the water. He is still laughing as he comes ashore, pygmy goose in hand, struggling through the sticky mud. His friends have seen something else and run out towards him, yelling in alarm. They drag him unceremoniously ashore, just as Ginga's jaws emerge from the water. All five run back to camp.

Hunting Ginga

At night, around the fire, the patriarchs talk for long hours about the crocodile's uncharacteristic boldness and fearlessness. Is he a special favourite of the spirits and therefore not to be killed or is he merely a cheeky fellow? One Murumburr elder, whose Dreaming is Ginga the crocodile, is consulted. They gently chide him, for he would have been partially responsible if the crocodile, his other self, had taken one of the boys. The man explains that normally if a crocodile came close to him he would feel that it was someone's spirit who had come to tell him something or to guide him somewhere. But this crocodile seems merely predatory, attacking a group that included his own grandson. He says he will go out on the billabong and talk to the crocodile.

A green pygmy goose like the one the boys caught.

The elder of Ginga's totem spends several days out on the billabong observing the crocodile closely. Carefully he notes its movements — where and for how long he basks on the bank, where he hunts for fish and turtles, how long he can stay underwater. Once or twice Ginga's head surfaces close to the man's bark canoe, but he sees no flicker of empathy in the reptile's glittering green eyes. There is no rapport of any kind. The man approves the hunt, though he himself will not take part.

The young men now look to their spears, especially long ones with hardwood tips barbed on one side. Each spear is painted with red ochre to give it greater potency. Nyalgan is taken out in a bark canoe, skilfully made by these water people and more manoeuvrable than a raft. He learns to adjust his technique. He has never thrown from such an unsteady platform.

A low mist hugs the water the morning of the hunt. The young men set out in three canoes with two people to each craft. They know where Ginga is lying on the bank, basking with mouth agape. The hunters approach stealthily from three directions. Nyalgan and his companion are in the centre. Slowly they drift nearer. When Ginga closes his mouth and twitches his mighty tail they fit their spears to their spear throwers.

Nyalgan concentrates as he rarely has before. He aims at the 4 m long crocodile's side at a place where the skin is not armoured with bony plates. He will try to pierce a lung so the animal cannot stay underwater long. Five other spears are also poised. When he judges the moment to be right, Nyalgan drives his spear home. He sees it penetrate the skin and is confident a lung is pierced. Three other spears find their mark, but two are deflected off the animal's back, their tips broken. Nyalgan and his companions have only a split second to assess the damage for Ginga explodes into the water with such force that Nyalgan's canoe capsizes and tips him and his friend into the water. His partner soon rights the canoe and bails it out. Quickly they clamber back on board. They follow Ginga's trail of blood and bubbles along the shallow edge of the billabong, confirming that the lung has been punctured. The wounded animal thrashes and rolls, throwing up a fountain of mud in trying to rid himself of the spears. He succeeds in snapping one of them. The men guide their canoes closer and closer to the turmoil, hoping to be able to drive home several more spears. Ginga's punctured lung and his very size work against him, soon he is exhausted and comes up to breathe. When his snout surfaces six more spears hit him at close range. He is finished. But being a reptile of immense strength it takes an hour or more before his heart stops beating and his legs and tail stop thrashing. Finally he sinks lifeless to the bottom. The men dive after him and getting hold of a barbed spear each, heave him onto the bank.

The elders cut Ginga up and the women put the meat into the stone-lined earth ovens. This afternoon there will be a feast for everyone except the young children, who would get grey hair if they ate Ginga's meat, and for the man whose Dreaming is the crocodile.

By late afternoon the stage is set for the dance. The raised treeless ground between the camps is the traditional ceremonial ground. It is cleared of sticks and rocks and anything else that might injure stamping feet. White clay is brought from dilly bags, ground on flat stones and painted on the men and women with bark brushes and bundles of grass. Children run in and out amongst the adults and get a lick of paint from one then another.

The didgeridoo player is ready first and sits down. The two song men, each with a pair of song-sticks, sit beside him. On the other side sit the women. Carrying spears the men

Burrungguy (Nourlangie Rock) and Anbangbang in the background and Nawulandja in the foreground. This was the country of the Warramal people.

arrange themselves opposite the musicians. The didgeridoo starts with a pulsating drone, the song men and their rhythmic clapping of sticks join in. The dancers' first movements are standard introductory steps. Warming to the celebration they begin re-enacting the day's hunt. One man mimics Ginga asleep on the bank, mouth open. The others approach him, spears poised, Nyalgan, a little unsteady in the canoe. They spear the Ginga-man. He holds several spears clamped under his arms and writhes about, upsets the canoe, tipping people into the water. So clever, so funny, so true is the acting that people fall over with laughter.

The sun goes down in a blaze of red, silhouetting the dancers. But on and on they go — refining their act and improvising changes. Each new twist brings more laughter. The children join in the dance, learning the steps and the mimicry. 'Nyalgan's hunt' may well pass into folklore.

Return Journey

Some weeks later the nests of the pied geese are well advanced. The waterlilies and spike-rush tubers have been harvested close to camp. Rains are less frequent and not so heavy. Gudjewg, the wet season, is drawing to a close, the monsoon has run its course. Banggerdeng, a short season of only about a month's duration, is upon them. Wamut notices the change in wind direction, it has turned from steady north-westerlies to light easterlies. Food is now abundant in the woodlands around their home. Yams and fruits are easily found, lizards and snakes are fat. The Badmardi must return to their own country.

The return journey is by a different route, via Flying Fox Dreaming near Anbangbang.

Paintings of dangerous and frightening spirits abound near Anbangbang rock shelter where the Badmardi camped. This painting shows Nabulwinjbulwinj who kills and eats women.

Walking almost due east for two days the family arrives at Anbangbang's cavernous shelter. The ceiling is about ten metres high and is the side of a monumental rock resting across two smaller ones. These rocks were split off Burrungguy's 265 m high bluff in a cataclysm that must have shaken the whole of Kakadu. Open at both ends, the cavern is cooled by constant breezes, a coolness the Badmardi are grateful for after their long hot walk. The cavern is in the Warramal clan's country but no Warramal are camped here now. Wamut had noticed their fires along the billabong at the Nawulandja outcrop.

The children stay close to their elders. Anbangbang's huge echoing caves and aura of mystery frightens them. A little way from the shelter paintings of dangerous spirits stare at them from rock walls through the foliage of trees — malevolent Namarndis and dangerous Nabulwinjbulwinj who kills and eats women. In hollows and shelves rest the skeletons of Warramal and Badmardi ancestors. It is no place for children.

The next morning the entire family walks the few kilometres to Nawulandja to see the three Warramal families to ask permission to hunt and to camp. The Badmardi children feel much more at ease here. The shelters are more open without any dark caves or frightening paintings. Laughing and shouting all the children, more than fifteen in all, run down the slope to the stream. Forming small canoes out of paperbark they have races in the swift flowing water, they have mock spear fights, they swing from vines and jump in the water.

There are enough fish, turtles and waterbirds in the billabongs and enough tubers and fruits in the forest to feed everyone in this time of plenty. There is time to make weapons and implements, to gossip and joke. A flying fox hunt near the bat's special Dreaming site is

An ancient rock painting of a flying fox.

planned for two days hence and the Badmardi are invited. Wamut, being of the Flying Fox Dreaming,* cannot take part in the hunt, but tomorrow he will visit the place on his own.

Relaxed and with a feeling of well-being the day slips into a clear evening. As the setting sun flickers through the weeping branches of the paperbarks, a haunting song drifts to the camp. Two boys, facing each other and leaning on sticks painted red and white, sing the song. All but the youngest immediately recognise it and the sticks the boys carry. The women reply in unison 'wait ba, wait ba, wait ba . . .', singing the words as often as they can without drawing breath.

One of the Warramal elders calls to the boys to come and join them and have some food. The painted sticks together with the songs indicate that the boys, about fifteen or sixteen years old, are ready to go through the second stage of their initiation. But first they must travel far and wide to broaden their horizons and to meet and get to know people who may have very different customs. The sticks guarantee their safe passage wherever they may go.

Flying Fox Dreaming

Wamut sets out alone the next day to visit Goluban Djang, Flying Fox Dreaming. He follows the watercourse upstream. After about a half-hour walk he can hear the querulous voices and smell the musky, penetrating odour of the large bats. His path stops at a sloping rock beside a billabong completely ringed by pandanus and silver-leaved paperbarks. The still water, its surface broken here and there by a leaping fish or surfacing crocodile, reflects the trees and has taken on a greenish hue. Where the stream drains out of the billabong, widely spreading paperbarks grow in marshy ground. Their branches are covered with large dark shapes: thousands upon thousands of roosting fruit bats. It is too hot this sunny mid-morning for territorial squabbles and nearly all the bats, hanging upside down, fan themselves with their wings. It is as if the trees have grown outsize black leaves to flutter in the breeze.

At the opposite end of the billabong Wamut stands by the flat rock with a round hole in its centre — Flying Fox Dreaming. This rock is Goluban, the ancestral Flying Fox, where he came to rest at the end of the creative period. The rock contains the flying fox's power and essence. It is a strong force for Goluban is a special being associated with the powers of darkness and the direct offspring of Almudj the all-powerful, ever-present Rainbow Serpent.

Even though Wamut is here on his own, unpainted and without anyone to perform a ceremony, he can feel some of Goluban's power enter him.

The next day's foray into the flying fox roost is less peaceful. Because of the sacred and somewhat dangerous nature of Goluban Djang only the initiated men can go on this hunt. The two visiting boys are old enough and are invited to join in. Eleven hunters set off, armed only with short, strong clubs. When they get to the marshy ground they quietly spread out and surround the roost. At a given signal the men rush forward clubbing any flying foxes hanging in the low branches. The hunters take advantage of the fact that the bats need room to take off, and also that they need to beat their wings till they are in a horizontal position. Screaming loudly in alarm the bats climb higher and higher into the trees but they are so densely packed on the branches that they get in each other's way. Some

* Each person has more than one Dreaming. In Wamut's case he has the giant python and the black flying fox.

Thousands of flying foxes take wing to escape the Gagudju hunters.

branches break under the weight of too many flying foxes and the men rush in and kill the fallen animals. Hunters climb rapidly up the trees and shake the branches so the flying foxes cannot take off, and losing their toeholds, fall to the ground. It is pandemonium. Thousands of bats shrieking in fear and alarm, people yelling and running about, and thousands more of the bats flying overhead.

Soon it is over. The people collect their spoils and the flying foxes settle down again in the same roost where they have been for hundreds if not thousands of years.

The day of the hunt sees a change in the weather. The wind suddenly turns from the east to the south-east. The elders know that it will bring the last storms; the storms of Banggerdeng. Wamut and his family stay at Nawulandja for the first of these fierce storms which tear limbs from trees and flatten the tall, yellowing grasses. These knock-em-down storms are the signal for the Badmardi to continue their journey home.

A Special Place

After two days' walking the family arrives at Golonjdjurr near the entrance to their enclosed valley. Deaf Adder Creek, still flowing strongly, passes close to the escarpment. The family does not cross the stream to go to Djuwarr, the current is still too strong for the children. Instead they travel up the valley to its eastern rim, to a special ravine cutting northwards into the escarpment. It is a place of great significance with many Dreaming sites and a flat stony ground where every few years hundreds of people gather to perform sacred ceremonies.

The Yuwenjgayay gallery is an important Dreaming site. It is here that Wamut and Nyalgan stopped to paint.

It is an ideal and beloved camping place with a clear stream, sandy banks and shady trees. Food of all kinds is plentiful. Wamut and Nyalgan feel a special affinity with a rock face on one of the cliffs that borders the stream. This is Yuwenjgayay gallery, a short walk up a bouldery slope. Before climbing up to it, Wamut as the senior man, calls out to the place where their clan's ancestors' spirits reside. He calls out in a clear voice: 'We are coming, Wamut, Nyalgan, Melpe, Berrep . . .' Rapidly he recites the names of all the family members. He continues: 'We want good hunting of wallabies, turtles, fish . . .' Only then do the men climb up to the rocks, where, on a 70 m long smooth surface, live animals and spirits in vibrant, exquisite paintings. There is one special painting for the Badmardi men, a large image of Djawok, the ancestral koel of the Dreamtime whose spirit is embodied here.

Both men feel compelled to stay here for some days and to paint. They retrieve their ochres hidden in crevices, make brushes from bark and their own hair and collect orchid stems to use their juices as a fixative. Carefully they add their work to that painted over the millennia before them. They become completely absorbed in what they are doing and the women and children must gather the food.

Nyalgan paints Garndagitj larger than life-size with a spear, his spear, through his chest, while Wamut repaints Djawok's image.

One evening as the family sits around the fire Wamut tells the story of Bamrudek and the origin of various animals. It happened in the very place they are now sitting, long ago in the Dreamtime. Bamrudek, the snapping turtle, came out of the waterhole beside which the family is now camped and walked up the ravine to a very sacred place. With his sharp stone axe he cut off a large branch from a tree. Water gushed from the trunk. Bamrudek could not stop the flow which grew stronger and stronger. He became frightened and ran away. Downstream in the sandy creekbed all the people from near and far had come together for an important ceremony. Suddenly they heard the roar of the floodwaters and soon saw the wall of water descend. The only way they could escape was to become animals. Some swam away as fish, some flew away as birds and some bounded away as kangaroos and wallabies. So, Wamut adds with emphasis, all the animals come from this important place and when you grow up you must look after it.

Soon the children go off to sleep, their heads perhaps full of dreams about raging waters and fleeing animals.

Once the storms of Banggerdeng have ended and the winds come steadily from the south-east, the land dries out quickly. The creeks are narrow and easily crossed, even by little Nabiwu. As the family arrives back at Djuwarr, Marrawuti greets them with his ringing call.

The grasses have shed their seeds and the stalks are brown and dry. Nights are cool and in the mornings mist drifts over the water and lies briefly in low-lying areas. It is the season of Yegge, the early dry. Grass-dwelling insects have matured. Black kites are increasingly numerous and glide low over the grasslands. Wamut, observing the signs, recognises that it is time to burn the country, to cleanse it. Dry grass and old dead trees are burnt bringing all kinds of benefits for man and many of the animals, for if fire never came the groundlitter and grasses would build up into dense thickets. Travel would then be more difficult for the people; wallabies would not have the fresh green shoots that come up after the fire; Dadjbe the king brown snake would have a place to hide and remain a danger; mosquitoes would have shelter well into the dry season; Gurrbelak the rock pigeon would not be able to find the ground seeds on which it lives; Barrk the black wallaroo would move to places where grazing and browsing is easier. Life would be more difficult all round. However, burning is not done willy nilly but in such a way that there is minimum damage to plants and animals. It follows precise rules, refined over the years. Only senior men are fire managers.

Early in the season, when the ground beneath the layers of dead grass is still damp, Wamut takes the children to selected places near the camp. He shows them how to make fire with fire sticks. One of the two sticks is flat and wide and has a small depression at one end. Holding this stick in place with his foot, Wamut sprinkles a dry powdery material from the trunk of a pandanus in the depression. Pressing the other stick into this hollow he twirls this rapidly between his hands. The friction soon makes the pandanus powder smoke and smoulder. He drops the glowing ember in a handful of dry grass and blows on it. Within seconds the grass catches fire.

Above
Dry spear grass is highly flammable and the fire races through it with fearsome noise and speed.

Above right
Fire was important to the Badmardis to clear the country and make travel easier. Fire management is as important today. This place was burnt too severely to have been done by traditional Aborigines.

Once the fire has started, the children, using flaming torches made out of bundles of paperbark, run lines of fire in all directions. The topmost layers of dry grass leap into crackling flames and race away on the south-easterly breeze. Everyone is ready to pounce on goannas, bandicoots or other animals driven from cover by the smoke and the flames. Innumerable kites and brown falcons appear as if from nowhere and snatch grasshoppers and lizards almost from the flames themselves.

Wamut keeps a tight reign on the children. He makes sure that in their reckless abandon they do not find themselves shut in by fire on all sides or engulfed when a sudden gust of wind makes the flames race.

Later when the cool weather of Yegge and Wurrgeng give way to the dry heat of Gurrung, burning-off is strictly man's business. Winds are observed and special habitats such as monsoon forests, protected. Families and clans will join together and in a carefully contrived plan use fire to flush kangaroos and wallabies towards strategically placed spearsmen. Always care is taken that fire does not rage uncontrollably and scorch the crowns of tall trees.

Djuwarr and across the Plateau

Woollybutt and grevillea trees now put on brilliant orange flowers laden with nectar. Wurrgeng, the cool dry season has come. Cloudless nights cause cool air to stream down the gorges and the night temperature drops steadily. The mornings are bitterly cold, and the family huddles close to the fire till the sun is well over the escarpment. Soon, Wamut says, they will set off on a long journey that will take them in a wide circle through nearly all the Gagudju lands. They will be away for several months.

It is a journey of teaching for Wamut and Melpe and one of learning for the others. Even though most have travelled these paths before, each time they learn more, expand their awareness of the land, the plants and animals and their oneness with the environment. Each journey will bring them closer to becoming full Badmardi men and women. On their journey they will follow the footsteps of the creator beings, they will learn where these spirit

Above
Detet, the red-collared lorikeet, whose feathers were used for decoration.

Top
An ancient Dynamic Figure Style painting shows a man stalking an emu from behind a bundle of grass he carries. Perhaps this is how Wamut and Nyalgan managed to spear one.

ancestors travelled, what they created, how they hunted, how human society was instituted, how and why man was charged with custodianship of the country. Everywhere they go the landscape and all living things will become part of them.

One morning when Wurrgeng is well advanced, and the dew is cold on their skins, they set off. They walk south past Jim Jim Falls, now only a trickle, through the woodland to the plain created by Alwandju the ancestral emu. Emus are plentiful here and Wamut and Nyalgan spear one of the birds. The catch frees the men from hunting for some days, time they spend at a special rock quarry. The rock is dark and fine-grained, very different from the quartzite. They fashion a number of stones which they later will grind into axe blades.

Never hurrying, camping a few days here, a few days there, the Badmardi family moves on. They follow a tributary of Barramundi Creek onto the high escarpment. In places the plateau rises to more than 400 metres in height and the people have commanding views over the country they will travel. For days on end they walk over the rough rocks which is hard even on their callused feet. When they reach the headwaters of the Katherine River they seek out Lambalk's family of the Matjba clan.

The two families stay together for a few weeks. The elders think that Nyalgan should take a second wife and decide that Lambalk's younger sister is the best choice. Nyalgan is pleased for he is very fond of this Matjba family, especially his mother-in-law, now quite elderly. He cannot show his fondness directly for tribal law forbids him to speak to her. But he goes out and catches an echidna and gives it to Lambalk who passes it on to her mother. The old lady in return sends Nyalgan a beautiful neck ornament decorated with lorikeet feathers and the red and black seeds of the abrus vine.

A gentle climb takes the family across the watershed to the headwaters of the East Alligator River. Before climbing down to the river the Badmardi stay a while with Melpe's family of the Borlmo Kadu clan.

Descent into the East Alligator gorge is steep in this most rugged part of the sandstone plateau. The river and its tributaries follow sheer, deeply incised fault lines. Down in the ravines are wonderful, large pools full of all kinds of fish, turtles and freshwater crocodiles. In tiny pockets of monsoon forest grow yams.

To ensure the future supply of these yams, the Badmardi join several Borlmo families to perform a ceremony at a Yam Dreaming in a rock shelter. Their bodies painted with yam designs, the people light a fire at the shelter's entrance. Green branches are used to create smoke which is made to drift across the yam paintings at the back of the cavern and then out over the woodlands. Wherever the smoke travels, yams will grow.

The Badmardi do not cross the East Alligator River, but continue along its western bank. Eventually the river issues from the rock country in a broad tidal stream full of large saltwater crocodiles. By the time the family reaches Malangangerr, the dry season has advanced and turned hot. The nights are also warm now and no longer is there any mist or dew. Native bees have gathered nectar from the flowering trees. The full sweet combs are collected and eaten with great enjoyment.

No one else is camped at Malangangerr, though ashes of recent fires show that people left only a few days ago. Wallabies and goannas are plentiful in the bush and Nyalgan spears huge barramundi in the river. Life is good at the cool shelter.

The view from Ubirr. It is from here that Nyalgan saw his first buffalo.

Late one afternoon a young man of about Nyalgan's age approaches their camp. He is tall and broad-shouldered, in contrast to the slightly built Badmardi, with curly black hair and flashing white teeth. Wamut invites him to share their food. He knows the young man from previous journeys. He is of the Bunitj clan whose country of floodplain and sandstone residuals lies a few kilometres to the north. They talk about things in general, using the Gagudju language, the language of the Bunitj and a few other clans.

The Bunitj man invites the Badmardi to join his family at Ubirr, a little way downstream. They want to burn a last piece of grassland. It is full of wallabies and two extra spears will ensure a good hunt.

Nyalgan becomes good friends with the tall man. A few days after the hunt the two leave

the camp under Ubirr's high dome and climb past several galleries of paintings to the highest point of the assemblage of the rocks. Sitting amongst the yellowing spinifex clumps, they look out over monsoon forest and floodplain. Further out are sacred rocks, Garrkanj, Warrayangal and Indjuwanydjuwa.

Strange Sights and Stories

Nyalgan is suddenly aware that out on the plain is a land animal larger than any he has ever seen. It is lying in the mud and from the side of its head grow what look like enormous bony growths. Nyalgan cannot believe his eyes. His friend explains that quite a few of these animals have appeared in Bunitj country over the last few dry seasons. He and some of his brothers and cousins hunted them and after spearing it many times managed to kill one. It is a grass-eating animal like the kangaroo, yet it is dangerous, for it does not always run away. Sometimes it charges straight at you, trying to spear you with the bones on its head. But the animal's meat is good and there is a lot of it.

The Bunitj man tells of other strange animals and also a strange people that have come to his mother's country by the sea to the north. The people especially are very strange, very different from the Macassan sailors that visit there each year. The new people have light coloured skin and pale hair and eyes. They wear lots of clothes, especially the women, and build shelters out of stones. They have large animals with long legs which they sit on and ride instead of walking. When they go hunting they do not take spears or throwing sticks but use something that makes a lot of noise and smoke and sends a round stone with such force that it will go right through a wallaby and kill it. These people, called Balanda, are not friendly. Often they shout at his mother's family.

The Balanda seem a strange and frightening people to Nyalgan, but just the same his curiosity is aroused. He asks his friend if he will take him to see these strangers. The Bunitj man agrees and the two set off the next day. Nyalgan will be the first Badmardi to see the Balanda, the white man.

The family does not wait for Nyalgan's return. After a few days they leave their Bunitj hosts and set off. The season of Gurrung is advancing and it is increasingly hot. Wamut is getting a craving for pied geese which are now congregating on the drying marshes. The best place to hunt them is back at Gummungkuwuy. In easy stages they make their way back. Wamut makes a special detour, going as close as he dares to the sheer cliff of Dadjbe* that faces the floodplain.

Wamut impresses upon everyone that this is a most dangerous place. During the creative period a titanic struggle between two giant serpents took place on the broken rock surface on top of the cliffs. Blood was spilt and ran down the rocks. You can still see the stains. One of the combatants was Dadjbe the king brown snake. He left his impression as a dark horizontal stripe across the entire width of the rock face. The serpents came to rest in pools on the escarpment where they still live today. If they are ever disturbed by any careless or drastic change to the land, these most powerful beings will rise up and split the rocks with such might that the whole mountain will collapse into the earth. The serpents will then come

* Mt Brockman.

Dadjbe, a dangerous place in Kakadu, where a titanic struggle took place between two Dreamtime serpents. The serpents are still there and if disturbed, will swallow up people and cause mountains to collapse.

out, swallow all the people and destroy the country. Be careful of Dadjbe.

A big gathering of clans has assembled at Gummungkuwuy to hunt geese. Hundreds of people are camped on a large expanse of dry ground. Out on the plain the shallow marshes are shrinking but in the deepest parts hundreds of thousands of pied geese are feeding on the tubers of the spike rush. Every morning and evening the geese leave the open plain to roost in the surrounding paperbark trees, only to be met by a barrage of short spears of the Gagudju people standing on platforms built in the tree tops. The Badmardi family joins in the enjoyment of the plentiful food and in the nightly social dances.

Once more Gunumeleng approaches, heralded by an increase in humidity and by wayward winds. Gummungkuwuy is oppressive and uncomfortable. When the first storm clouds build up over the plain, the clans disperse, each family returning to its own country.

Shortly after the Badmardi family is back at Djuwarr, Nyalgan returns to great rejoicing. Seated on the rock beside the water he tells of a new and fascinating people. He talks about the people's habit of inhaling the smoke of a dry, sweet smelling herb. Nyalgan says his Bunitj friend gave him some to try. At first it made him cough and feel nauseous, but in the end it gave him a most pleasant and relaxed feeling. Nyalgan has brought some tobacco with him and he passes it around to the others. Till long after dark he tells of all that he saw.

Apart from minor changes, for no society is static, the Badmardi lived like this for many thousands of years. Archaeological research has shown that Nawulabila, like Malangangerr, has been inhabited by people for the last 23,000 years or more. If left to themselves the Badmardi and other Gagudju clans would, no doubt, have lived in harmony with everything around them for many more thousands of years. But that was not to be. In 1987 the last two senior Badmardi men, Nipper Kapirigi and George Namingum, died. Like Wamut they were fully initiated into all the Badmardi lore and wisdom, and like him had been on the journeys described here. The two men were half-brothers, their remains and their spirits rest at Djuwarr. Fewer than six Badmardi people are left and only two of them are male. As neither of them have male heirs, and as according to Aboriginal law the clan can only be perpetuated through the male line, the Badmardi may cease to exist. This is a fate that has already overtaken the Warramal people of Nawalundja and several other clans of the region.

One of the surviving Badmardi men lives at the Cooinda Motel, not far from Gummungkuwuy, where he is a nominal gardener sweeping paths and mowing lawns. Every day, all around him people from many parts of the world rush about in cars, buses, planes and powerboats — intent on their own pursuits and oblivious of the man's heritage. This lone Badmardi has become a stranger in his own land. The other Badmardi man has made his life a long way from his clan's homeland and never visits there.

In truth there are no more Badmardi people to take up custodianship of the land, to look after the country, to see that Djawok is properly repainted, that Garndagitj ceremonies are carried out, that Almudj rests undisturbed in her pool.

And who will now pacify Dadjbe, that most dangerous force? A large hole has been dug by the Balanda at the base of his mountain to extract uranium. Dadjbe's spirit, embodying the power of the Dreamtime, may well have entered the uranium and through it could still wreak havoc by making mountains collapse and by swallowing up people.

8 ~ LOOKING AFTER THE COUNTRY — THE GAGUDJU WAY

THE GAGUDJU MEN AND WOMEN, as we have seen, could gather their food with comparative ease. They were able to do so because of their intimate knowledge of the land and all living things and because of their great skill with their implements and weapons.

The people's skills, knowledge and spiritual attachment to their environment were refined over more than 2500 generations of keen observation and cumulative experience. Slowly over a long span of time this quite precise body of knowledge was given cohesion and authority, in fact a force of its own, and so became the Dreamtime. It became enshrined in the laws of the people.

In the mythology of the Dreamtime ancestral beings came to a blank unknown country, just as Australia was to the minds of the first Aborigines to arrive here. Then the ancestral beings gave shape to the land just as the accumulated experience finally gave shape to the environment in the minds of the people. The great spirit ancestors hunted, chanted, danced, painted, made artifacts, lived in rock shelters and had human foibles and weaknesses exactly like the traditional Aboriginal people do.

The traditional Gagudju live like the original, mythical creator beings; they obey their laws and live their way of life. As long as they perpetuate those values the people, the land and the life it supports will endure in harmony. Paradise for the Gagudju is here and now and on earth — something that in Kakadu is not difficult to accept. There are no rewards in the hereafter, maintaining the integrity of the life force is its own reward. But man plays a special role in this natural order of things. Only he, by constantly keeping in touch with the life force, can ensure its continuation and conversely only he, by neglecting his duties, can cause its disruption.

This was decreed at the end of the creative period of the Dreamtime when the great spirit ancestors, before becoming part of the landscape, charged the people with the custodianship of the land. They said: 'Now that we have created the land and showed you the laws you must live as we did and look after the country for all time.' The creator beings set a pattern for a way of life that will last for all time, provided man plays his part.

The Gagudju call their custodianship 'looking after the country'. It is a subtle, all pervasive motivation that governs the people's entire lives. The most important part of any traditional person's life is to 'look after the country'.

Like 'Dreamtime' and 'story', 'looking after the country' is an inadequate expression for so deep a responsibility. But it is a phrase the Gagudju themselves have coined and like to use.

Ceremonial dances are an important part of looking after the country as decreed by the spirit ancestors. This dance was held at Cannon Hill.

Previous pages

Neidjie's son, Yarramarna, surveys his traditional lands in Kakadu National Park.

The English language is generally not equal to the task of explaining the Gagudjus' attachment to the land and the complexity of their spiritual lives. It is a deficiency many elders feel keenly, for they firmly believe that if what are to them the self-evident truths of their 'story', their culture and philosophy were properly explained, the white people would understand the Dreamtime imperatives and would not be in conflict with them so often.

Over the millennia the vast amount of knowledge and wisdom that was gathered was synthesised into a complex network of interrelationships, not only between man and other living things, but among the individual people themselves. For the Gagudju this rich tapestry of insights was never written down. It always only existed in the minds of the elders, who passed it on to the new generations in a sequence of initiation ceremonies. It takes most of a person's life to learn, absorb and understand their complete 'story'. Only when all the ceremonies have been gone through, is the person a complete man or woman and the possessor of all the knowledge and wisdom of the Dreamtime.

There are only a few Gagudju elders who still know their people's full story, and they are old now. All the Gagudju's lore, traditions and laws, all their accumulated knowledge, now remains only in the minds of these few men. They are the library of the Gagudju. Only they can maintain the integrity with the life force and so look after the country properly. As has happened with so many Aboriginal groups, the younger generations have not been initiated. This is because the disruptions to the people's lives split the clans and dispossessed them of their lands. As a result the initiates were removed from their ceremonial heartland. The ceremonies could not be performed; they would be meaningless away from their own land, their own country. For the Gagudju their land has now been restored, but it may well be too late to enable them to restore ceremonial life.

'Looking after the country' is a many faceted obligation. It can be as simple and unobtrusive as visiting a sacred place in order to maintain communion with a special spirit. Or it can be a potent, active force such as burning the grasslands. Hunting for and gathering food according to the guidelines laid down by the spirit ancestors, is also part of looking after the country. Ceremony is perhaps the most important part of the process. This includes song cycles relating activities of the Dreamtime and dances that dramatically re-create great deeds of the past. The act of painting, be it on rock, bark or the bodies of people, is a vital link in the endless chain that binds people and nature together.

By definition fully initiated men know and understand all aspects of the Gagudju story and have the skills necessary to make their artifacts and to create paintings. They all know the stories about the plants and animals and the secret and secular ceremonies. But because of the great intricacies of the complete 'story' and, human nature being what it is, some elders are more active and interested in maintaining the traditions than others. In theory there are no specialists in Gagudju lore, but in practice there are. One person may have a greater facility in retaining the knowledge of secret ceremonies, another is perhaps more skilled in making spears and didgeridoos while a third may be a great bark painter.

The Last Traditional Elders

Fewer than a dozen traditional elders now live in Kakadu — they are the last repository of a story that began 50,000 years ago, and the heirs to the legacy of Malangangerr. They are a

Big Bill Neidjie is a Gagudju man of the Bunitj clan and most passionate about keeping the Dreamtime alive.

Top
Felix Iyanuk, of the Limilngan clan, is the keeper of many Gagudju ceremonies.

remarkable group of people for in their lifetimes they saw their society change from the stone age to the atomic age; in their youth they felt the stone knives of initiation ceremonies and as elders they had to decide whether to allow uranium mining on their lands. All the elders are concerned about preserving their culture and four of them especially have articulated their fears about the future. Two are Gagudju men, the other two are from neighbouring areas but have close ceremonial and marital links. All live in Kakadu.

As a child Nipper Kapirigi lived in the bush in the traditional way. Kapirigi is of slight build but of an upright bearing. He has a full, greying beard. None of the elders know how old they are. Going by known events such as the building of a road or railway or the activities of certain white buffalo hunters, it is sometimes possible to guess how old they are. Kapirigi must be in his late seventies. He belongs to the Badmardi clan. His knowledge of the lives of the creator beings, where they left their marks on the land, the stories about and uses of the plants and animals is unsurpassed in scope and detail. To walk with him in Kakadu and to be told its stories, is to enter another and vital world. An irrepressible sense of fun often hides Kapirigi's growing worries about the future of his tribal lands. Kapirigi is the repository of the Dreamtime stories and their application to everyday life.

Bluey Ilkirr is the youngest of the four, he is in his mid-fifties. Though balding and with a greying stubble beard he is strong and vigorous. Ilkirr belongs to the Gunwinggu tribe and was brought up in the traditional way in Arnhem Land not far from Kakadu. His wife, Susan Aladjingu, however, is a full Gagudju. Ilkirr and his wife live in the bush where they still gather much of their food. Despite the fact that Ilkirr, like all of his people, is always ready to pull somebody's leg and have a good laugh, he is essentially a serious person. Ilkirr communicates the Gagudju story through his intricate paintings and as a result is now generally accepted as one of the people. He is Kakadu's principal artist.

Eldest of the four is Felix Iyanuk, a tall, slender man with a full head of curly grey hair and a luxuriant beard. He must be close to eighty years old. Kindly and generous, soft-spoken and with a warm smile, Iyanuk is always ready with a good-humoured joke. He is of twofold importance in Kakadu's culture. While he is the manager of many important Gagudju ceremonies, he himself is of a different group, the Limilngan clan, whose country adjoins Kakadu to the west. Iyanuk is the only person who still knows the Limilngan language; it will die with him. He is also one of perhaps five or six people who still speak the Gagudju language. But he alone, no-one else, can still perform the songs and dance steps of the Gagudju's funerary rights, still knows the complete song cycle, in the Gagudju language, about Indjuwanydjuwa one of the most important spirit ancestors. He is the only one who can still look after that part of the country properly. Iyanuk is the keeper of ceremonies.

Iyanuk's close friend, Big Bill Neidjie, is a true Gagudju man of the Bunitj clan. He is the custodian of the same sacred places for which Iyanuk is the ceremonial manager. Neidjie is probably in his early seventies. He is a tall, powerful man. His face reflects an inner strength and his stern demeanour and deep rumbling voice inspire respect. Neidjie's concerns, his passion, is to preserve the Gagudju story. Not only to pass it on to the new generations of his own people, but to explain its subtle and vital wisdom to other peoples of the world. He is convinced that if its lessons, which have a universal application, are not heeded it is not just the Gagudju who will suffer but all of mankind. Neidjie thinks about the totality of the

Right
Nipper Kapirigi, an elder of the Badmardi clan and keeper of Dreamtime stories.

Below right
Bluey Ilkirr belongs to the Gunwinggu tribe and is Kakadu's principal artist.

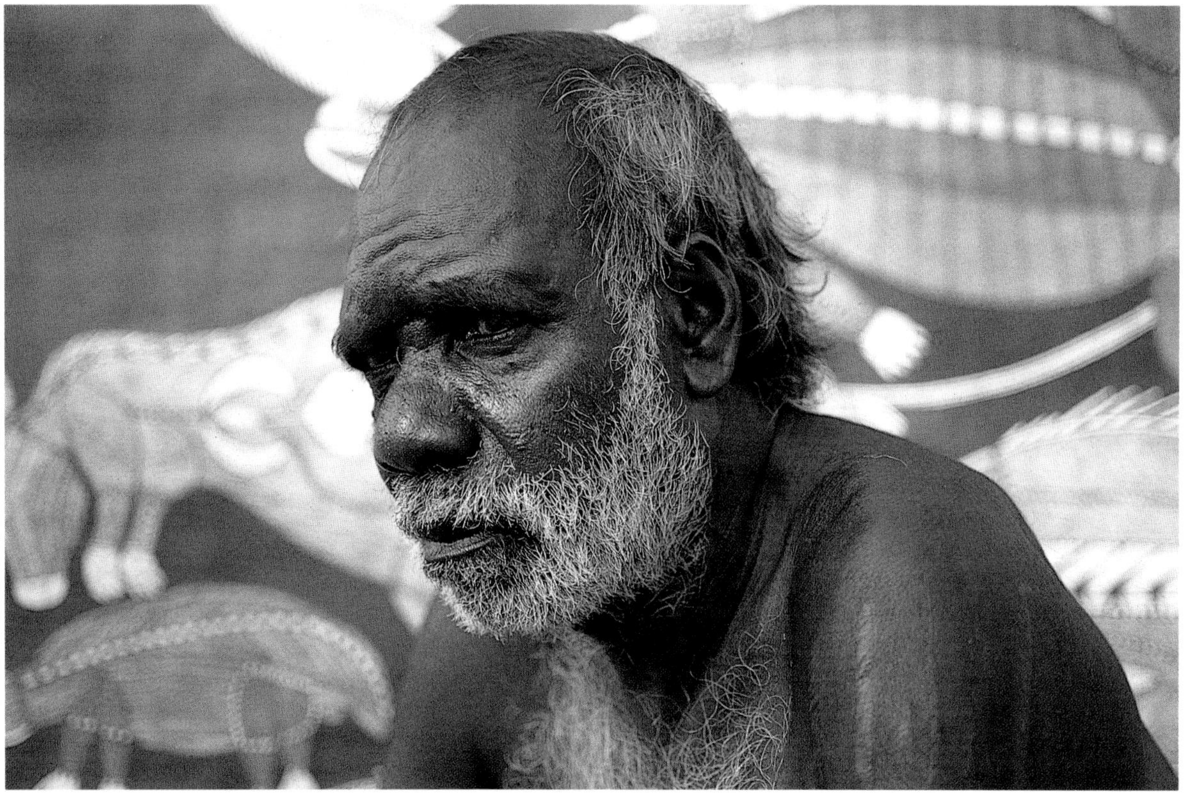

Above
Nipper Kapirigi and Minnie Gapindi camped at Djuwarr Rock. Kapirigi must make periodic trips to his country to fulfil his obligations as custodian.

Right
Kapirigi follows Djuwarr Creek on his way to address Almudj, the Rainbow Serpent.

Gagudju's philosophy and religion. Like a Buddhist or Hindu sage he searches in a people's accumulated wisdom for the meaning of the interconnectedness of living things. One of his great frustrations is that he is unable to express his thoughts fully in English. Yet like many Aborigines he can speak with a simple poetic directness that has great power. Neidjie is the philosopher of the Gagudju.

Keeper of Dreamtime stories, artist, custodian of ceremonies and philosopher all look after the country in their own way.

Djuwarr's Custodian

Nipper Kapirigi is camped deep in the escarpment near the headwaters of Deaf Adder Creek. His companion is Minnie Gapindi. The sun colours the eastern sky as Gapindi blows on the embers of last night's fire and restarts it. Kapirigi sits up on his swag and wraps his blanket tightly around himself, for even in this season of Gurrung, the beginning of the hot season, early morning is cool.

The camp is on a grassy flat beneath shady paperbark trees, growing on the edge of a deep waterhole. This permanent water is fed by a stream flowing out of a narrow ravine. A low mist swirls over the water, hiding the long legs of a ghostly black-necked stork foraging in the shallows. A barramundi slaps the water with its tail. Up in the ravine a jungle fowl crows and cackles. Across the 20 m of water is a white sandy beach and towering above it is the rugged face of Djuwarr Rock.

Kapirigi has been coming to Djuwarr since he was a small child and he must return periodically to keep in touch with the forces and spirits of the Dreamtime that live in this sacred place. He must do so both for himself and as the chief custodian of his clan. He does not like to come alone for he says the place is haunted by too many frightening spirits.

The sun rises, evaporating the mist, and soon it is warm enough for Kapirigi to discard his blanket. He and Gapindi talk quietly about what they will do during the day. While they talk Marrawuti the white-breasted sea-eagle lands in a tall paperbark and eyes their camp as well as the waterhole for food. Kapirigi straightens a wooden spear he has been working on while Gapindi heats some fish she caught last night. When they have eaten, Kapirigi suddenly gets up, picks up his spear and walks off briskly. He follows the water's edge some distance downstream to where it is shallow and where he can walk across. On the other side he scrambles up the scree slope, to a huge, flat-topped block of stone. He climbs on top of it. After pausing for a few moments to catch his breath, he stands up and, spear in hand, faces the escarpment; a slight, but straight and vital figure dwarfed by the escarpment and the giant boulders cleaved from its surface.

Speaking rapidly in a clear ringing voice, gesticulating with both hands, Kapirigi addresses Almudj. He announces his presence and that of Gapindi and recites the places he will visit. His voice, echoing off the rocks also echoes down the millennia, perhaps as much as 10,000 years, when someone very like Kapirigi spoke to the Rainbow Serpent. Kapirigi is perhaps the last of the Gagudju to speak to Almudj, here in the place where she lives.

There is a deep gash that splits the escarpment where Almudj forced her way through the rocks before moving up the ravine. This ravine, its entrance guarded by Djuwarr rock, ends at a bottomless pool beneath a waterfall. This pool is where Almudj took up residence 'altogether for good' and that is where she lives today. She can still vent her anger on people if she is suddenly and carelessly disturbed. But if approached, as Kapirigi does, by first announcing his presence, she is pacified. Kapirigi still smiles at the time he brought a 'white fella archaeologist' to Almudj's pool. He told the young man not to throw stones into the pool or bathe in its waters. But the scientist laughed at such superstition and threw a large rock into the water. That night a storm blew up bringing torrential rain that washed the archaeologist's camp away. And that was in the dry season.

In his younger days Kapirigi would have climbed up to the split in the rock. But he is old now and his legs, and particularly his lungs, will not allow it. He would have visited an important gallery of paintings, of barramundi, kangaroos, echidnas and ancestral spirits and especially the 5m long painting of Nawaran the giant Oenpelli python. Some of these paintings were done by Kapirigi's cousin Najombolmi about thirty years ago, the same man who painted Kakadu's last major rock art at Anbangbang.

Slowly Kapirigi climbs down the slope again, passes beneath Djuwarr, walks a short

Above
The deep pool where Almudj lives.

Above right
Kapirigi looks at the painting that is the embodiment of Garndagitj, the ancestral kangaroo, on a rock near Djuwarr.

distance up the ravine and enters a patch of dark, dense forest. The tall spreading trees and darkness follow a steep-sided gully. Pausing frequently to keep his breathing under control, Kapirigi makes his way slowly to a smooth wall of rock. It is at the base of a cliff which bulges outward before rising to a height of about sixty metres. The sun never reaches here. Through the tracery of leaves at the shelter's entrance Kapirigi can see two giant images of kangaroos outlined in white. These are Garndagitj, the ancestral kangaroo, and his mate Garnday painted larger than life-size. To Kapirigi these *are* the ancestral kangaroos and this place is where their spirit resides. The images contain their essence and power, which when looked after and tapped through ceremony, will be transmuted into living kangaroos. In the past Kapirigi took part in such ceremonies, but now all he can do is to go to this place invested with the power of Garndagitj and ensure the images are intact and therefore their power still potent.

Kapirigi does not like to stay alone in such a dark place and soon heads back to camp. Once out of the rainforest he hears the hissing, churring, scratching calls of Djuwe the great bowerbird. The sounds are of the bird displaying at his bower. Djuwe, who builds an elaborate ceremonial ground which he decorates and at which he sings and dances, is of special significance to the Gagudju people.

Kapirigi has known this particular playground for many years. He now squats down beside it and examines the ornaments the bird has collected. These are mostly bleached bones of

Kapirigi examines the bones at Djuwe, the great bowerbird's, playground. Djuwe is a dangerous bird who will 'steal your bones'.

kangaroos, possums, birds and even a freshwater crocodile but also snail shells, some pinkish flowers and round green fruits the size of marbles.

Kapirigi says this about the bird:
Djuwe, that bird, he keep ceremony,
Special ceremony for business*
He dance and sing like ceremony,
He build special hut to keep bones.
He keep our special initiation ceremony;
That's his job.
But you gotta be careful.
That bird dangerous,
He kill you and steal your bones.

It is hot by the time Kapirigi returns to camp. Gapindi has also been busy. She has caught a turtle and some black bream in the waterhole and is cooking them.

After they have eaten Kapirigi sits down, his back against the broad trunk of a paperbark tree. His venture into the dark forest has rekindled his awareness of the spirits that live here.

* The word 'business' refers to anything secret in Aboriginal ceremonial life.

Susan Aladjingu with a young agile wallaby she is rearing and a basket she has woven out of pandanus fronds.

Top
Kapirigi with the eggs of the freshwater crocodile which Gapindi had dug up. The eggs are good bush tucker.

He thinks about the slender and fragile Mimis which he can sometimes feel watching him from small caves high up on Djuwarr. But they come out only at night when they leave messages for the Gagudju such as a special arrangement of leaves or a new painting. But he knows that they do very few paintings nowadays. He explains:

Mimis can't do paintings when people around.
Only after about five years there might be a new painting.
You'll go back and find a good painting.
Mimis don't like white fellas.
Maybe they're frightened.
But if they see them lots of times, it's all right.

In the afternoon, when the paperbarks' shadows lie darkly across the water, the two old friends walk over to the white sandy beach on the other side of the waterhole. They had noticed the tracks of freshwater crocodiles leading up the bank. As this is the season of egg-laying they thought the tracks were of females who had buried their eggs in the sand during the night. Gapindi probes the sand with a pointed stick and soon finds a clutch and digs up the twelve pure white, hard-shelled eggs.

During Kapirigi's and Gapindi's absence, Marrawuti has raided their camp, taking a great many of the small fish Gapindi had caught. Both people laugh in delight. 'That's all right,' says Kapirigi, 'Marrawuti, he is the boss around here.'

As Gapindi puts the crocodile eggs on to boil in a blackened billy, the usually effervescent Kapirigi is in a reflective mood. At the end of a day spent in his country he is more than ever aware of the Dreamtime and its obligations. He greatly fears the retribution of Almudj if the country is not looked after. Not so much for himself, for he is old now, but for his people and the country itself; his country, his spirit.

Speaking half to himself and half to Gapindi he talks about the younger people:

My children and grandchildren not interested.
When I go away, when I pass on, no-one will know these stories.
I know them myself, that's all.
Kids go to school now, they learn white fella stories.
They don't learn our stories, our culture.
Maybe when they finish school
I'll bring them out here and teach them.

After a few moments he adds:

'I can teach a good man, but there is nobody.'

It is almost dark now. Tiny bats wheel and turn after insects. One catches a mosquito that hovers centimetres from Kapirigi's face. Down in the ravine Marrawuti and his mate call from their nest. Kapirigi's face brightens. For the time being at least Almudj rests in her pool, the Dreamtime continues. By just being here, living here and looking after the country Kapirigi reaffirms a 50,000 year continuity, the longest in human history.

A Tradition Continues

Rock painting virtually ceased in Kakadu during the 1970s and early 1980s. Nothing of the scale and artistry of Najombolmi's 1964 masterwork has been done since. However, the ancient painting traditions continue. But now the paintings are only on bark. They are of

A Gagudju boy with Al-mangeyi, the long-necked turtle, a favoured item of bush tucker.

Above right
Gagudju women make a string game pattern of a turtle. The Gagudju know about 250 patterns. On the right is Ilkirr's wife, Susan Aladjingu.

the same X-ray style of the most recent rock paintings and are unique to Kakadu and the adjacent areas of Arnhem Land.

The chief practitioner of the art in Kakadu is Bluey Ilkirr. He has lived in the bush for most of his life. This is what he tells of his early years:

I lived in the bush, not white man's place.
Only when I grow up I learn white fella lingo.
My family used to hunt kangaroo.
The women, my mother and grandmother,
They used to go hunt wild yam,
Cheeky yam, all kinds of fruit.
All bush tucker: sugarbag, goanna, possum.
My family they teach me how to hunt.
You go hunting, they tell me,
Then you can find your own food when you are big.
And I learned to hunt.
It was a good life when I was young.
But not now I think.
Too much serious.
Young people won't go hunting
Because too much serious. Too weak.
My wife brought me to Gagudju country.
She was born here, she belongs to this place.

Ilkirr cuts bark from a stringybark tree for his painting. © National Geographic Society.

He carries the large and heavy sheet back to his camp.

Ilkirr and his wife Susan Aladjingu still live in the bush. For long periods they live by themselves for Ilkirr needs the tranquillity of a quiet camp for his painstaking work. Relatives sometimes come to stay. They like to gather as much bush tucker as they can. It is their preferred food. Their camp centre is a large canvas stretched over a rough timber frame.

The making of a large painting is a long and arduous process. First of all the bark must be collected. This has to be done during Gudjewg, the wet season from January to March, when the sap is rising and when the bark is flexible and will not crack. The favoured tree is Manbaddgurr, the stringybark (Darwin stringybark, *Eucalyptus tetrodonta*), which provides a thick, smooth surface to paint on.

On an overcast day in late March Ilkirr and Aladjingu go out to a favoured spot where the stringybarks grow straight and true. Dew lies heavily on the grass which has grown so tall that it dwarfs the two people. After some spirited discussion they select a tree that has escaped severe damage from fire and termites.

Using a small steel axe, Ilkirr cuts through the bark, right around the tree, at about waist level. Next he cuts down a sapling that has a fork at about three metres height. He leans this against the stringybark, climbs up it and stands on the fork. Reaching as high as he can he ringbarks the tree again. Back on the ground he removes his ladder and pulls off a narrow strip of bark between the two cuts. Inserting his axe where the wood is exposed he now levers the bark away. It peels off easily and Ilkirr has a beautiful new 'canvas' about four metres long and a metre and a half wide. The whole process took only a few minutes. Except for the fact that Ilkirr used a steel axe instead of one made of stone, he collected the bark in the same way as his ancestors did, perhaps for thousands of years.

In the past the bark was primarily used to build shelters during the wet season particularly by people like Ilkirr, who were from places some distance from the escarpment. Instead of painting on rock walls they painted on the walls and ceilings of their simple bark structures. Today bark is used only for painting.

The long piece of wet bark is heavy and it takes all of Ilkirr's considerable strength to carry it back to his camp. He immediately flattens it out, very carefully so as not to split it, and weighs it down with heavy stones. Over the next six weeks or so Ilkirr works on the bark intermittently. He removes its rough, flaky outer layer and when the drying process is well advanced, he turns it over and works on the inner surface, the one to be painted on. He scrapes it carefully with a knife and sometimes with a metal file (in the past he would have used a stone scraper), to remove small bumps and other imperfections. To achieve the final smoothness, Ilkirr still prefers to use the traditional 'sandpaper', the rough leaves of the sandpaper fig (*Ficus opposita* and others).

By the time the season of Yegge is well advanced, the bark is finally ready. One morning Ilkirr cuts about a one and a half metre length from it, trims the edges and carries it to a bough shelter. He has built this specially, some distance from the rest of the camp. The ground has been swept and covered by a tarpaulin. Ilkirr sits down, cross-legged, and puts the bark on his knees. Beside him, already laid out, are his brushes made of bark and of grass, his colours — red and yellow ochre, black manganese oxide and white clay, a small tin with water mixed with a fixative and several flat stones on which to grind the colours. He pours a little water on one of the grindstones then vigorously rubs a piece of red ochre, a

Top left
A small piece of bark is trimmed into a brush.

Top centre
Ilkirr paints a red background on a carefully prepared piece of bark. The red ochre will give the subjects life.

Above
Once all the animals are outlined, their shapes are filled in, also with white paint.

fairly hard rock, on it till he has a blood red paint. Using a piece of bark, frayed at one end, as a broad brush, Ilkirr quickly covers the entire surface of the bark with the red colour. Red ochre represents blood in paintings and ceremonies and blood in turn is the symbol for life itself. The red surface will give life, vitality, to the subjects to be painted on it.

While the paint dries, Ilkirr lights his pipe and as he smokes he thinks about what he will paint. Before he begins he must clearly visualise how the finished painting will look. He must compose it in his mind so that all the elements will have proper emphasis and together will form a well-composed whole. He must also think of the story to be told and of the designs and patterns which will cover the subjects. He is limited in the designs that are available to him. He can use patterns inherited from his father and grandfather and certain clan designs. But he can use other people's designs only with permission. The unauthorised use of a design is a serious breach of tribal law, in the old days punishable by death.

Above left
The animals are first painted in white outline with the bark brush.

Left
Ilkirr then covers the animal shapes with patterns of very fine lines in red, yellow and black pigments.

Above
Ilkirr puts the finishing touches to his painting; East Alligator Djang. This painting is only of animals, but spirit figures and people are also painted.

Above right
Details on the barramundi are painted with a brush consisting of a grass stem reduced to a few fibres.

The choice of subject matter must also be carefully considered. The combination of pattern, subject and the actual act of painting together reflect the Dreamtime, a tangible visualisation of the people's philosophy. The artist, by painting, draws on the powers of the Dreamtime and maintains, through the symbolism of his designs, the people's oneness with nature and the life force. When painting totemic animals he ensures, as in some other acts of looking after the country, that the life essence of that species as vested in the Dreamtime, flows to living species. So painting is as much a spiritual act as an artistic one. It keeps the Dreamtime alive and relevant.

It is not a simple task. As Ilkirr says:

You think, you think all the time in your mind,
And at night before you sleep
You think how to do that.

Ilkirr decides he will paint some of the mythical animals of the East Alligator region — he calls it East Alligator Djang. A djang is a sacred place, often a dangerous one, and its associated story. It usually involves secret ceremonies and frequently is the point of origin of a species of animal.

Using a fresh grindstone Ilkirr grinds the chalk-like white clay and mixes it with water till it is the consistency of a runny smooth paste. With deft, deliberate strokes of his bark brush, he outlines a crocodile. Its shape takes up the entire length of the bark. Then he draws a barramundi, a wallaroo and finally an echidna, with assurance, without hesitation or mistakes. Once the outlines are completed, the animals' shapes are filled in with white paint. Ilkirr comes from a long line of painters:

I learnt to paint from my father and grandfather.
When I was little boy I watched them paint.
They used to sit out in the bush
A little bit long way from the camp.
My father used to go to quiet place.
I couldn't talk.
My father said: "Don't talk, watch and you will learn."
Then he stopped and tell me:
"Do like that, slow and not rough."
That way they teach me different lines and patterns.
Young people they can't do it.
They bit rough.
Only if they learn properly they can do it.
But it take long time
To be slow and not be rough.

Once the animals are painted in white, the most difficult and painstaking part begins — their forms must be filled in with an intricate pattern of very fine lines. It is these patterns, which have very special meanings, that will give the work its spiritual power. The cleaner and more precise, that is 'not rough', the painting is, the greater its power.

But before beginning this phase, Ilkirr must prepare the special brushes. Some Aboriginal artists use a twig, frayed by chewing to a fine point, or a part of a pandanus frond. Others use a brush fashioned out of human hair. But Ilkirr prefers a brush made from the stem of a particular kind of grass that grows in only a few places.

He has soaked a number of these grass stems for several days in water. Now he rubs them between finger and thumb till he frees the individual fibres. He then strips away all but a few at the centre. That is his brush, a few long fibres from a grass stem.

Ilkirr now begins with the crocodile, painting long, fine, red lines the length of its body with enviable assurance. Painting with such a simple brush on a comparatively rough surface demands great skill and concentration. For hours on end Ilkirr works on his painting — calmly, deliberately, rarely needing to change or correct a line.

While the basic framework of the designs that an Aboriginal artist can paint are dictated by tradition and law, there is room for improvisation. Each major artist, and Ilkirr is one of them, has his own distinctive style and flourishes.

Ilkirr says:

I look to my father's line and pattern.
That old line. I paint that first,
That my father's line.
But this line I paint alongside,
That my idea.

Just as Ilkirr begins the cross-hatching on the crocodile's head, a breeze springs up. It is only a slight wind, but it is enough to disturb the long fibres of his brush. He can no longer put the lines down straight and true. He has to stop.

After working intermittently for several months, Ilkirr finishes his painting; a masterly work of technical finesse, traditional design, philosophy and artistic innovation. The painting fulfils the artistic criteria of compositional balance and the harmony of its earth colours. But it is more than that for it also fulfils a spiritual need. This spiritual aspect can only be completed with the performance of the appropriate rituals. This is rarely done now. In the past once the ceremonies were completed, the painting lost its power and was discarded. If it was secret, it had to be destroyed. Nowadays it is sold.

'East Alligator Djang' can be looked at, admired and contemplated by anyone. But the exact meaning of the patterns and the stories about the animals can only be revealed to the initiated.

Ilkirr comments:

The outside [non-secret] story everyone can see.
They can look at that painting and say,
"Ah — that's a good painting" and feel happy.
They can like this painting.
But they cannot know inside [secret] story.
You just look, think yourself, think about it.

Of all the traditions and expressions of the Dreamtime, bark painting is most likely to endure — a form of expression that began 30,000 years ago.

The Law and Indjuwanydjuwa

Neidjie and Iyanuk, when looking after their country, usually do so together. The two are very close.

Neidjie says:

In white man way they say we are cousin.
But we are Aborigines. We are brothers.
No matter different mother or different father,
We are brothers.

The areas which are sacred and important to them are close to where Neidjie lives, where he says he is 'camped'. This 'camp', near Cannon Hill, is a group of four small houses built in a clearing close to a grove of shady trees. The two old men like to sleep in the open, under the trees, well away from the houses where Neidjie's large family lives.

This evening they sit on their swags beside a small fire where they make their tea. Their conversation, as it so often does, turns to their 'story', the Gagudju culture. They are

Felix Iyanuk and Big Bill Neidjie (right) at Warrayangal.

worried that the laws laid down by the creator beings, their spirit ancestors, are ever more difficult to comply with. Often they are overcome by an ineffable sadness.

Iyanuk expresses these feelings this way:

Nobody else know our law, our traditions
Only few old men now.
All others been pass away,
That's all finished.
Now everybody forget our law.
At night we sit down and think,
Think about ourselves.
Sometimes I cry before I go to sleep.
In the morning we get up, and I cry again.
When I'm crying my brother he listen to me.
He get up and boil a cup of tea.
We are sorry nobody follow after us,
That's the truth.
Then we talk together till everything settle down
And we say: "come on we go,"
We go and walk around, all around this country and have a look.

Neidjie adds:

We very much worried now
Because we don't know if young people
If they can hang on to this story.

That night the two sleep fitfully. They are awake at first light, rekindle the fire and make some tea. They look to the east where the sun already casts its colours across the sky. Before them is a grassy plain that stretches to the East Alligator and beyond to the escarpment in Arnhem Land. A white mist hugs the ground and slowly turns to gold as the sun rises. Not far out on the plain stand sandstone outcrops in stark black silhouette; Ngamarr-kanangka, Warrayangal and that most sacred of places for the Bunitj, Indjuwanydjuwa. After a contemplative cigarette the two friends drive the 2 km to Warrayangal in a battered old utility. In their younger days they would have walked. They leave the car at the rock outcrop and slowly walk up a wide expanse of sloping rock, their callused feet scraping on the rough stone. On one side there is a precipitous drop to a narrow strip of marshy ground beyond which the rock rises sheer again to a height of sixty metres or so. On the other side is a lower cliff made of a softer stone. Its surface is sculpted into columns, shelves and small caves by the wind and rain. The two elders stop at one such cave. In it lie the skulls and other remains of four people, ancestors and relatives of Neidjie. Some of the bones still bear traces of red ochre from the ceremony during which they were placed in the cave. Even though the remains are of Neidjie's Bunitj clansmen, it was Iyanuk who sang and danced the funerary rites. Iyanuk explains how it was done:

We take bones out of the ground and dry him up.
When dry we paint him with red ochre.
We paint ourselves too.
First with red ochre,
Then we use white paint,
And paint lines along legs and arms and fingers.
To sound of song-sticks we go like that,
We put hands like that, dance like that.
I am singing man and I sing . . .

Iyanuk's soft, yet clear, voice chants as at the funeral here, perhaps twenty or thirty years ago, the last burial at Warrayangal.

He continues:

All the men been hiding in grass.
Then they come out and start song.
All the other mob sitting down,
They want to run away, but can't run away.
We must sit down and look, altogether.
The old people bring the bones,
Some bones they have in hands,
Other bones carry in mouth.
They cannot get poison because painted with red ochre.
They sing like that, dance like that.
And the people put the bones in the cave

Iyanuk and Neidjie sit beside the lagoon in front of Indjuwanydjuwa, the creator-being turned to stone. The rock is Indjuwanydjuwa and still contains his spirit and his power.

Then they say "goodbye" and go home,
Never stopping on the way.
Only me and Neidjie know what song, what dance.
That Gagudju song. Nobody else know.
I am more weak and weak now
When I pass away they can bury me any place, no matter.
But must take my bones from there,
And bring them back to this same cave.
No matter if no song, no dance
As long as I am in cave, this cave here.

Neidjie adds:

That spirit, you know, that bone,
He must go back to his own country
Spirit and bones got to stay there in cave
That's the law of Gagudju.

For some time the two sit on a rock shelf close to the cave and talk about other occasions they have been here. Their sadness slowly fades as they talk. Cheering each other up they recall funny incidents and old gossip. Smiles and quiet laughter soon return.

Warrayangal is such an important burial site for the Bunitj and those close to them, because the place is suffused with the spirit of their principal creator being, Indjuwanydjuwa. The people's spirit after death will join that of their great spirit ancestor if their bones are placed here, where his essence lives.

Neidjie and Iyanuk leave Warrayangal's caves and rock slopes and walk along a small lagoon filled with the flowers and large leaves of the red lotus. The plants wave gently in the breeze. Egrets lift off lazily but soon settle down again. Turtles dive from exposed rocks back into the water. Black kites fly figures of eight overhead and a goanna raises itself on its hindlegs, watching over the grass as the two men walk by. At a fractured and fissured rock outcrop adjoining Warrayangal the men climb to the top of a rise and sit down, cross-legged, in a rock shelter overlooking the lagoon. Behind them, on the cave wall, is a painting of a man holding sacred objects in his hands. Directly below them, in the lagoon and framed by palms rustling in the wind, stands a white rock. Red lotuses surround it, egrets and darters stand on its summit. Some distance out on the green plain stand other, smaller piles of rocks. Neidjie and Iyanuk are sitting at the centre of one of the most sacred places in Kakadu and *the* most important for the Bunitj. They are at the focus of the life force, Indjuwanydjuwa.

The rock shelter is where Indjuwanydjuwa camped with his family. The painting on the wall is his image. Across the plain are the very secret places where no women or young boys were ever allowed to go. There, surrounded by paintings and rock formations as dramatic as any man-made architecture, young men were initiated. To the accompaniment of the drone of didgeridoos and the sharp rhythm of song-sticks they entered manhood as their elders, painted in sacred designs and decorated with feathers, performed the dances and rituals. And it was done in the presence of the great spirit ancestor himself — for the white rock standing amongst the flowers in the lagoon is Indjuwanydjuwa, today and forever.

Neidjie tells the story:

Indjuwanydjuwa came at the beginning, the Dreamtime.
He been fly, that man,
Across plain, across river.
He made this world.
He sit down in this cave with family.
He hunt: turtle, file snake, duck, fish, goanna . . .
Women get red lily.
One day Indjuwanydjuwa, the old man,
He come to this billabong
He stops and has drink of water.
"Good place this," he says.
He decide to stay, he become stone.
That stone there that is Indjuwanydjuwa
That very big man, solid man.
His family not stay here, go to other place.

Iyanuk plays a slow rhythm on the song-sticks he has brought. Eyes shining he begins to sing in his gentle voice the song cycle of Indjuwanydjuwa. Iyanuk is the last man to know the full cycle. This may be the last time the song resounds in Indjuwanydjuwa's cave.

For as Iyanuk says:

Me and Neidjie are only people who know this song.
But he [Neidjie] is without voice you see.
That's why I'm singing it all the time
Taking his place
To keep this thing good, to hang on to this story.
When something wrong with me then got nobody.
I may never sing this song here again.

The worry about losing their story, not being able to look after the country and the frustration at not being able to pass it on, weigh heavily on their minds.

Neidjie says this:

I worry about this place,
About Indjuwanydjuwa and his painting in cave.
He got to be looked after.
My father, grandad, mother been looking after him well
So this time I'm bit afraid . . .
Someone might rub off that painting.
New generation coming up maybe not look after it.
But no matter what generation,
That painting got to be there.
Looking after this country worry me.
But to look after country you have to live here,
Hunt here.
Hunting is good life, but it is little bit hard.
If children and grandchildren don't look after Indjuwanydjuwa,
Look after country,
They will go funny, get paralysed, eyes swell up —
They may die.
They got to hang on to this story.

Neidjie and the other Gagudju elders say that the young people are not interested in their story, in the laws and traditions of their culture because they are too soft and cannot cope with the hard life of the old days. They say that the new generations are too lazy and so preoccupied with the material objects of the white people's culture that they have lost interest in their own, their ancient Gagudju heritage. That may be true for some, but it is not the case for a small group of young Gagudju men and women who are vitally concerned with looking after their country. These are the Aboriginal rangers of Kakadu National Park, their own tribal lands. Among them is Neidjie's son, Jonathan Yarramarna.

Yarramarna is a strongly built young man with somewhat stern features which mostly hide a shyness. But once the ice is broken he has a ready smile. Whenever he can he goes to his tribal lands to hunt and to learn from his father. He loves the freedom and the spaciousness. He can feel what it must have been like in the old days. To go fishing with a spear along a billabong is to leave the everyday frustrations and problems behind. He is aware too, that to

Iyanuk sings the Indjuwanydjuwa song cycle, a vital part of looking after the country and maintaining the Gagudju story.

Yarramarna spears barramundi in the traditional way at a billabong on his clan's land.

go hunting is part of looking after the country, it is an activity taught the people by the spirit ancestors of the Dreamtime. As Yarramarna says:

> We must keep hunting, for we must be able to live off the foods of our country, the fish, geese, kangaroos, and goannas. We have to live by those rules. It keeps us close to the land and we get to know the place really well.

But like it does to the elders, modern times have put heavy and uneasy burdens on Yarramarna's broad shoulders. As he says:

> There are two sets of laws for us here, Aboriginal law and government law. As park rangers we learn both of them and live by both of them. That means we have to look after the country in two ways. The old people depend on us to look after the country in the traditional way, while the Park Service wants us to be rangers like the others. That's pretty hard for us — but we can do it.

The New Generation

Due to his age Neidjie does not climb the rocks of Garrkanj, Hawk Dreaming, any more. But because of Yarramarna's interest he will make the effort one more time. Neidjie has not been here for many years and probably will never go again.

Halfway up the imposing rock massif Neidjie and Yarramarna stop at an extensive gallery of paintings of special mystical significance but also of a personal importance to Neidjie. He speaks at length about the spirit of Garrkanj, the brown falcon, which resides here. About how the bird, at the beginning of the Dreamtime, showed the people how to catch the different kinds of fish and how to prepare them for eating. Tucked away amongst the images of fish is a small hand stencil outlined in white. Neidjie points to it, smiling: 'I made that when I was a little fella, maybe eight, nine years old when I came here with my father.'

Above right
Neidjie places his hand beside a hand stencil he made as a child at Hawk Dreaming.

Neidjie and Yarramarna sit in the heart of Bunitj country at a place that overlooks all their traditional lands.

The two climb higher onto the rocks. Neidjie's breathing is laboured but he struggles on right to the summit. A cool breeze now fans their perspiring faces. Below them, all around, is a panoramic view of their clan's lands: the plains, forests, billabongs, Indjuwanydjuwa and Warrayangal. Snaking through it is the East Alligator River. It is their life and their beliefs at a glance. Seated on a rock Neidjie looks around him for long, savoured minutes. Then slowly he points out the landmarks one by one and explains their significance to Yarramarna.

Several days later Yarramarna, accompanied by his father, puts his hand stencil on rocks close to Hawk Dreaming, a symbolic commitment to his Aboriginal heritage.

Buoyed by his son's interest Neidjie decides to take some of the Aboriginal park rangers deep into the bush to a special place few white people go. He asks Kapirigi and Ilkirr to come along also. Iyanuk is too frail to make the journey.

One hot day in the dry season, during Gurrung, they all set off for Djirringbal, a place where the Gagudju once made stone implements and where Ginga the saltwater crocodile

Above
Neidjie and Yarramarna prepare to make a hand stencil. © National Geographic Society.

Right
Yarramarna making a hand stencil on rocks near Hawk Dreaming. © National Geographic Society.

Far right
Yarramarna's completed hand stencil.

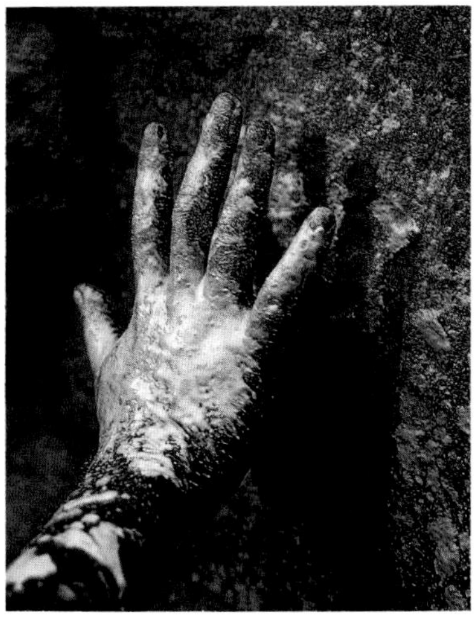

Ilkirr and Kapirigi make stone knives at Djirringbal.

forced a passage through the rocks. To all of them it is a journey into their living culture. Their boisterousness and good natured humour bubble over. Today sadness and worry slip away from these naturally joyous people.

They drive along a faint bush track for about an hour, but the last few kilometres they must walk. Neidjie leads them through a small patch of rainforest to the base of a quartzite rock wall that rises sheer to a height of about two hundred metres.

All are awed and silent as they first look up the tall cliff and then at the paintings in front of them. An exquisite painting of a kangaroo is surrounded by sacred designs. The irrepressible Kapirigi is the first to rush forward and to exclaim about the paintings. Soon all are in a deep discussion.

Below the paintings is a scattering of what appear to be freshly chipped stones. It is a kind of quarry where the Gagudju came to make their stone scrapers, knives and spear points for hundreds of generations. It looks as if the last toolmakers have only just left, but in fact the place has not been used for about fifty years. Core rocks, from which the implements were struck, are still at hand. Ilkirr, with some advice from Kapirigi and Neidjie, shows Yarramarna and the other rangers how to strike this core rock with another stone to make a sharp knife. Kapirigi demonstrates how such a knife was used to pierce his nose. Ilkirr traces the scars of initiation marks on his chest and shoulders and explains how they were made. Newly made knife in hand he turns to Yarramarna as if to make the marks. 'Now it is your turn,' he smiles. The laughter bounces off the rocks. But Ilkirr has the last word: 'If you got no mark you got no story.' Without being initiated you cannot know the full ramification of the culture.

On the way back the group stops at a cool circular pool fringed by white sand. A waterfall trickles down at one end. When all are seated in the shade, Neidjie says:

See that waterfall?
That's where Ginga, the big crocodile
Cut through the rock to get to East Alligator.
That's just one of many stories
Three of us [elders] know and you must learn.
All these stories
Tell of earth, animals, Gagudju people.
Our blood, animals' blood and sap of plants.
It all the same, we all the same.
The old people they know this,
That why for thousands and thousands years
This country not change.
This is our culture, our story,
Your story.
We learned from our fathers and mothers.
They said you sit down and listen, listen that story.
If we move, we talk or try run away we get spear.
We sit. We listen.
Slowly it all came into our heads.
As years go by we learn more and more.
At first we think, this does not make sense.
But as we grow up, go through ceremonies,
The stories come together.
At last ceremony when you proper man or woman,
Then that last story we are told,
It bring everything together.
Then we know our story and our culture.
We true Gagudju people.
That you must learn, that what we losing.
We old men now, soon we pass away.
We the last of Gagudju who can tell you this story.
So you listen, listen.
You must hang on to this story.
Never mind motorcar, never mind money —
This your true story.
If you don't learn now, in twenty years' time you cry
Because you don't know your story.
Too late then.
We'll be gone.*

* During the preparation of this book Kapirigi died. His remains, wrapped in bark, rest high in a tree at Djuwarr; his spirit has gone back to his country.

End of the Story?

By observing the laws and traditions of their society, the Gagudju ensured that their unity with all living things continued. As long as they looked after the country the life force would endure. But only the fully initiated men and women know their entire story and so can perpetuate the Dreamtime. As Ilkirr said if you are not initiated, if you 'have no mark', you have no story. And to have no story is the worst that can befall an Aborigine. One leader put it this way: 'Without our culture and our law we are nothing. We have no spirit. We are wobbly without any foundation like a little plant that has withered and then blows away in the wind.'

To the elders the loss of culture means oblivion. The people will survive as human beings, but there will be no more true Gagudju people. Neidjie said that if the links with the life force are broken the people will sicken and die. To them that is true in a spiritual sense.

The Gagudju's full story may well disappear with Neidjie, Iyanuk, Kapirigi, Ilkirr and the small number of other elders. It has already happened to many other Aboriginal groups. It would be a tragedy of epic proportions made all the more poignant because it plays itself out in a place of compelling beauty and power. A 50,000 year partnership with nature will have come to an end.

The Gagudju left no great monuments, no pyramids, no palaces, no forts. But for 2500 generations they and their ancestors lived in harmony with their environment. *That* is their monument and in the long term may be the most important of all for it contains the wisdom necessary for the ultimate survival of all humankind.

To the traditional Gagudju, to go contrary to nature, to defy its laws, is not only sacrilegious, but also flies in the face of sound economic sense. From their point of view the new people, the white people they call Balanda, who have invaded their lands, who destroy, gouge, dig, trample and over- populate large areas of country, are irresponsible on a scale beyond comprehension. They pity the newcomers for they see them destroying not only the land but ultimately themselves. They see this from a 50,000 year perspective, as a people who have lived on this land for 99.6 per cent of the time it has been occupied by humans. What they have seen happening around them during the last 200 years will not sustain life for another 50,000 years, perhaps not even 1000.

They put it simply:

White man got no dreaming,
him go 'nother way.
White man, him go different.
Him got road belong himself.

It is a road often contrary to nature and one they see leading to the destruction of all people.

The Gagudju's lands have now been leased to the Balanda. The pressures of 200,000 visitors a year are beyond the resources of a small group of people to deal with. Now the Balanda must look after the country.

Yarramarna and the three elders at Djirringbal.

9 ~ LOOKING AFTER THE COUNTRY — THE BALANDA WAY

THE BALANDA DID NOT BEGIN WELL in looking after the country; not in Kakadu and not in any other part of the continent. Their practice was to alter the country to their will and to exploit recklessly whatever they could find of value. The clash between the exploitative ways of the Balanda and the philosophy of humans being an integral part of nature held by the Aborigines, was brutal. Aboriginal society collapsed under the combined onslaught of aggressive intrusions, routine dispossession of their lands and the introduction of infectious diseases to which they had little or no resistance. But in all this the Gagudju people were more fortunate than most Aboriginal groups. They survived, where many, many did not. They did not suffer any organised massacres nor wholesale poisonings and the country they lived in defeated the Balanda's early efforts at colonisation. There were times when the two races lived side by side with tolerance. In recent years the Gagudju's lands have been restored to them, but they had to compromise with the Dreamtime; their country is now mined and is visited by more than 200,000 Balanda each year.

Europeans Arrive

It all began in the 17th century when Dutch seafarers skirted the northern coastline. The Dutch made few landfalls in northern Australia and were not tempted to establish themselves on what they considered to be inhospitable shores. They saw no prospect of either trade or exploitation. Phillip Parker King was the first Balanda to have a close look at Kakadu. He was British. He came by sea in HMS *Mermaid* in 1818 to explore and map the coastline. He followed the Arnhem Land coast, crossed Mount Norris Bay and surveyed the shores of Cobourg Peninsula. At a deep inlet, which he named Port Essington, King and his men met with a group of Aborigines. He called them Indians. He had set off in a small boat to investigate what appeared to be a passage through the mangroves, when:

> . . . about half-way towards the mouth, we found the boat impeded by the roots of a mangrove bush; whilst the boat's crew was busily employed in clearing the rudder, we were suddenly startled by the shout of a party of Indians, who were concealed from our view by a projecting bush, not more than eight or ten yards from us: our situation was rather alarming, from the boat being so entangled, and the river not being broad enough for the oars to be used. No sooner had the natives uttered the shout, than they leaped into the water armed with spears and clubs; but the moment they made their appearance around the tree, two muskets loaded with ball, and a fowling-piece with small shot, were fired over their heads, which had the desired effect, for they gave up their premeditated attack, and quickly disappeared . . . (King's diaries, 1827.)

Monsoon forest bordering the East Alligator River. The Alligator rivers were named by Phillip Parker King in 1818 in response to the many crocodilians he saw there.

The attack was later resumed: 'Happily, however,' King reports, 'we received no damage, although the spears and stones fell about us very thickly, and several of the former struck the boat. A volley of musketry was fired into the mangroves, but we could not ascertain whether any of the balls took effect, since we could not see our assailants.'

King later vented his anger on the Aborigines' canoe:

> . . . their canoe was observed secured to the beach by a small rope, which offered so good an opportunity of punishing these savages for their treacherous attack, that we landed and brought it away . . . The canoe was nearly new, it measured eighteen feet in length, and two in breadth and would easily carry eight persons . . . The canoe was made of one sheet of bark, but in the bottom, within it, short pieces were placed cross-ways, in order to preserve its shape, and increase its strength.

If there had been Gagudju people amongst the 'Indians' who attacked King, though this is unlikely, this was the first 'meeting' between Gagudju and Balanda.

King continued his voyage, rounded Cobourg Peninsula and 'discovered' and named the East Alligator and South Alligator Rivers. As he explained, 'the name Alligator Rivers was bestowed upon them' because of the large number of crocodilians. King also named Field and Barron Islands, at the mouth of the South Alligator River. Both islands are now part of Kakadu. King sailed up the two rivers, to a distance of 58 km on the South, but pronounced the land flat and uninteresting, though teeming with wildfowl. He did not meet any more Aboriginal people and did not see the stone country.

Previous pages

Toby Gangele, wearing a hat, is one of the few Gagudju elders to have lived most of his life in Kakadu. With Ian Morris, sitting on his left and for many years training officer for Aboriginal Rangers, he discusses Park management with trainees. The Gagudju lands, though owned by the Aboriginal people, are now looked after by the Balanda as a National Park.

Leichhardt had to cross rugged terrain like this to reach Kakadu.

Six years later, in 1824, Captain James Bremer took formal possession of Kakadu and the adjacent lands for the British crown. He did so at Port Essington. Twice the British tried to establish settlements in this part of Australia, once at Raffles Bay and once at Port Essington, both on Cobourg Peninsula. The attempts failed because of attacks by Aborigines, isolation and frequent sickness. In 1849 the last settlement was abandoned and the British left the north. As already mentioned, they left behind their domestic animals, of which the buffalo and the pig were to create havoc in Kakadu.

During the time of the settlements, in 1845, the first European entered and crossed the Gagudju's lands; a Balanda who was neither Dutch nor British but German. He was the explorer Ludwig Leichhardt.

Leichhardt Explores in Kakadu

Leichhardt wrote at some length about his travels and he recorded many details about the first encounters between Gagudju and Balanda on Kakadu soil (Leichhardt's Journal, 1847). It must be borne in mind, however, that Leichhardt was in the final stages of a most arduous journey that began fifteen months previously, at Moreton Bay in Queensland, 4800 km down the track. He did not come specifically to look at the Alligator Rivers region and, as he himself observed, he had to overcome '... the irresistible impatience to come to the end of our journey'; and an '... inconsiderate, thoughtless desire of pushing onwards'. Also Leichhardt and his nine companions had had frequent encounters with Aborigines throughout their journey. There had been several skirmishes during one of which John Gilbert, the noted naturalist, had been speared and killed.

Leichhardt was an explorer motivated by curiosity and the desire to be the first European to traverse this remote part of Australia. He was not driven to seek material gain nor religious converts.

To his travels through Kakadu he brought a sensitivity and appreciation unmatched by other early explorers and exploiters. He had time to note the animals and plants, the songs of birds, the scents of the bush and to make friends with the Gagudju people. And this despite the fact that the going was always hard, that pack animals died around him and that he and his party often went hungry. Also, he had to contend with the heat and humidity of Gunumeleng in November and December.

Before reaching Kakadu, Leichhardt struggled for many days to cross the rugged Arnhem Land Plateau which he considered a:

> . . . disheartening, sickening . . . tremendously rocky country. A high land, composed of horizontal strata of sandstone, seemed to be literally hashed, leaving the remaining blocks in fantastic figures of every shape; and a green vegetation, crowding deceit- fully within their fissures and gullies, and covering half of the difficulties which awaited us on our attempt to travel over it.

Finally, on 17 November 1845, Leichhardt stood on the edge of the escarpment when:

> . . . suddenly the extensive view of a magnificent valley opened before us. We stood with our whole train on the brink of a deep precipice, of perhaps 1800 feet descent, which seemed to extend far to the eastward. A large river, joined by many tributaries . . . meandered through the valley.

They were the first Balanda to gaze over the expanse of the South Alligator River and see nearly all of Kakadu spread out below them.

The precipice, the escarpment, prevented them from descending. In his search for an exit onto the 'beautiful valley, that lay before us like a promised land' with lush green grass for their footsore horses and bullocks, Leichhardt found time to note a special insect:

> . . . a great number of grasshoppers, of a bright brick colour dotted with blue: the posterior part of the corselet, and the wings were blue; it was two inches long, and its antennae three-quarters of an inch.

Science knows this insect as Leichhardt's grasshopper, *Petasida ephippigera*, and it was not recorded again until 1972. To the Gagudju the grasshoppers are Aldjurr, the Lightning Man's children on earth.

For three days the party searched for a way down, but at every turn they found their way blocked by 'deep chasms, down which the boldest chamois hunter would not have dared to descend'. It was a difficult and depressing time. But one morning after a thunderstorm during the night Leichhardt saw:

> . . . all nature . . . refreshed; and my depressed spirits rose quickly, under the influence of that sweet breath of vegetation, which is so remarkably experienced in Australia, where the numerous Myrtle family, and even their dead leaves, contribute so largely to the general fragrance.

With the horses and bullocks thin from the rock country's poor grazing, they finally found a

Jim Jim Falls after heavy monsoon rain.

The voice of the sandstone, the white-lined honeyeater, whose haunting song so pleased Leichhardt.

way down into the 'promised land' of forest and tender grass. They had arrived at Jim Jim Creek, close to the falls in Murumburr country, and only a few kilometres from the Badmardi homeland. Leichhardt noted:

> The melodious whistle of a bird . . . frequently heard in the most rocky and wretched spots of the tableland . . . a slow full whistle . . . which was very pleasing and frequently the only relief while passing through this most perplexing country.

This was no doubt the wonderful song of the white-lined honeyeater, a bird endemic to the rock country.

Leichhardt Meets the Gagudju

The next day while camped along Jim Jim Creek, four Gagudju men came to see Leichhardt at sunset. The Aborigines gave the visitor some red ochre, which they value highly, and a spear tipped with a quartzite point. In return Leichhardt gave them some nails and his geological hammer. He remarked that, 'one of the natives was a tall but slim man; the others were of smaller size, but all had a mild and pleasing expression of countenance'. There is no record of the Aborigines' impressions of the first meeting between Balanda and Gagudju. The Gagudju men were probably of the now extinct Warramal clan. Continuing the journey, Leichhardt reached the South Alligator River on 24 November and for the next week or so continued north, almost to the sea. On 26 November at sunset 'a whole tribe of natives', probably of the Murumburr clan, visited the Balanda's camp:

> They were armed with small goose spears, and with flat wommalas [spear throwers]; but, although they were extremely noisy, they did not shew the slightest hostile intention . . . I made them various presents: and they gave us some of their ornaments and bunches of goose feathers in return, but showed the greatest reluctance in parting with their throwing sticks.

The next day:

> The natives returned very early to our camp, and took the greatest notice of what we were eating, but would not taste anything we offered them. When Brown returned with our bullock, the beast rushed at them, and pursued them for a great distance, almost goring one of their number.

During that day's travel, Leichhardt found that 'the natives were very numerous'. He noted 'a noble fig tree, under the shade of which seemed to have been the camping place of the natives for the last century'. Beyond this Leichhardt came upon a billabong on the floodplain that could have been Gummungkuwuy or otherwise a place very much like it. But the floodplain impressed Leichhardt most, a marsh that:

> . . . extended beyond the reach of sight, and seemed to form the whole country, of the remarkable and picturesque character of which it will be difficult to convey the correct idea to the reader.

'Several times,' that day Leichhardt, 'wished to communicate with the natives who followed us, but, every time I turned my horse's head, they ran away.' The Gagudju probably did not trust the horses any more than the bullock. Leichhardt continues:

> . . . finding my difficulties increased, whilst attempting to cross the swamp, I dismounted and walked up to one of them, and taking his hand, gave him a sheet of paper, on which I wrote some words, giving him to understand, as well as I could, that he had nothing to fear as long as he carried the paper. By this means I induced him to walk with me, but considerably in advance of my train, and especially of the bullock; he kept manfully near me, and pointed out the sounder parts of the swamp, until we came to a large pool . . . We encamped at this pool, and the natives flocked around us from every direction. Boys of every age, lads, young men and old men too, came, every one armed with his bundle of goose spears, and his throwing stick. They observed, with curious eye, everything we did, and made long explanations to each other of the various objects presented to their gaze. Our eating, drinking, dress, skin, combing, boiling, our blankets, straps, horses, everything in short, was new to them, and was earnestly discussed, particularly by one of the old men, who amused us with his drollery and good humour . . .

The next day, 28 November, Leichhardt was well out on the South Alligator River floodplain. He notes in his journal:

> Our good friends the natives were with us again very early in the morning . . . After having guided us over the remaining part of the swamp to the firm land, during which they gave us the most evident proofs of their skill in spearing geese, they took their leave of us . . .

The exploring party travelled on northwards. Wildlife was prolific and Leichhardt noted:

> No part of the country we had passed, [presumably referring to the entire journey from Moreton Bay] was so well provided with game as this . . . The cackling of geese, the quacking of ducks, the sonorous note of the native companion, and the noises of black and white cockatoos, and a great variety of other birds, gave the country, both night and day, an extraordinary appearance of animation.

Far left
Pied geese at sunrise. Leichhardt noted in his journal how numerous these birds and other wildlife were.

Left
Agile wallaby mother with large young.

There are numerous references to the abundance of wallabies, flying foxes, crocodiles, fish and edible fruits.

By 2 December, Leichhardt and his men had entered Bunitj country and soon met Bunitj people who had obviously spent some time at the Victorian settlement at Port Essington. The Aboriginal people were familiar with and no doubt amused by, the habit of the Balanda to give orders. Leichhardt describes the meeting:

> . . . a fine native stepped out of the forest with the ease and grace of an Apollo, with a smiling countenance, and with the confidence of a man to whom the white face was perfectly familiar. He was unarmed but a great number of his companions were keeping back to watch the reception he should meet with. We received him, of course, most cordially . . . we heard him utter distinctly the words, " *'Commandant!' 'come here!!' 'very good' 'what's your name?!'* "

At the Yuwenjgayay gallery there is a painting of a Balanda that is believed to be Leichhardt.

The Bunitj people stayed with Leichhardt for some days, guiding him across swamps along the East Alligator River and feeding him and his companions on the nutritious and palatable spike-rush tubers called An-gurlatj. Leichhardt appreciated their kindness:

> The natives were remarkably kind and attentive . . . They remained with us the whole afternoon; all the tribe and many visitors, in all about seventy persons . . . They were fine, stout, well-made men, with pleasing and intelligent countenances . . . We had to take great care of our bullock, as the beast invariably charged the natives whenever he obtained sight of them . . .

On the morning of 3 December, the largest gathering of Gagudju ever seen by a European, and not seen again, came to Leichhardt's camp. 'There could not have been less than 200 of them present.'

On 6 December Leichhardt came to the place where the East Alligator issues out of the escarpment and was moved to write:

> The valley of the Upper East Alligator, which I should rather call Goose River (for nowhere we observed so many geese — and what is called alligator is no alligator but a crocodile) is one of the most romantic spots I have seen in my wanderings. A broad valley, level, with the most luxuriant verdure, abrupt hills and ranges rising everywhere along its east and west sides . . . lagoons forming fine sheets of water, scattered over it; a creek . . . winding through it.

That same day Leichhardt crossed the East Alligator and left Kakadu and the Gagudju people. He reached Port Essington at 5 p.m. on 17 December 1845.

The first extended contact between the Balanda and the Gagudju was characterised by natural and sincere attempts at mutual understanding. The Gagudju showed great hospitality and curiosity, the Balanda, Leichhardt, was appreciative and equally curious. Such meetings of mutual goodwill were a rarity during the next 130 years.

Leichhardt, however, was in too great a hurry to learn much about the Gagudju. Had he, for example, accepted any of the frequent invitations to visit the poeple's camps, he might have learned something of their art. But he never saw any paintings either on bark or rock. Ironically, Leichhardt himself may well be immortalised in a rock painting not far from where he descended the escarpment. At the Yuwenjgayay gallery in Badmardi country is a painting, in the X-ray style, of a European wearing a long-sleeved shirt, trousers, boots and a tie. The man carries a firearm, faithfully painted, but is throwing it like a spear. One of the reasons why the painting is thought to be of Leichhardt is that no-one else but this very correct German, would have travelled here in such formal attire.

Based on Leichhardt's observations, it has been estimated that there were at least 2000 Gagudju people in 1845. As the only possible contact with white people could have been at faraway Cobourg Peninsula, it is reasonable to assume that this was a population as yet unaffected by the darker forces of the Balanda's invasion. But 100 years later this population had been reduced to only about 4 per cent of their former numbers.

Other Explorers

Stimulated by land speculation, that eventually saw nearly the whole of the Northern Territory taken up by leases of one kind or another, periodic explorations came to the Gagudju lands. In 1862 John McDouall Stuart reached the northern coast not far from Kakadu at the end of a cross-continental journey from Adelaide. His report, perhaps over-estimating the grazing potential of the region, was the spur for the top end development.

South Australia gained control over the whole of the Northern Territory in 1863 and the next year established the first settlement, at Escape Cliffs at the mouth of the Adelaide River. Impatient with the slow progress in their new territory, the South Australian Government sent John McKinlay to select the best site for a capital and to report on the lands, including those of the Alligator Rivers region. McKinlay arrived at Escape Cliffs in November 1865 and his first act was to condemn it. 'A greater scene of desolation and waste could not be pictured . . . as a seaport and city this place is worthless.' He recommended that the capital should be built at Port Darwin well to the west.

On 14 January McKinlay set off for the Alligator Rivers. By the end of March he found himself along the escarpment not far from the East Alligator River when the wet season struck with all its force. He and his party were marooned, shut in by endless swamps on one side and steep cliffs and impenetrable mazes of rugged sandstone on the other. Horses died and food was running out. By early June he had insufficient resources to return to Escape Cliffs overland.

There is no record of McKinlay's encounters with the Gagudju people while he was marooned. But a rock painting at Djirringbal, close to where he was camped, may well be of his party. The paintings, only a few centimetres high, form a frieze of seven riders on horseback. The horses are somewhat kangaroo-like and the majority are shown carrying bells around their necks.

McKinlay decided to return by sea. Killing his horses, and drying their meat, he used their skins to build a raft. He launched his strange boat in the East Alligator River, close to Indjuwanydjuwa in Bunitj country, and sailed it back to Escape Cliffs, arriving back on 5 July.

Gold and Disease

In 1869 Darwin, then called Palmerston, was founded and a few years later in 1872 was connected to the rest of Australia by the overland telegraph line. So far none of this had impinged greatly on the Gagudju. But from now on change would be rapid.

The first traces of gold were found at the Finniss River south-west of Darwin in 1865. Small finds were discovered at Pine Creek in 1871. These discoveries slowly grew and became a gold rush in the 1880s. People came from all over the world and the population exploded. By 1880 there were 4358 Chinese at the gold diggings, more than twice as many people as there were Gagudju at the time of Leichhardt.

The mining towns and capital of Palmerston needed to be fed. Market gardens became established around the Adelaide River. The pastoral industry, anticipating a demand for beef, spread eastward, taking up leases right to the East Alligator. But only a handful of those leases were occupied, and even they were soon abandoned in favour of the Katherine area. No cattle reached the Alligator Rivers at this stage.

But the activities along the Pine Creek-Palmerston axis brought curious Aborigines from far and wide. In the mid and late 1880s 'Alligator tribesmen' were noted in some numbers at the Jesuit mission at Rapid Creek, now a suburb of Darwin. No doubt Gagudju people had also made their way to Pine Creek and the other mining towns. Initially the people must have been drawn to the towns and encampments out of curiosity. Why many stayed and others returned again and again is more difficult to explain. For it is this contact with the settlements that set in motion the catastrophic decline in the Gagudju numbers and the disintegration of their society. It is all the more puzzling when it is realised that they left the abundance and idyll of Kakadu for the hustle, squalor and degradation of frontier towns. As the newly introduced diseases created such havoc among the people, it may well be that they returned to the Balanda in search of a cure. Tobacco and opium were also attractions.

Foreign diseases were terrible killers of Aboriginal people throughout Australia almost from the day the First Fleet landed in 1788. As early as April 1789 an epidemic of smallpox was taking its toll on Aborigines in the Sydney area. Epidemics of one kind or another raged across the continent from then on, claiming countless lives. In Victoria only 2000 Aborigines remained in 1863 out of the 11,500 that lived there in pre-contact days. Around the town of Bourke in New South Wales the population fell from 3000 in 1845 to fewer than eleven in 1884. The influenza pandemic of 1919 is said to have claimed 25—50 per cent of the Aboriginal population.

The Gagudju, like all of Australia's Aborigines, were not resistant to the diseases bred in the congestion of European and Asian cities. The diseases included smallpox, measles, influenza, typhoid, whooping cough, diphtheria, leprosy, tuberculosis, pneumonia, mumps and venereal diseases. Later prostitution, malnutrition and alcoholism were added to the list of woes. An official report at the turn of the century states that 130 Aboriginal people out of a group of 190 died over a six-year period in an area close to Kakadu. In 1860, there was a protracted epidemic of smallpox along the Northern Territory's coast, presumably including

Feral buffalo by their wallowing, movements and grazing, used to reduce the floodplains to bare hard-baked soil long before the end of the dry season. Now that the animals have been largely eradicated, the marshes remain green all year round.

Kakadu. In 1902 'scores' of people died of influenza south of Oenpelli. Venereal disease, which was not immediately fatal, caused sterility and so further contributed to the decline of the population, a decline that continued into the 1960s.

However, throughout these grim times of death, disease and disorientation, a core of Gagudju people always remained in the bush on or close to their traditional lands. These groups and individuals carried the Gagudju through the horrendous times into the 1980s when once again they were secure in their own lands. Their numbers are now increasing.

At the same time as the Gagudju's society was ravaged by European and Asian influences, another virulent force began to make inroads into the environment — the pigs and buffaloes left to fend for themselves in the 1820s and 1840s on Cobourg Peninsula. In an ironic contrast to the Aboriginal people, the animals found themselves in an ideal habitat rich in grass to eat and black mud to wallow in and one, to begin with, free of disease and predators. Soon the pigs and buffaloes were trampling and uprooting the wetlands from the East Alligator to the Adelaide Rivers. The buffaloes especially were soon so numerous that their well-worn trails and constant wallowings altered the nature of the marshes. They breached the levees that had maintained the delicate balance between the freshwater and saltwater habitats. The incursions of saltwater destroyed large areas of marsh. Trails were worn so deep that they became drainage channels and where once vast areas of the floodplain remained as swamps throughout the dry season, now they were cracked, bare earth by the middle of the dry. Species of native reeds, sedges and grasses could not cope with these artificial droughts and disappeared. Lotuses and waterlilies were eaten out of many billabongs. Pied geese, once so numerous at the East Alligator River that Leichhardt called it Goose River, became scarce and ceased to breed there.

In the 1880s all these buffalo began to attract attention as a cheap source of very tough hides. The stage was set for the first major penetration of Gagudju land by the Balanda. By about 1920 buffalo shooting and culling became a major industry and has continued as such into the late 1980s. It had a drastic effect on the Aboriginal people. But before buffalo shooting became fully established in Kakadu, the Aborigines had an important visitor.

Spencer's Kakadu

In 1912 Baldwin Spencer, a pioneering ethnologist, came to the Gagudju for a prolonged visit in the late dry season. As in the case of Leichhardt's travels sixty-seven years previously, it marked a milestone in the modern history of the Gagudju. But unlike Leichhardt, Spencer was not hurried and he readily accepted invitations to visit the Aborigines' camps and observe their ceremonies. Spencer made his observations around Oenpelli and was greatly aided in his research by Paddy Cahill, a buffalo shooter who had taken up residence there. Cahill spoke Gagudju fluently and had a good rapport with the people.

What Spencer achieved in a comparatively short time is quite extraordinary, providing as it does nearly all that is known of the Gagudju's material culture and major ceremonies. Spencer noted rituals, customs, social organisations and some of the Gagudju language. He collected weapons, implements, ornaments, dilly bags, belts and ceremonial objects. His collection of about 200 Gagudju bark paintings is still the most important of its kind, preserving this artform from a time before European influence. Spencer was meticulous in compensating the people for all he collected. These collections are housed in the National Museum of Victoria in Melbourne. He also took cinefilm and photographs, with a cumbersome plate camera, of the people and their ceremonies.

'All in all,' Spencer remarked, 'I am kept pretty busy. What with managing . . . two cameras and watching what takes place and taking notes I have rather more to do than I can manage. But it is all very interesting.' It is also an irreplaceable and invaluable record of a vanishing culture.

During his stay in the Northern Territory's top end in 1911 and 1912, Spencer was asked by the Commonwealth Government to report on the condition of the Aboriginal people and to make recommendations for their welfare. Today his report would be considered racist and paternalistic. He said for example that:

> The Aboriginal is, indeed, a very curious mixture; mentally about the level of a child who has little control over his feelings and is liable to give way to violent fits of temper, during which he may . . . behave with great cruelty. He has no sense of responsibility and, except in rare cases, no initiative . . .

But he also noted the people's highly developed memory, their art of mimicry and their sense of fun. It was an attitude of the times, but even so, difficult to reconcile with the sensitivity of the observations in his other writings.

Many of Spencer's recommendations such as healthcare, the setting up of large reserves

A rock painting of a Balanda, probably a buffalo shooter, with guns. In the early days, buffalo shooters were dependent on the Gagudju people.

and preventing the Aborigines' drift to degrading lives at the settlements, were sensible and humane. If implemented they could have prevented much misery. But they were not. One of his recommendations was prophetic: '. . . the care of the Aboriginals of the Northern Territory should be made a national responsibility and any scheme devised for the purpose of preserving and uplifting them should be under the control of the Commonwealth Government.'

Buffalo Shooters

But it was the buffaloes that were unwittingly instrumental in keeping many Gagudju on their lands. The rapidly multiplying animals attracted a band of adventurous Balanda who hunted them for their skins.

By the early part of this century the whole of Kakadu was taken up by shooters' leases, from Kapalga on the west bank of the South Alligator to Oenpelli on the east bank of the East Alligator.

Rock painting of a Balanda at Ubirr. Referring mostly to buffalo shooters, Neidjie said: 'And soon the Balanda, standing with hands in pockets told us what to do.'

In 1920 a buffalo shooter by the name of Carl Warburton took up a shooting lease at Cannon Hill in Bunitj country. When he first rode into the area he came to a narrow passage through the rocks, somewhere near Hawk Dreaming, where:

> Immediately through the small opening appeared about thirty blacks, fearsomely painted, and armed with spears. A chill of fear swept over me . . .
>
> Before I could think what next to do, they rushed toward me, fitting their spears into their wommeras . . .
>
> Howling and grimacing, the blacks rushed to within a few feet of me, and came to a dead halt, with an ominous grunt . . .
>
> I endeavoured to appear unconcerned, but I was as scared as a rabbit.
>
> They were the finest specimens of natives I had ever seen or have seen since . . . they were all about six feet and over, and they were marvellously muscled. Their hair had a reddish tinge in it, through the cartilage of their noses were stuck teeth of animals, pieces of sharpened shell or carved wood and they were painted in red and white stripes across the belly and chest, and down the thighs and face.
>
> . . . as I stared at them, they stared back at me for some moments. Then happened one of those extraordinary things which one dreams of. They all burst out laughing.

After their fun:

> One of them stepped from the rest and came closer. He was the pick of a splendid bunch; perhaps not quite as tall as the others, but more powerfully built, and I could see the muscles rippling under the skin of his thighs and arms. He carried a grim-looking jagged spear, and I noticed that it was tipped with iron. He . . . had an air of authority about him which told me plainly that he was the leader . . . In a musical bass voice, he said with a grin: "Good day!"

The Bunitj man introduced himself to the indignant Warburton: 'My name Koperaki . . . This my country. I sit down here.'

Koperaki was Dolly Yanmalu's father and Big Bill Neidjie's uncle.

A typical buffalo shooter's establishment of the early days would consist of one or two white men, a Chinese cook and anything up to forty Aborigines. They led a nomadic existence moving every few weeks to find new herds.

The Gagudju people took readily to this life. The nomadic movements, the use of their great hunting skills and the exhilaration of fast and dangerous work, suited them. At the onset of the wet season the intruders would pack up their spoils and leave, not to return for five or six months. The Gagudju would then attend to their ceremonies and other aspects of their traditional lives. The Aboriginal people benefited from this arrangement to the extent that they remained on their lands in cohesive clans, maintaining their ceremonies and avoiding the worst effects of disease and degradation, though they did not escape them entirely.

The European shooters benefited from the Aborigines more materially and directly. They had a large, able and reliable workforce that cost them almost nothing: the Aboriginal men shooting and skinning the buffaloes and the women washing, salting and drying the heavy hides. The women and children also supplemented the unlimited supply of buffalo meat with a wide variety of bush foods. The European 'bosses' had to do little more than supply the horses and rifles. They paid the Aboriginal people in kind — clothes, tea, sugar and, above all, tobacco.

The remarkable Dolly Yanmalu, Neidjie's sister, is the only person left who speaks fluent Gagudju.

The boom years of buffalo shooting were in the late 1920s and 1930s. Many of the Gagudju who were young men in those days lived on into the 1970s and 1980s. One of these hunters said the following about his white employer:

> Him little bit good boss. Bit rough. Some people didn't work properly . . . He go crook about the work. Sometime people used to run away. He'd get rough with that boy, you know. Chase him around with horse. Bring 'em back, start work again.

Charlie Whittaker, of the Murumburr clan, who now lives at Humpty Doo near Darwin, held the record for the most buffaloes shot in a single horseback pursuit. He shot forty-two buffaloes by running after a herd at full gallop, bringing his horse within a few metres of each target, shooting it in the spine and then avoiding the falling beast. Reloading also had to be done at a gallop. Often the rider would find himself in the middle of a running herd when he would have to shoot animals on either side of him and at the same time be ready for any buffalo that might attack his horse.

Another Murumburr elder, Butcher Night, now living on his tribal lands in Kakadu, describes how it was done:

> On foot we got long rifle .303. You got to shoot from five hundred yards . . . get about five or six buffalo on foot. Get hide, skin it, take all the hide back home. Have supper, have tea. Get up three o'clock in the morning and muster all the shooting horses . . . Go out and shoot again. Horseback this time. Leave long rifle home; take short rifle for horseback shooting . . . at five o'clock we see how many buffaloes are running on the plain. Hold the bridle on the left, hold the gun in the right hand . . . Horse got to gallop, you see. Shoot with right hand, then get gun up quick, quick load. One gallop for ten shots. Ten shots, ten bullets, ten buffalo, one gallop. Use short .303 rifle. Skin 'em up, go back home. Give horses a spell from the running.

Few Europeans developed these skills. Some leaseholders did not do any shooting themselves.

Balanda a Bit Rough

Relations between the two races varied immensely. Some of the Europeans, like Paddy Cahill, were regarded with trust and affection by the Gagudju. Others were 'a bit rough', a phrase that hides a multitude of sins from verbal abuse to physical violence and even murder. Big Bill Neidjie well remembers being shot at by a white adventurer. His sister, the diminutive Dolly Yanmalu, was held a prisoner in the hut of one of the white buffalo shooters for two years. Little Dolly, as she is known, is a remarkable person. She never left Kakadu, living her entire life there. She was the last person to live at Malangangerr and she is also the last person left who speaks fluent Gagudju. Her comment about the old days is: 'the Balanda did wild and rough things, not like now, eh.'*

In 1925 Oenpelli became a mission run by the Church Missionary Society. A school was started and the children were encouraged to leave their families and live in dormitories. Up to one hundred Aboriginal people lived at the mission and were maintained by them. Hundreds of others came and went. Clans and tribes were mixed up as much as possible with a resultant breakdown in traditions. The Gagudju were probably always a small minority at the Oenpelli mission. In 1931 Arnhem Land was declared an Aboriginal Reserve and became an important refuge for the Aboriginal people, which it remains to this day. Meanwhile the population continued to decline. The number of nomadic Aborigines in the Territory's top end fell from 10,000 in 1930–31 to 4000 in 1937–38.

* In January 1989, as this book went to press, Dolly Yanmalu died.

World War II, which the Gagudju call the Japanese War, brought a major disruption. The administration of the north was taken over by the army. Their policy was to remove all Aborigines from the coastal areas, including Kakadu, and take them to camps along the Stuart Highway from Mataranka to Pine Creek. In 1943, 1157 Aborigines worked in these camps in return for rations and clothing. Luckily many Gagudju families eluded the army and others escaped from the camps to live in the bush, maintaining the traditions and the population. They painted sorcery figures with animal heads, elongated, twisted and even severed limbs. But even their most potent magic could not turn the inexorable tide of change.

After the war, buffalo hunting resumed and once again became the focus for the Gagudju people. Gradually the emphasis moved from the supply of hides to that of meat. The horse was eventually replaced by the four-wheel drive vehicle. The car, combined with the aeroplane, made Kakadu less isolated. More and more Balanda came to look for adventure and to see its wild beauty. Crocodile shooting was taken up but involved few Gagudju people. Buffalo shooting camps were now less nomadic and became centred on the pastoral leases of Munmalary and Mudginberri, which between them took up nearly all the floodplains along the Alligator Rivers. Aboriginal people were employed there and later also at Gimbat and Goodparla Stations to the south, which are now also part of Kakadu National Park.

At first the stations supported many Aboriginal people. Toby Gangele, a Gagudju elder of the Mirarr clan now living at Nourlangie, was head stockman at Munmalary for many years.

When equal wages for Aborigines were introduced in the 1960s most jobs at the cattle stations were lost to the Gagudju. They were discouraged from going to Munmalary and soon left that area. They were welcome, however, at Mudginberri and a camp with about 130 Aboriginal people (not all Gagudju) remained there throughout the 1960s and 1970s. Other Gagudju went to live at Oenpelli, Pine Creek and Darwin. Few lived in the bush.

Land Rights and Uranium

The Gagudju may well have left their lands altogether, never to return, but for a strange combination of events — the discovery of uranium in Kakadu in the late-1960s and the passage of the *Aboriginal Land Rights (Northern Territory) Act* in 1976. These two events and their consequences stirred the Gagudju people to a movement back to life in the bush and efforts to revive their traditions and beliefs. The minerals in themselves actually posed a dire threat to the Gagudju, for if they had been allowed to be mined unfettered and uncontrolled they could well have destroyed vital areas of Kakadu and pushed the people finally and irrevocably from their country. But in the Australian community at large an awareness had grown that mining should not always be given a free reign and that other values might take precedence. Also, because of easier access more and more people visited the region and came to appreciate its compelling beauty and historical significance.

So under the *Environment Protection (Impact of Proposals) Act* of 1974 the Commonwealth Government set up an inquiry into the potentially hazardous uranium mining in the top end — covering areas of Arnhem Land as well as the Alligator Rivers. It looked into social as well as environmental issues. The inquiry was headed by Mr Justice R. W. Fox.

Among the Gagudju people there had not been a grassroots land rights movement such as

Mick Alderson, Gagudju Association Chairman and National Park Ranger, shoots feral buffalo from a helicopter as part of the Park Service's feral animal eradication program.

there had been among the Gurindjie people at Wave Hill. The Gagudju were widely scattered; most of them lived away from their spiritual homeland. They had come to accept what seemed the inevitable, that the Balanda would push them off their land. But when the Fox inquiry was set up the Gagudju were consulted about their fate and their lands for the first time. Their response was unequivocal and positive.

The commission was called the *Ranger Uranium Environmental Enquiry* and began hearings in September 1975. Even though it is called the Ranger Inquiry, Ranger being just a single deposit, it dealt with the entire uranium province. This includes Jabiluka, believed to be the world's richest deposit of uranium ore, and Koongarra.

The Gagudju themselves, and at times through people speaking on their behalf, gave evidence at the inquiry. Their position and also their difficulties at giving evidence, were eloquently expressed by Silas Roberts. He was the first chairman of the Northern Land Council, an organisation that coordinates matters for the top end Aboriginal people, and a most able and perceptive man. He was a full-blood Aborigine of the Alawa tribe of the Roper River area. He was the first Aborigine to become a magistrate.

The following is part of a statement Silas Roberts made to the Fox Inquiry:

It is true that the people who are belonging to a particular area are really part of that area and if that area is destroyed they are also destroyed. In my travels throughout Australia, I have met many Aborigines from other parts who have lost their culture. They have always lost their land and by losing their land they have lost part of themselves. By way of example, they are like Christians who have lost their soul and don't know where they are — just wandering. We in the Northern Territory seem to be the only ones who have kept our culture.

We are worried that we are losing a little bit, a little bit, all of the time. We keep our ceremony, our culture, but we are always worried. We still perform our ceremonies.

We are very worried that the results of this Inquiry will open the doors to other companies who also want to dig up uranium on our sacred land. There are so many I find it hard to remember them all but I can remember Ormac, Queensland Mines, Union Carbide, Reynolds Mining, B.H.P. and Pancontinental. We think if they all get in there and start digging we'll have towns all over the place and we'll be pushed into the sea. We want a fair go to develop. We are human beings, we want to live properly and grow strong.

We see white men as always pushing. We know white men think differently from us, and they are not all bad. But even this Commission is pushing in its own way. I must explain this because it is very important that our difficulty in this is understood. The trouble is the Aborigines did not run their business the same as the white men. We did not and do not reach decisions in the same way. Our people are not as free to make decisions and give evidence as white men seem to be. If you add to this that most Aborigines are very frightened of white men; you will have a lot of trouble getting much straight talk from Aboriginal people and you will have a lot of trouble getting them to come back to give evidence more than once. These problems are always faced by our field officers. Let me explain a little bit more. We have got to make decisions in respect to land our own way.

It is a long hard road to final answer. Sometimes a person or group will say 'yes' then talk a little bit more and then say 'no'. Then more talk might take place after a few months and still no final answer. Then all the people who really belong to that country will go over it all again until everyone is sure of his answer and then the answer is given. That may be years after the first talks if the question is a hard one.

The Ranger uranium mine, with Dadjbe in the background.

The whole process of inquiries and land claims was to the Aborigines a strange, elaborate, costly and convoluted ceremony to establish something that is really quite simple. For many months, the Fox Inquiry sat and listened to evidence and to lengthy and esoteric exchanges between lawyers. It ran to 13,525 pages of transcripts, cost close to a million dollars and produced a 622 page report. All to establish what to the Gagudju is a self-evident truth, eternal and immutable, vested in the Dreamtime. For them there was only one conclusion possible: no digging up of any land. As one elder said, 'We don't want them to kill our land,' and, by inference, the people.

The Fox Inquiry recommended that the Alligator Rivers region, the lands of the Gagudju, be made into a National Park, to be declared in three stages, for, the report says: 'Aboriginal interests have much in common with those of conserving the environment'. Two areas were to be excised from the National Park — the Ranger and Jabiluka uranium deposits in one and the Koongarra deposit, near Nourlangie Rock, in the other. Mining was to go ahead only after negotiations with the traditional owners, the Gagudju people, had been concluded.

The mining industry, supported by the Northern Territory Government, was opposed to the forces of moderation and conservation set in motion by the Commonwealth Government and the battle for Kakadu was joined. It still rages on. For periods in the mid-1980s Kakadu was on the front pages of national newspapers and on television news bulletins almost daily. The bitter fight is mostly between opposing groups of Balanda, leaving the Gagudju bewildered and frustrated in the middle.

The Gagudju are opposed to mining, but they realise that they are powerless to stop it. They agreed to the Ranger uranium mine going ahead, but the Dreamtime was compromised. To compromise it no further, the Aboriginal people insisted that the Commonwealth Government manage the rest of their lands as a National Park, to be called Kakadu.

Kakadu Becomes a National Park

Land claims, made on behalf of the Gagudju by the Northern Land Council, have resulted in the people being given title to large areas of their country. Further claims are still pending.

The results of the inquiry and land claims were profound and changed the Gagudju's lands and way of life forever. An all-season highway was built linking Darwin with the heart of Kakadu. The road from Pine Creek was upgraded. A township, called Jabiru, was built to serve the Ranger mine which now supplies uranium to the world.

In 1978 the traditional owners leased their lands to the Director of the Australian National Parks and Wildlife Service (ANPWS) for 100 years to be managed on their behalf. Stage 1 was declared in 1979, Stage 2 in 1984 and Stage 3, with certain provisions for possible mining, in 1987. The total area is close to 20,000 square kilometres.

Gagudju elders have expressed their satisfaction with the National Park concept. Toby Gangele, who lived most of his life in Kakadu, working there as buffalo hunter, crocodile shooter, stockman, tourist guide and National Park adviser, has this to say:

> We are happy to have this National Park here. Tourists can come up here and enjoy themselves — have a good look at birdlife, go to Jim Jim Falls, look at cave paintings, but they can't go to ceremony places. They've got a lot of places to go but they can't go to sacred sites, dreaming places and burial places.
>
> That's where National Parks help us with management . . . They help us 'cause they've got more knowledge to control tourists. European and Aborigines work together here — no worries . . . In some ways the old days are gone but we are still living on the land — we've still got tribal law, ceremony, funeral. We never give it away us blokes . . .
>
> So we've still got to have country to hunt in and live in. But we don't want to have to worry about tourists. We get a bit frightened if tourists go down to our hunting place . . . We don't want to worry them when we go hunting . . . We've got to have a big National Park so there is place for everybody to go. That's the way we want it — places for us to hunt and live. We've got to look after all our sacred places and still let tourists come and have a good time. That's where National Parks help us. I remember I went to a lot of places — America, New Guinea, Sydney, Canberra. I think we've got a good Park here.

And Nipper Kapirigi:

> Aboriginal people still want to come back to their country. Might be they come back to Nawulabila, Dangurran or Kubowo. They have to hunt kangaroo with gun and sometime still with spear. We still get that long yam, bush potato and waterlily too. We living that way, that our life. That first mob [creator beings] showed us what to do, how to hunt and light fire, we didn't make it up. Us second mob have to do these things to look after the country.

Yarramarna, Neidjie's son, is a National Park Ranger. He burns the country as part of the Park Service's management scheme.

> It's good those young Aboriginal boys and girls work for the Park [as rangers]. They come back to their country that way . . . It's good for . . . visitors to go to places like Cooinda and Yellow Waters, but they can't go everywhere. They would get lost or go to a dangerous place and get hurt. If tourists want to go into the bush they have to have an Aboriginal or ranger with them to show them the way and keep them out of trouble.

Kakadu in the Future

With all this development, what the Aborigines feared most, that is large numbers of people, strangers, coming to their country, has eventuated. About 2000 have come to stay to work the mine and service the tourist industry. But the vast majority are visitors — 47,000 in 1982, 200,000 in 1987 and if the trend continues 700,000 are expected each year by the mid-1990s.

The Gagudju fear that their hunting grounds will be trampled, their sacred places desecrated. It is something they themselves would not have had the resources to prevent, but they are now able to control it through the Australian National Parks and Wildlife Service. The traditional owners have placed their trust in the Commonwealth Government. For its part, the government has recognised Kakadu's significance, not as a tourist resort or a mine, but as one of the world's most important places in terms of human history and culture and as one of the last spectacular and unspoilt parts of Australia.

As such Kakadu National Park met all the criteria for listing with the World Heritage Convention in full measure. This international convention, under the auspices of UNESCO and the International Union for the Conservation of Nature, seeks to identify, list and protect all the world areas which have a unique cultural heritage, are of exceeding scientific value and have an unspoilt environment. These places are not just of national importance but are vital to the world community as a whole. Few areas are better qualified to meet these standards than Kakadu.

The Commonwealth Government proposed Kakadu's Stage 1 for World Heritage listing and it was accepted in 1981. After a bitter wrangle with the Northern Territory Government, Stage 2 was proposed and accepted in 1987. The battle for Stage 3 continues. Deposits of gold and other minerals have been discovered there and it may well be that parts of this area will be excised from the park so that mining can go ahead. Uranium mining at Jabiluka and Koongarra is also still possible.

Both uranium and gold mining pose serious threats to Kakadu's environments, especially the extensive wetlands. Despite the stringent safeguards imposed the industries have or would have highly toxic wastes poised on the South Alligator River and Magela Creek drainage systems. If the poisonous substances were to enter the waters they would kill all organisms in them, destroying the billabongs and floodplains perhaps forever.

The Gagudju people, the traditional owners of Kakadu, benefit materially from the mining. Each year they receive about $3.3 million in royalties from the Ranger uranium mine. At the suggestion of the field officers of the Northern Land Council, the traditional owners formed an association to administer these funds and to generally look after the welfare of their people. In July 1979 they formed the Gagudju Association Inc. In the late 1980s the Association had 330 members (120 children). All of them are Gagudju.

Big Bill Neidjie: 'Listen! Listen! Listen this story.'

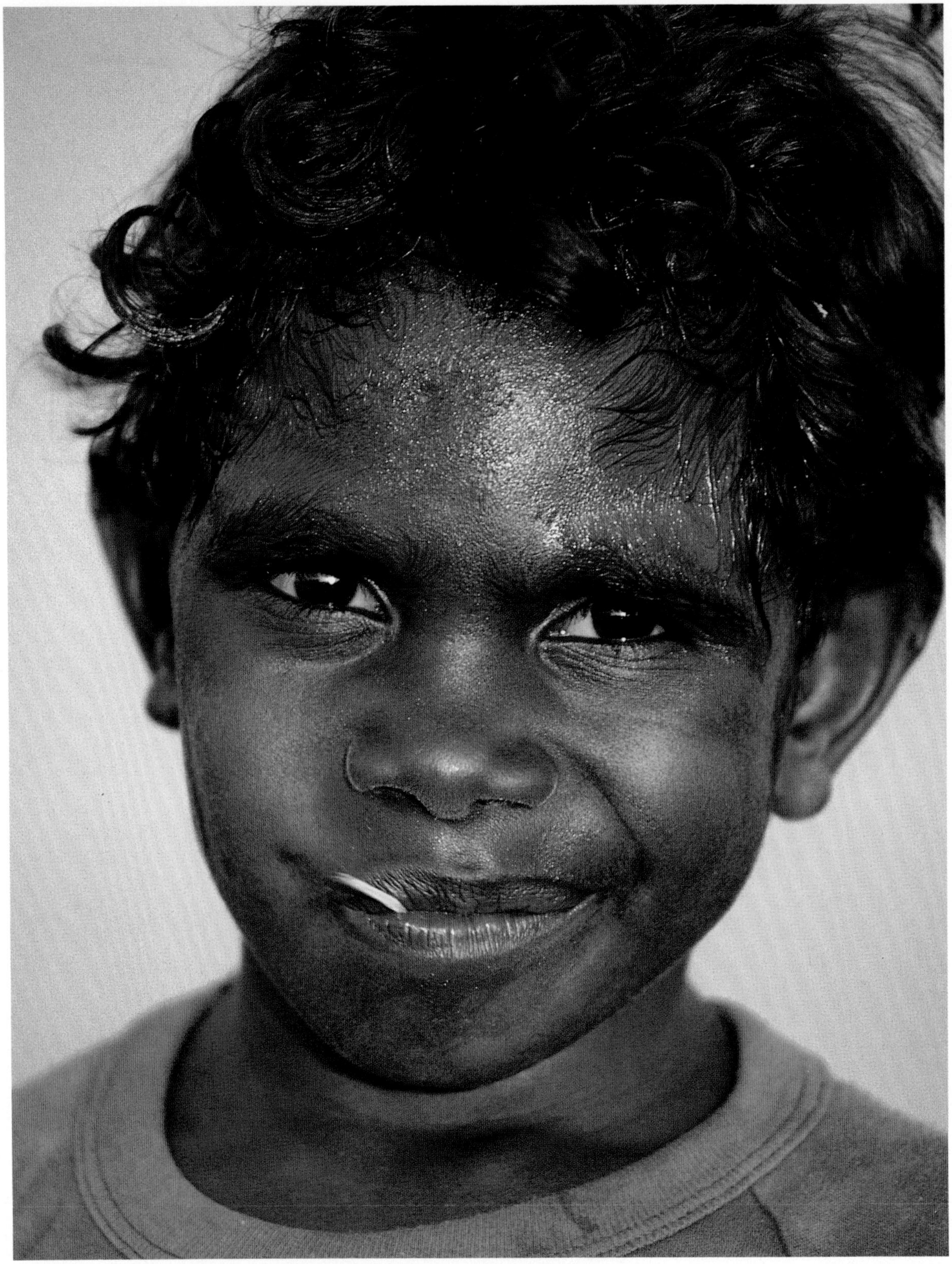

Big Bill Neidjie's grandson Simon. Will he and his generation be able to 'hang on' to the Gagudju story?

The Association is administered by a committee of Gagudju, but its day-to-day affairs are run by a small group of Balanda. The royalty money is used in many ways. Each member receives a small cash payment annually. The children's money is put in a trust fund till they are eighteen. A sizeable amount is used in looking after the welfare of the members; their health, housing, education and transport, and in administrative costs. The remainder is invested against the days when the mine will be worked out. As part of that investment the Association has bought the Cooinda Motel and has invested in a new motel in Jabiru. The Association owns the Border Store and has a share in the South Alligator Motor Inn. The Gagudju have an interest in nearly all the travellers' accommodation in the National Park.

These developments have enabled the Gagudju to return to their land and resume contact with their culture. However while they are secure on their land, there are now other pressures. New and alien ways of thinking are forced upon them. Ownership of land was a foreign concept to them; land was not something anyone owned, it was what had to be looked after, of which the people were custodians. In traditional times the Gagudju accumulated no wealth and personal possessions were only of the simplest kind. Everything was shared. The new ways of thinking create tensions and disputes.

The task of looking after the country has now fallen to the ANPWS. Inevitably emphases and perceptions have changed. In traditional times it was essential, in looking after the country, to be there, to be part of it, to know all the names of all the places. Now it is necessary to control people, for them *not* to be in certain places. The sacredness of names is often forgotten.

When the ANPWS was first asked to administer Kakadu, in late-1977, it was a small organisation ill-prepared for such an enormous task. Much groundwork was done by a few dedicated staff members during 1978 and early 1979. They were people who had a close rapport with the Aboriginal people and with each other. They worked closely with the traditional owners of Kakadu and devised management plans with their full co-operation and understanding. In those early days human relations were what mattered most. Much was accomplished in a short time. When Kakadu was officially declared a National Park on 5 April 1979, a sound foundation had been laid. The first Aboriginal ranger training program was already in its third month.

The ideal was to train sufficient numbers of Aboriginal rangers so that one day they could run Kakadu on their own. But because of the phenomenal number of visitors this does not now seem possible. ANPWS's original handful of dedicated workers has swollen to a large organisation. Human relations have suffered. Aboriginal rangers are still few and have not been promoted very high up the hierarchy. ANPWS has become, perhaps inevitably, a somewhat impersonal bureaucracy. Looking after the country is no longer a sacred life and death obligation. It is now governed by the impersonal and implacable rules of a government department.

In the late 1970s and early 1980s the stage was set for Gagudju and Balanda to live in harmony with each other and the environment. Instead Kakadu has become a political battlefield and will no doubt continue to be so for decades to come. Kakadu was made a social and environmental experiment without precedent or guidelines, that for the most part is in a continual and unsettling state of flux. Yet there are white 'managers' and Aboriginal

Pied geese at sunset.

managers within the bureaucracies who have not lost their vision of Kakadu's original concepts and ideals and who will never cease to struggle for their fulfilment. In Kakadu, more than anywhere else, they deserve to succeed.

In the controversies, in keeping hundreds of thousands of visitors under control, in trying to reconcile all the interests, the essential message that the Gagudju have to offer the rest of the world is often obscured by bureaucratic obfuscation or smothered by wrangling over mining rights.

But the true Gagudju people never lose sight of what is at stake — man's harmony with

the natural world, his being an essential and indivisible part of it. This is what they call their story and ultimately it may be the key to the survival of all mankind.

As Big Bill Neidjie says:

This story not for Aborigine only,
This all over Australia story.
But white man he don't listen,
He only worry about money.

Neidjie, with all the passion at his command, implores the world to:

Listen! Listen! Listen this story.

ABORIGINAL WORDS

The following list of names evolved as we worked with various people in Kakadu. No orthography was in use with the Aboriginal languages of the area. Linguistic studies are in progress and in time these spellings will no doubt change.

MAMMALS

ANTECHINUS, SANDSTONE, *Parantechinus bilarni* — **Dokun**
BANDICOOT, NORTHERN BROWN, *Isoodon macrourus* — **Yok**
BAT, GHOST, *Macroderma gigas* — **Bumapuma**
ECHIDNA, *Tachyglossus aculeatus* — **Gowarrang, Ngarrabek**
FLYING FOX, *Pteropus* sp., general term — **Goluban**
BLACK, *Pteropus alecto* — **Na-ngamu**
LITTLE RED, *Pteropus scapulatus* — **Na-gayalak**
GLIDER, SUGAR, *Petaurus breviceps* — **Lambalk**
KANGAROO, ANTELOPE, *Macropus antilopinus* — ♂ **Garndagitj,** ♀ **Garnday**
NATIVE CAT OR QUOLL, NORTHERN, *Dasyurus hallucatus* — **Djabbu, Nyanjma**
PHASCOGALE, BRUSH-TAILED, *Phascogale tapoatafa* — **Wumbu**
POSSUM, NORTHERN BRUSHTAIL, *Trichosurus arnhemensis* — **Dugula, Djebuy**
ROCK, *Pseudocheirus dahli* — **Djorrkkun**
RAT, ROCK, *Zyzomys* sp. — **Godjberr**
WATER, *Hydromys chrysogaster* — **Yirrku**
THYLACINE, *Thylacinus cynocephalus* — **Djangerr**
WALLABY, AGILE, *Macropus agilis* — **Gonobolu,** ♂ **Warradjangal,** ♀ **Melpe**
SHORT-EARED ROCK, *Petrogale brachyotis* — **Badbong**
WALLAROO, BLACK, *Macropus bernardus* — **Barrk**
EURO OR COMMON, *Macropus robustus* — **Galkberd**

BIRDS

BOWERBIRD, GREAT, *Chlamydera nuchalis* — **Djuwe**
BROLGA, *Grus rubicundus* — **Al-gordu, Gurdurrk**
COCKATOO, RED-TAILED BLACK, *Calyptorhynchus magnificus* — **Garnamarr**
SULPHUR-CRESTED, *Cacatua galerita* — **Ngarradj**
CORELLA, LITTLE, *Cacatua pastinator* — **Ngaleklek**
CURLEW, BUSH, *Burhinus magnirostris* — **Gurrwerlu**
DUCK, PACIFIC BLACK, *Anas superciliosa* — **Nawangku**
WHISTLING, *Dendrocygna* sp. — **Djurrbiyuk**
EAGLE, WEDGE-TAILED, *Aquila audax* — **Wamut**
WHITE-BREASTED SEA-, *Haliaeetus leucogaster* — **Marrawuti**
EGRET, *Egretta* sp. — **Al-gurndurr**
EMU, *Dromaius novaehollandiae* — **Al-wandju, Gurdugadji**
FALCON, BROWN, *Falco berigora* — **Garrkanj**
FINCH, CRIMSON, *Neochmia phaeton* — **Al-maykordu**
FRIARBIRD, SANDSTONE, *Philemon buceroides* — **Gawolk**
GOOSE, PIED, *Anseranas semipalmata* — **Bamurru, Manimunak**
GRASS WREN, WHITE-THROATED, *Amytornis woodwardi* — **Yilding**
HERON, PIED, *Ardea picata* — **Miniwalmat**
WHITE-NECKED, *Ardea pacifica* — **Gulabakku**
HONEYEATER, WHITE-LINED, *Meliphaga albilineata* — **Bindjanok**
KITE, BLACK, *Milvus migrans* — **Buluydjirr**
WHISTLING, *Haliastur sphenurus* — **Na-wurrkbil**
KOEL, *Eudynamis scolopacea* — **Djawok**
KOOKABURRA, BLUE-WINGED, *Dacelo leachii* — **Barradja**
LORIKEET, VARIED, *Trichoglossus versicolor* — **Djurrih**
RED-COLLARED, *Trichoglossus haematodus* — **Detet**
LOTUSBIRD, *Jacana gallinacea* — **Demdorrkedorren, Garrayguwyeng-guwyeng**
OWLET-NIGHTJAR, *Aegotheles cristatus* — **Natjik**
OWL, BARN, *Tyto alba* — **Mobiny, Mowirn**
PARROT, HOODED, *Psephotus dissimilis* — **Djikkilirritj**
PELICAN, *Pelecanus conspicillatus* — **Makkakkurr**
PIGEON, BANDED, *Ptilinopus cinctus* — **Bogung, Adjmu**
CHESTNUT-QUILLED ROCK, *Petrophassa rufipennis* — **Gurrbelak**
SPINIFEX, *Petrophassa plumifera* — **Bamgarnagarnamalk**
PLOVER, MASKED, *Vanellus miles* — **Berrep perrep**
PYGMY GOOSE, GREEN, *Nettapus pulchellus* — **Bewutj**
ROSELLA, NORTHERN, *Platycercus venustus* — **Djadbelhbel**
SCRUB FOWL, *Megapodius reinwardt* — **Gulguldany**
STILT, BLACK-WINGED, *Himantopus himantopus* — **Amurak, Nginark-nginark**
STORK, BLACK-NECKED, *Xenorhynchus asiaticus* — **Djagarna**
WILLIE WAGTAIL, *Rhipidura leucophrys* — **Djikirdi-djikirdi**

REPTILES AND AMPHIBIANS

CROCODILE, FRESHWATER, *Crocodylus johnstoni* — **Muwuydjalki, Gumugen**
SALTWATER, *Crocodylus porosus* — **Ginga**
DEATH ADDER, *Acanthophis paelongus* — **Bek**
DRAGON, CHAMELEON, *Chelosania brunnea* — **Al-walngurru**
GILBERT'S, *Lophognathus gilberti* — **Matjdjandemit**
FILE SNAKE, *Acrochordus arafurae* — **Na-warndak, Gedjebe**
FROG, GENERAL TERM — **Djati**
GREEN TREE, *Litoria caerulea* — **Godburkmi, Belkanghmi**
GECKO, KNOBTAIL, *Nephrurus asper* — **Belerrk**
GOANNA, MERTENS' WATER, *Varanus mertensi* — **Burarr**
SAND OR GOULD'S, *Varanus gouldii* — **Galawan**
KING BROWN SNAKE, *Pseudechis australis* — **Dadjbe**
LIZARD, BLUE-TONGUED, *Tiliqua scincoides* — **Gurri**
FRILLED, *Chlamydosaurus kingii* — **Gundamen, Ngalangak**
PYTHON, BLACK-HEADED, *Aspidites melanocephalus* — **Matjdjun**
OENPELLI, *Morelia oenpelliensis* — **Nawaran**
OLIVE, *Liasis olivaceus* — **Mandjurdurrk**
WATER, *Liasis fuscus* — **Bolokko**
TREE SNAKE, BROWN, *Boiga irregularis* — **Ramberambe**
TURTLE, LONG-NECKED, *Chelodina rugosa* — **Al-mangeyi**
SNAPPING, *Elseya dentata* — **Bamrudek, Arderrhwu**

FISH

ARCHER, *Toxotes chatareus* — **Nyalgan**
BARRAMUNDI, *Lates calcarifer* — **Na-marngol**
CATFISH, FORK-TAILED, *Arius leptaspis* — **Anmakkawarri**
GRUNTER, SOOTY OR BLACK BREAM, *Hephaestus fuliginosus* — ♂ **Agetmi,** ♀ **Galarr**
RAINBOW, RED-TAILED, *Melanotaenia splendida* — **Djelabang**
SARATOGA, *Scleropages jardini* — **Guluybirr**

INSECTS

ANT, GREEN TREE, *Oecophylla smaragdina* — **Gabu**
BEES, NATIVE (SUGARBAG), GENERAL TERM — **Nabiwu**
HIGH NEST, BIG EGGS — **Garddirri**
HIGH NEST, SMALL SPECIES — **Manyalk**
GRASSHOPPER, GENERAL TERM — **Djatete**
LEICHHARDT'S, *Petasida ephippigera* — **Aldjurr, Namarrkun**
PRAYING MANTIS, GENERAL TERM — **Malindji, Anngorel**
WASP, MUD, GENERAL TERM — **Gurlurrmumu**

PLANTS

BLOODWOOD, SWAMP, *Eucalyptus ptychocarpa* — **An-ngal**
FISH POISON TREE, *Owenia vernicosa* — **An-barnatja**
FRESHWATER MANGROVE OR ITCHY TREE, *Barringtonia acutangula* — **An-galngki**
GREVILLEA, DRYANDER'S, *Grevillea dryandri* — **An-djamgu**
FERN-LEAFED, *Grevillea pteridifolia* — **Manbulu**

LILY, RED, *Nelumbo nucifera* — **Urrumarnginj**
WHITE WATER-, *Nymphaea gigantea* — **Barrdjungga, Wurtidjiledji**
PANDANUS, *Pandanus* sp. — **Manbelk**
PAPERBARKS, *Melaleuca* sp. — **Baratjbarr**
PLANCHONIA PLUM, *Planchonia careya* — **Mangonggu**
SPEAR GRASS, *Sorghum intrans* — **Manbidje**
SPIKE-RUSH, *Eleocharis dulcis* — **An-gurlatj**
STRINGYBARK, DARWIN, *Eucalyptus tetrodonta* — **Manbaddgurr**
WOOLLYBUTT, DARWIN, *Eucalyptus miniata* — **An-djalen**

PLACES

BARRAMUNDI GORGE — **Makuk**
CANNON HILL — **Ngamarr-kanangka**
GRAVESIDE GORGE — **Galarrngakngak**
HAWK DREAMING — **Garrkanj**
JA JA — **Djarrdjarr**
JA JA ESCARPMENT — **Djawumbu**
JABIRU DREAMING — **Djagarna**
JIM JIM FALLS — **Barrhmarlam**
LITTLE NOURLANGIE ROCK — **Nawulandja**
MOUNT BROCKMAN — **Djidbidjidbi, Dadjbe**
NANGALOR — **Na-nguluwurr**
NARRADJ — **Ngarradj warde djobkeng**
NOURLANGIE ROCK — **Burrungguy**
NOURLANGIE ROCK SHELTER — **Anbangbang**
TURKEY DREAMING — **Imagirrk**
TWIN FALLS CREEK (ABOVE FALLS) — **Gun-gurdul**
YELLOW WATERS — **Naranggul**

MISCELLANEOUS

BILLABONG — **Anlapal**
CLOUDS — **Gun-ngol** (large), **Gun-gotjngol** (small)
CREATOR BEING — **Warramurrungundji**
FIRE — **Gunak**
FLOODWATER — **Gung**
LIGHTNING MAN — **Namarrkun**
MOON — **Dird**
RAIN — **Na-gurl**
RAINBOW SERPENT — **Ngalyod, Almudj**
SPIRITS, BAD — **Namarndi**
ROCK-DWELLING — **Mimi**
STARS — **Al-gokkarrng**
STONE KNIFE — **Lawuk**
SUN — **Gun-dung**
THUNDERSTORM — **An-djewg**
WHITE PEPOLE — **Balanda, Watjpala**

ABORIGINAL SEASONS

WET SEASON (JANUARY TO MARCH) — **Gudjewg**
KNOCK-EM-DOWN STORMS (APRIL) — **Banggerdeng**
COOL, EARLY DRY SEASON (MAY AND JUNE) — **Yegge**
COLD WEATHER (JUNE AND JULY) — **Wurrgeng**
HOT, DRY SEASON (AUGUST AND SEPTEMBER) — **Gurrung**
HOT, PRE-MONSOON STORM SEASON (OCTOBER TO DECEMBER) — **Gunumeleng**

SELECTED BIBLIOGRAPHY

BLAINEY, G., *Triumph of the Nomads*, Sun Books, Melbourne, 1976.
BREEDEN, S. AND K., *Australia's North*, William Collins, Sydney, 1975.
BRENNAN, K., *Wildflowers of Kakadu*, K. Brennan, Jabiru, 1986.
CHALOUPKA, G., *Burrunguy Nourlangie Rock*, Northart, Darwin.
— *From Palaeoart to Casual Paintings*, Northern Territory Museum of Arts and Sciences, Darwin, 1984.
— *The Traditional Movement of a Band of Aborigines in Kakadu*, Kakadu National Park Teachers Resource Book, A. Stokes ed., ANPWS, 1982.
EDWARDS, R., *Australian Aboriginal Art*, Australian Institute of Aboriginal Studies, Canberra, 1979.
FLOOD, J., *Archaeology of the Dreamtime*, William Collins, Sydney, 1983.
GILLESPIE, D. (ed.), *The Rock Art Sites of Kakadu National Park*, ANPWS Special Publication No. 10, Canberra, 1983.
ISAACS, J. (ed.), *Australian Dreaming*, Lansdowne Press, Sydney, 1980.
JONES, R. (ed.), *Archaeological Research in Kakadu National Park*, ANPWS Special Publication No. 13, Canberra, 1985.
KING, P.P., *Narrative of a Survey of the Intertropical and Western Coasts of Australia*, 2 vols., John Murray, London, 1827.
LEICHHARDT, L., *Journal of an Overland Expedition in Australia, from Moreton Bay to Port Essington*. T. and W. Boone, London, 1847.
MCKINLAY, J., *Expedition of Northern Australia* (South Australian Parliamentary Paper No. 131), Government Printer, Adelaide, 1866.
MULVANEY, D.J. and CALABY, J.H., *So Much That is New*, University of Melbourne Press, Melbourne, 1985.
NEIDJIE, B., DAVIS, S., AND FOX, A., *Kakadu Man*, Resource Managers, Darwin, 1985.
SPENCER, W.B., *Native Tribes of the Northern Territory*, Macmillan, London, 1914.
WARBURTON, C., *Buffaloes; Adventures and Discovery in Arnhem Land*, Angus and Robertson, Sydney, 1934.

CREDITS

Text by Stanley Breeden. Photographs by Belinda Wright except for the following: Ian Morris pages 4–5, 12, 14, 18 (r), 32 (top), 40, 44, 46, 48, 49 (r), 56 (top l), 62, 66, 67, 73 (bottom), 76 (r), 81, 83 (l), 86 (top, bottom l), 95, 97 (l), 99, 101, 102, 113, 114 (r), 121, 127, 130, 137, 140 (r), 141 (bottom), 184, 191, 193, 197. Stanley Breeden pages 2–3, 22 (top), 28 (bottom l), 37 (top r), 42, 45, 51, 70 (top l, r), 71 (top l), 73 (top l, r), 74 (bottom), 75 (top l, bottom l), 79, 80, 83 (r), 84, 86 (r), 88, 90 (l), 91 (r), 92, 93, 108 (l), 110, 134. Back jacket flap photo of Belinda Wright by Ian Morris, and photo of Stanley Breeden by Belinda Wright.

INDEX